SNIPORIES

Little Stories, Big Lessons

A.K.A.

LEDRSHHIP

(No, I did not misspell that.)

Gerald A. Thornhill Jr.

CPT USAR (RET)

ISBN 978-1-0980-0199-5 (paperback)
ISBN 978-1-0980-0200-8 (digital)

Christian Faith Publishing, Inc.
832 Park Avenue
Meadville, PA 16335
www.christianfaithpublishing.com

Printed in the United States of America

This book is dedicated to my wife, Sheila, who has stood by my side through so many smiles and so many trials. Everything as a man that I am is because of you. I know God loves me because he gave me you.

Warning

Reading this book may cause the reader to experience a myriad of emotions for no apparent reason. These could possibly include but are not limited to any of the following: inexplicable joy, happiness, anger, sadness, depression, relief, anxiety, guilt, remorse, mood swings, great satisfaction, and sudden outbreaks of laughter.

Each of these emotions may be experienced simultaneously, individually or not at all. Additional side effects may also include life-altering behavioral changes. Read this publication at your own risk.

Author's Note

To use this book properly, substitute your name for mine. This book is about you and your family. The chronological order of this manuscript is inconsistent because events described fit the book outline instead of the order in which they occurred. Parts of "Snipories" were written while I was working and others were written after retiring.

Disclaimer

The contents described in this book, to the best of the author's recollection, are based on actual events. Any errors or misstatements are either intentionally made due to family requests or attributable to the fallibility of my memory.

FOREWORD

For as long as I can remember I have had a difficult time trusting people. It seemed that once I let someone into my circle, it was only a matter of time before they betrayed me, or metaphorically "threw me under the bus" so they could get ahead. I started thinking this was just human nature in a fractured society. I withdrew from people, always keeping a professional distance and never letting the true me out. I lived this way of life for many years. After a series of really bad situations *(the death of my father, and being in a serious motorcycle accident, etc.)* I started turning things around. I met my awesome wife and my life has been improving ever since. This is the subject for a different book, but you the reader need to know my perspective and why I agreed to write this forward.

In October 2005, I began working as a flight instructor and lecturer at Southern Illinois University Carbondale (SIUC). A short time later, while in the process of being promoted to an Assistant Chief Instructor, I met Gerald Thornhill, or should I say, began hearing more about him. Through the years, I would send flight students to checkrides and a few would end up scheduled with Gerald. Usually when the checkride was over, I would hear interesting stories about how the process went. Most of the time my students passed, but occasionally, one would fail and have to make another attempt. I began hearing my students and others referring to this one Assistant Chief as *"Mr. T."* I became curious as I could not recall any large-build, gold necklace wearing, African Americans with a mohawk working in the aviation program. I thought it was odd. In fact, I began to think *"Mr. T"* resembled Tommy Lee Jones more than Lawrence Tureaud *(a.k.a. Sgt. Bosco "B.A." Baracus—A-Team NBC 1983–1987).*

One particular student I sent to "Mr. T" *(Gerald Thornhill)* told me "That guy always seems so serious, he needs to just relax and smile." It seemed quite funny to me at the time. After this student took his checkride with "Mr. T", in the debrief, apparently my student told "Mr. T" he needs to have a happy face; to which "Mr. T" replied, "This is my happy face." The humorous part is he said it with the same inflection and tone as Tommy Lee Jones in the movie "Man of the House" *(Sony Pictures 2005)*. This solidified for me that Gerald should have been known as Mr. Tommy and not as "Mr. T." I later discovered an interesting fact. Mr. T. *(Lawrence Tureaud the bouncer, actor, wrestler)* seems to have more in common with Gerald than I originally thought. Lawrence Tureaud said in an interview with Beliefnet.com that this was one of his prayers during his battle with cancer:

"Father, give me strength today, not
strength so I can lift 500 pounds,

but give me strength, Lord, so when I
speak, my words might motivate,

might inspire somebody, Lord, when they see me,

let them see you. When they hear me,

Lord, let them hear you. In your holy name I pray."

Part of the process for me to become an Assistant Chief was to choose a current Assistant Chief to serve as my mentor. I deliberated on that decision with great angst for some time. As I write this, I don't recall if I ever actually told "Mr. T" *(Gerald Thornhill)* this, but he knows now as I'm sure he has read this before using it as the forward in his book. I chose "Mr. T" as my mentor for two reasons. First, his integrity as a military officer, and second, the reason behind the sometimes-strange stories I would hear from my students. "Mr. T" was trying to keep them alive for their entire career, not just the checkride. I would often tell my students, "I won't always be there, so you have to be able to make good decisions yourself. My job is to help you learn so the decisions you make won't ultimately end in disaster." "Mr. T" seemed to have the same purpose in mind.

It has been some time now since I left SIUC and Gerald has retired. Whether it was an article he wrote, or a conversation we had, his support and assistance have been invaluable. Needless to say, when he asked me to read the draft of his book, I was very curious. Was this going to be reflections of a life spent in service? Was the book going to explain why he is the way he is? Or was this going to be a literary disaster meaning I would have to be creative with my response? I truly didn't believe the latter, but it was a thought. What I wasn't expecting was the impact this book had on me. I am proud to admit, "Mr. T" went from that guy I heard didn't come with a volume control *(he got loud a lot)*, to one of the most respected educators and mentors I have ever had *(who did actually have a volume control but knew when to turn it off)*.

So why should you continue past my ramblings and read "Snipories, Little Stories Big Lessons: aka LEDRSHHIP"?

Sir Richard Branson has a quote I have come to appreciate: "Train people well enough so they can leave, treat them well enough so they don't want to." Whether "Mr. T" was motivating troops under his charge in the military or dealing with sometimes whiny college students, he is a leader. There is a funny thing about leaders. You can disagree with me if you like, but my belief is true leaders are created, not naturally born. Some people tend to take charge more than others and some tend to follow more than others. It is experience in life, mistakes made and remedied, a fair amount of luck, and most certainly divine intervention that molds people into who they become. Some take that lesson to heart and share their knowledge. Some choose to dismiss it or perhaps drink it away. Others still, pay attention and lead the less knowledgeable to be able to make decisions on their own. This is the true leader. "Mr. T." is the true leader. The experiences we have in life, good or bad, make us into who we are. It is those experiences that you will read about in this book. As you read it, you may laugh, you may cry, or you may be numbed. I believe the point "Mr. T" is trying to make by sharing his experiences from loyalty, empathy, duty, respect, selfless service, honor, humility, integrity, and personal courage, can shed new light on your own struggles.

I can honestly say, compared to some of the stories shared in this book, my life has been uneventful. But even I could relate to what "Mr. T" has to say. Some of the family struggles and pain, strike familiar memories from my life. Some of the humorous times remind me to not take myself so seriously. As they say in various self-help publications, you have to learn to laugh at yourself. That laughter could be just the cure to solving a problem or two. One of the many take-aways I gained from this book is, nobody has the perfect family. If you think you do, you are only deceiving yourself. Quite a few times it may seem this family or that family has it all together. Each member may even have the same outward story to tell, but when the doors close, and they are all alone reality surfaces. What each of us must do is take what life has handed us and use it for the greater good of God's family. Just like we all have different giftings, we all have different experiences. God not only uses us to help others, but he uses others to help us.

You may never meet "Mr. T," but by learning his story, and living yours you might be able to improve your story. You may love this book, you may hate this book, but rest assured, you will have a reaction to it. That reaction, will add to your life story.

I am thankful of the honor to write this forward for my friend Gerald. I am even more thankful for the time I had getting to know him. Rick Warren said the greatest gift you could ever give someone is your time, because you will never get it back. I am thankful for the time spent with my friend and brother. Perhaps as you meet Gerald through his book, you will gain an appreciation for his struggle and a new appreciation for your own.

Kevin M. Krongos
April 27, 2019

ACKNOWLEDGMENTS

A project like this does not happen because of one person's effort. In the words of Mrs. Hillary Clinton *(who was quoting an ancient African Proverb)*, "It takes a village." There are so many people to thank that I am certain I will forget some. Let me apologize to those I do.

First and foremost, I am grateful to my Lord and Savior, Jesus Christ, for a love that I cannot begin to fathom and for blessing me with the life I have lived. Sometimes the road has been rocky, but you never promised I would always have blue skies and tailwinds. You did promise to take care of me, and you have. Without the experiences you have provided me with, I would not be the man I am today, and this book would not exist. The words of this manuscript are a reflection of those experiences. My Jesus, I love you more than anything.

Within the short span of a single paragraph, it is impossible to express my appreciation and the gratitude I feel for the love of my life, Mrs. Sheila Ann Thornhill, so I will not try. Sweetheart, I will simply thank you for believing in me when I probably didn't deserve it, for loving me when I know I didn't, and for always making me a better man. Thank you for showing me what really matters. Thank you for being the sweet wonderful woman you are and choosing me to share your life.

I am grateful to my three children, Magen Joy Erickson, Jarred Andre Thornhill, and Lindsay Jean Seals for letting me be your father and for your unconditional love. Each of you has taught me lessons without which my life would not be complete. Any man can be a father, but it takes someone special to be a dad. Though I have often been undeserving of the honor, I am proud and grateful that each of you allowed me to be your dad. I am even more proud of the people you have become. It has been such a delight to watch you grow from childhood into the remarkable adults you are. I love you unconditionally.

I am so thankful for my siblings and the way we were able to weather the storms of our family life. Somehow, instead of tearing us apart, against all odds, they only brought us closer. I am even more grateful for your continued support and to know the amazing thoughtful people each of you has become. Your poignant stories have had a huge impact in making this book become what it is.

Thanks to Dr. Charlie Rodriguez for your keen insight, your wonderful ideas, and grammatical corrections. Your thoughts and suggestions have made this book so much better than it would have otherwise been. I am grateful to you for the discussions we had about this project as it was painstakingly completed. They were delightful and thought-provoking. My sincere hope is that I have been able to do your ideas justice. Thank you for your incredible friendship. It is an honor to know you.

Thanks to my numerous SIUC colleagues, friends, and students for the trust you have placed in me and allowing me to guide you throughout my career as you pursued your own. There isn't enough space to name each of you, but never doubt that I remember you fondly, think of you daily, and pray for you constantly.

Thank you, Pastor Kyle Idleman. We have never met, but you have been an inspiration to me in so many ways through your amazing publications and videos. I have been blessed by them, and the world is profoundly better because of you. Your writing style has influenced mine, and I am more grateful than you could ever realize.

Thank you to the many pastors, particularly Brother Larry Shacklee, whose sermons I have heard throughout the years, the teachers who have offered so much of themselves, and my First Baptist Church of Zeigler, Illinois, family for your prayers when I or someone in my family was sick. Thank you for accepting me as I am. I felt your love for me the first time I walked through the door, and it has only gotten better. I love each of you more than you could ever know.

CONTENTS

1

Introduction and More

A friend of mine recently reminded me of something which I'd not thought about for years. It is quite likely you are familiar with the concept. My friend reminded me of the most important lesson my tenth grade high school English Literature teacher taught me. It was seemingly her life's mission to stress the importance of learning to become "visually literate." She often told us visual literacy was infinitely more important than knowing who wrote something, being able to recite lines from a poem, or the moral a particular author may have thought important.

Visual literacy isn't simply reading the words on a page and comprehending their meaning. It amounts to forming a mental picture of what is happening. It requires you to close your eyes for a moment, mentally place yourself in the situation, and think about the story you're reading. It requires using your imagination, which is perhaps the most wonderful thing about reading, because a good book can take a visually literate person anywhere. You will get much more from this book if you read it with an eye toward visual literacy. This book is about you. Place yourself in it as you read.

I've noticed public speakers will often begin with an anecdote in order to get the attention of their audience, and ultimately, it will emphasize the main point they are trying to make. I'm not sure if that holds true for books *(I have read and digested quite a few of them)*; but regardless, let's begin with a story about my father.

I was blessed to grow up in a Christian home with two loving, church-going, God-fearing parents. Dad was a military man and a preacher. As a young child, I was dragged (almost literally) to church and heard my father preach nearly every Sunday. What wouldn't I give to hear my dad preach one of his sermons again?

Occasionally, in the middle of one of his messages, he would stop, usually midsentence, hold up a raised fist, take one step backward, then take one step forward and loudly exclaim, "Behold, I come!" It was not something he did on a regular basis, but it was often enough that one day, curiosity got the better of me, so I asked him why he did this. I suppose I was perhaps nine or ten years old at the time, and it struck me as somewhat unusual behavior.

Dad told me he did this whenever he lost his train of thought and was trying to remember what to say next. This little catchphrase could be worked into whatever he was preaching about, and nobody was ever the wiser, but he was also reluctant to use that tactic anymore. Notice my use of the word *anymore*, the implication being he had used this ploy on numerous occasions but to a degree had discontinued the practice.

Of course, that led to my next question: "Dad, it works. Why not use it?" One thing you have to understand about my father is that he was a master at telling a good joke, even corny ones, and the printed page could never do him justice. Try to use your imagination as you hear this story. This is how he answered my question.

"Son, I was preaching one day, got off-track, took a step back, loudly proclaimed 'Behold, I come' as I took one step forward. Well, it didn't work, and as I looked out at the congregation, I knew I had to do something. I took two steps back, raised my fist, and even more loudly than the first time, took two long steps forward, proclaiming, 'Behold, I come!' I still couldn't remember what to say next, so I took three steps backward this time, raised my fist again, shook it vigorously, spoke as loudly as I could *(believe me that Dad could get really loud if he wanted and did so as he told me this)* and took three giant steps forward while I shouted, *'Behold, I come!'*

"Then I just don't know what happened, son. My shoelace may have become untied and I tripped over it. Perhaps I misjudged my step. Maybe I ran out of room on the stage about the time I took that third step. All I know is that just about the time I shouted 'come,' I tripped, fell off of the stage, and ended up on my knees with my face in the lap of a young lady who was sitting in the front pew *(Author's note: It is somewhat rare for a Baptist to sit in the front pew)."*

This, of course, led me to another question. "Dad, that had to be embarrassing. What did you do?"

He replied, "Well, son, I got up and did the only thing I could do. I straightened the knot in my tie, smoothed down my sport coat, and apologized profusely."

"What happened then, Dad? What did the lady say?" I asked.

Wait for it! Wait for it! Dad said, "She told me not to worry about it. I warned her three times."

There is a reason I told you this story, but you are going to have to read a little more before the big reveal.

Think about everything you have learned thus far in your life. Now think what it would be like if you could go back in time, remember it all, and start over. What would elementary or junior high school be like? How about high school or college? Your grades would be incredible! You would likely win any scholarship you applied for. You could have your pick of any Ivy League university you wanted with a full ride—Harvard, Princeton, Yale, Dartmouth, you name it.

What about the mistakes you have made in your relationships, your investments, your career choices? Life would be a breeze. You would be wealthy and successful in all of your heart's desires. I can't send you back in time. I can't make your life a breeze, but I can give you some insight which you may find almost as useful. No doubt, you're thinking that is a bold claim; but in many respects, that is what this book is about.

I have been blessed with two simultaneous wonderful careers. One was serving as a US Army reservist as an enlisted soldier and then as an officer. There were many more years with stripes on my sleeves than there were with brass on my collar. Several deployments amounted to a total of six-and-a-half years' active duty time in service to this great country. My military service began in 1974 and lasted until 2013. I was fortunate enough to have both the responsibility and challenge of being a company commander on two separate occasions. One of my last duties as a company commander was to attend the YTB. What is the YTB, you ask? Let me explain.

The YTB is when all the company commanders and 1SG's, along with the BN Cdr and SGM meet in an undisclosed location *(which is usually a large banquet room at a hotel)* to brief the CG and CSM along with S1 through S6 so they can crosswalk their YTC's in order to report DMOSQ, PMCS, APFT, weapons qualification rates and equipment stats. The reason for this annual gathering is the CG might be tasked by his up trace to send a down trace unit to the FOB in the sandbox. CG's need to know that nobody will violate the ROE when they arrive in theater, and everyone is going to be ready for deployment after a brief train-up. I'm glad I could clear that up for you.

My second career was as a faculty flight instructor at Southern Illinois University Carbondale, a major state research university. The main reason I decided to pursue aviation as a career is the jargon sounds so cool and is really easy to understand *(that might be wee bit of sarcasm coming across, but pilots are never sarcastic)*.

Becoming qualified for my job was actually rather simple. All I had to do was get my BS, my MS, then pass the FAA, PAR where I learned how to flambé tomatoes without taking much FLAP, the IRA *(no, not your retirement account)* where I learned how to GRAB the right CARD, and that compulsory always isn't; the CAX where I learned that all CFI's are named TOM, then the FOI which was a little challenging because this guy named REEPER kept me from finding the correct domain; the FIA, not to be confused with the AIF which I also had to pass, and let's not forget the IGI exams so that I could fill out a few 8710s and then go take some check rides,[1] administered by various DPE's and FSDO's *(pronounced fisdo)*.

---

[1] A check ride is also referred to as a practical test or practical exam. After completing the required and appropriate flight training in order to earn certification pilot applicants must first pass a Federal Aviation Administration (FAA) written test. While technically not considered a part of the practical exam the written test must be passed prior to taking the practical test, which can be administered directly by a qualified FAA examiner or someone who has been

All of this made it possible to get my Private, add on my IR, then my Commercial, followed up by the GI, the AGI, the IGI, and my CFI. Then I was able to qualify for my CFII and MEII, all according to the PTS which is now the ACS because special emphasis was being overlooked. By that point, I was a bit tired and didn't bother to take the ATM *(not the machine you put your debit card in to get cash from, which is different)*, because I thought, *Who wants to become an ATP that badly anyway?* When you next board a jet, remember the pilot has an ATP. That means he took the ATM and added a type rating to go with it along with the other things I just told you about. The copilot did all of that too but probably only has an RATP which is why he is the copilot and why your ticket is so expensive.

No, I'm not going to explain all the acronyms. Their meaning isn't the least bit important, but you'll understand my reasoning for listing them in a moment. To make matters worse, the military and aviation often use the same acronym. Even though spelled identically, the same acronym can have two entirely different meanings.

Of course, I'd be remiss if I failed to mention those rare acronyms which cross the boundaries of aviation, military, and civilian life, one of which is ASAP. In the aviation world, ASAP means Aviation Safety and Accident Prevention; in the army, it means Army Substance Abuse Program; and in the civilian world, it means "as

---

designated by the FAA to give the exam. They are known as Designated Pilot Examiners (DPE). The practical test consists of two phases. These are an oral exam where the applicant must demonstrate appropriate knowledge, followed by a flight exam in the aircraft where the applicant must prove his ability to fly safely, make appropriate aeronautical decisions and perform various tasks. The guidance which examiners use to administer their test is published by the FAA in the Airmen Certification Standards (ACS) formerly known as the Practical Test Standards (PTS). After successful completion of the practical exam the pilot applicant is awarded the appropriate certification. The process is repeated each time the applicant earns a new certificate or rating i.e., private pilot certificate, (PPC) instrument rating, (IR) commercial pilot certificate, (CPC) airline transport certificate, (ATP) etc. It is called a "check ride" because the DPE is "checking" the abilities and "riding" with the applicant during the process. Each new certificate or rating has its own unique written exam, i.e., Private Pilot Airplane (PAR), Instrument Rating Airplane (IRA), Commercial Pilot Exam (CAX), Airline Transport Pilot Multi-Engine (ATM).

soon as possible." This means you might occasionally hear the ASO (Aviation Safety Officer) say, "We need to improve our ASAP ASAP" or the BC (Battalion Commander) say something like, "Let's get PFC Smith enrolled in the ASAP ASAP." There have been numerous occasions when I've had to look at the clothes someone was wearing so I could figure out what they were attempting to tell me, all of which is enough to make me consider PHAWMOB (pounding my head against walls made of brick).

If you didn't follow very much of that, don't be concerned; there isn't a test at the end of the book, but if you come to 246G in the TEC at SIUC, I'll happily explain. If you can't make it to Carbondale, Illinois, then refer to note 1. It won't completely clarify things, but it should at least help.

There is a point, though. Based on what you've read so far, it is only logical that an acronym came to my mind as I began writing. The US Army uses "LDRSHIP" to describe army values. The overlying purpose is to promote leadership characteristics and admirable personal qualities. LDRSHIP represents Loyalty, Duty, Respect, Selfless Service, Honor, Integrity, and Personal Courage. These core traits, army values, are invaluable characteristics for leaders and soldiers alike. If adhered to, they will carry anybody far in life and greatly contribute to one's success, no matter what avenues are pursued. More importantly, they represent the model of how I desire to live my life, but I don't think of them as army values. To me, they represent Christian values.

You do not have to think of them as Christian values if "God" isn't your thing. Regardless of how you think about them, they are important enough for me to spend considerable time analyzing and writing about them. While thinking about them, the idea for this book began to form in my mind.

A good soldier is always striving to improve, preparing to take on ever-challenging roles, and learning to lead their subordinates when called upon. That attitude should be something everyone aspires to, regardless of a chosen profession. I'm going to take some liberties and modify the military acronym LDRSHIP by adding two more terms, which are Empathy and Humility. Then I'll attempt to explain "LEDRSHHIP" from my perspective.

It is necessary to share personal experiences with you to accomplish my goal. If you will allow me to slightly alter the English language and make up a word, it is what I refer to as *Snipories*, hence the title of this manuscript. It seems ironic to me that seemingly mundane events which I gave very little or sometimes no thought to, when they occurred, have resulted in small snippets of memory *(snipories)*. My snipories have taught me some treasured and valued lessons which I believe epitomize life's education. All of us have these little stories. It is likely you'll recognize yourself or perhaps others you know as you read some of them.

We have all known the school bully, the boss, or coworker we just can't get along with no matter what we do, experienced the accident that seemed devastating at the time, the unexpected loss of a loved one, or the unfairness of a situation we have lived through. My belief is these events mold us into the person we become. I have *partially* learned what being a Christian and being a leader means because of them.

Let me paraphrase something Dr. Martin Luther King Jr. said. I am not the man I should be or the man I someday will be with the help of Jesus Christ, but thank God I am not the man I once was. Let me remind you, I did say *partially*.

Perhaps you have been out to eat or attended an office party with your spouse and their work colleagues. No doubt you experienced a moment of boredom when your spouse began talking shop with a coworker. Engineers talk about construction projects. Doctors talk about patients and diseases. Teenage boys talk about teenage girls, and teenage girls talk about clothes, makeup, and hairstyles, which is really an excuse to talk about teenage boys.

Brace yourself. I am going to talk about God in this book and not just a little. A Christian talks about God. It's what we do. LEDRSHHIP represents quintessential Christian core values to me. If the word *God* or *Christianity* bothers you, substitute it with LEDRSHHIP. The concepts taught by Christianity and LEDRSHHIP are virtually interchangeable.

I've done some pretty dumb things in my life. You likely have as well, but hopefully you've never done things as stupid as I have. Like the GEICO Insurance commercial used to tell us, "We all do dumb things *(Really? Another acronym? The lizard works for the Government Employees Insurance Company)*." Perhaps one of the dumbest was climbing a water tower on a dare. Fortunately, I didn't kill myself. I'm pretty sure the reason is because God was keeping a close eye on me and protecting me the entire time. I didn't realize how high it was until I got to the top *(FYI, the top of a water tower is really high when you're a twelve-year-old)*. I received a quarter for my efforts which was promptly used to purchase an ice-cream sandwich. I learned from that experience that God protects us, even when we do dumb things.

I also jumped from the roof of a two-story house using an umbrella as a parachute. My brother Robert and I had been watching a movie about combat pilots—*12 O'Clock High*[2] as I recall—forced to parachute from their damaged aircraft. I'll introduce you to the rest of my siblings within the next few pages. We thought we would use an umbrella and pretend to bail out of an airplane. Robert insisted I jump first *(I've always thought Robert was smarter, but don't tell him I admitted it)*. My "parachute" worked perfectly well until I was about halfway to the ground, which is when a chain reaction of events worthy of a Hollywood movie stunt began.

Robert was watching me and concluded jumping off of a roof using an umbrella as a parachute was a perfectly normal and safe thing to do. He jumped right behind me. About the time he jumped, my umbrella turned inside out. The wind pulled it out of my hand. It flew up as Robert was coming down which resulted in a midair collision. While attempting to remove my umbrella from his eye, Robert let go of his own. I landed on the ground, lying on my back with a broken umbrella on top of me. Robert landed on top of me and my umbrella. He was lying on his chest with a broken umbrella on top of him. Everything hurt for a week *(The previously described*

---

[2]   *12 O'Clock High*, film, Release date: December 21, 1949, Screenplay by Henry King, by Sy Bartlett, and Beirne Lay Jr. Produced by Daryl Zanuck, Distributed by Twentieth Century Fox, Based on *12 O'Clock High*, the novel written by Sy Bartlett, and Beirne Lay Jr., 1948.

stunt was performed by children. It was not performed by professionals. Do not attempt.).

We learned several things from the experience. Brothers will follow you, even if you do something stupid, especially if they trust you and it looks fun. The sudden stop when you hit the ground after jumping from the roof of a two-story house can be quite painful. It's a wonder children grow up.

I'm not sure how the two of us weren't hospitalized or impaled. Perhaps God makes kids resilient because he knows how silly they can be. We never told anyone how the umbrellas got mangled, but I'm certain everyone wondered about it for a while. Don't follow your brother unless you know where he is going and are absolutely positive you want to arrive in the same place. Following your brother might get you hurt. In case you missed the inference, we're not really discussing siblings, silly things children do, or umbrellas. Who are you following? Is it your brother when he jumps off the roof? Or is it Jesus? It might look like fun, but umbrellas don't make good parachutes. Take mine and Robert's word for that!

My daughter's birthday is the first of December. Her mother and I knew we were having a daughter and decided on her name before she was born. I used glitter and glue to write her name on her Christmas stocking before she came home. When she arrived, I put her in her Christmas stocking with her name showing and took one of her first pictures. This was before digital cameras and cell phones, when you actually had to use film, mail it off, and wait for your pictures to be developed; even before one-hour photo development stores *(I know that sounds archaic).*

When we received our pictures in the mail, her stocking photograph was adorable. We wanted copies for friends and relatives, but something happened to the negative. We were unable to print additional copies. I attempted to put her back in the stocking to take another picture, but she no longer fit. This all happened between December 1st and Christmas day. If you are a parent, this isn't an Earth-altering shattering news flash. Children grow fast.

I didn't notice the daily change in Magen as my daughter began to grow during her first weeks of life. Upon placing her in the stocking the second time, the difference became more than noticeable. It was dramatic.

To be a Christian leader, to truly serve God, we have to grow spiritually each day. God expects it. He doesn't want us standing still in our relationship with him. It is unlikely we will recognize the daily changes in ourselves, but the changes do happen. Eventually, we become a different person.

> Therefore if anyone is in Christ he is a new creation; the old has gone, the new has come! (2 Corinthians 5:17, NIV)

There is only one story in the Bible about Jesus's childhood. It tells us about when he was twelve years old and got left in the Temple. As a young boy, Jesus was teaching the teachers, and they were amazed at his level of knowledge. His ministry did not begin for another eighteen years at the age of thirty. The Bible is quiet about him for the next eighteen years of his life. With the exception of the Temple story, it doesn't mention anything about his childhood, adolescence, teenage or young adult years. You might conclude this to be strange, but I disagree. There is a single and very short verse in the entire Bible which addresses the time frame.

> And Jesus grew in wisdom and stature, and in favor with God and man. (Luke 2:52, NIV)

The implication is we should realize how critically important it is for us to grow spiritually each day. It was my responsibility to provide for my daughter's physical needs, but I had nothing to do with making her grow or change each day. She didn't either. However, it is our *own* responsibility to work on our spiritual growth and maturity as long as we are allowed to live.

God expected it from Jesus, and he expects it from us. I'm not nearly the same man now that I was when I began writing this book. Don't take my word for that. Ask anyone who knows me. I am not nearly the person I want to be either, but thank you, God, that I am not the person I was. Well said, Dr. King.

Why write my personal life experiences down on a piece of paper and air my dirty laundry in public? I'll answer that question, but first let me eliminate some false assumptions you might have—and clarify what you might believe—about why I am writing this manuscript.

Maybe you're thinking my motivation is to become the author of a bestselling book in order to become wealthy. It would be nice if that happens, but you couldn't be more wrong. As this project begins, I seriously doubt its publication or know what this project will become upon completion.

My hope is a book that can help anyone who chooses to read it, but it's not like there is some great story line in my mind. Many authors have published works, books, poems, or songs, but can't pay the rent. If this should become published and any proceeds come my way as a result, the vast majority of money earned from my efforts will be donated to charity, starting with a van for the children's ministry at First Baptist Church in Zeigler, Illinois. The one currently in service was manufactured in 1983.

Notoriety or fame perhaps? Again, you're absolutely wrong. I don't desire either of those and tend to think of myself as a shy man. However, almost everyone who knows me *(particularly my students)* would likely argue the point.

Am I trying to convince you of something? Sorry, but once again, you are incorrect. You are so far in left field, you can't even see the ballpark. No, I'm not a baseball fan either, but my mother-in-law is a St. Louis Cardinals fan *(actually, she is more like a Cardinals fanatic. Don't tell her I said that. Sorry, Mom)*.

Scare you about the possibility of going to hell? *Puhhleease!* Not even close. Give me a break already. Hell doesn't scare me. It really shouldn't scare anyone. I'll tell you what terrified me for a long time, though. It was the thought of leaving this earth one day and spending an eternity separated from God. You don't believe in God, heaven, hell, or eternity? Let me remind you, I'm not trying to convince you of anything, but let me ask you this question: Are you completely convinced, without any shadow of a doubt, that all there is to this life is the few meager years we're allowed to spend on Earth?

If you really believe that, rob a bank and move to a country without extradition. My suggestion is Russia. What is the point of going to work every day, driving through rain and snowstorms, fighting with the boss who really doesn't seem to care about you, the rude customers who are trying to nickel and dime you to death, the guy who tailgates you or cuts you off in traffic, only to slam on the brakes and turn onto the next street if all we have is the few meaningless years we have on this planet? Why worry about anything except yourself and today? By the time you can retire, you're too old, too sick, too tired, or too feeble to enjoy it. What possible reason is there for considering anyone else? Why bother? Just grab all you can, make it easy on yourself, and damn the consequences.

Let's be straight with each other. We both know you don't believe that. Perhaps you don't want to admit it, but the reality is you know there is more to your existence than the limited amount of time you are privileged to inhabit planet Earth. As you consider those questions, think about one more. If you are wrong, how long do you think eternity will last? It's called eternity for a reason.

I have experienced God in the crimson moonrise casting exquisite colors you cannot imagine over the horizon on a clear cold night from the window of my airplane. I've experienced him in the joyfulness of my life. I've seen his artwork in the perfection of a brilliant rainbow showing the entire color spectrum palate set against the backdrop of a vibrant billowy white cloud carpet below me and a dazzling crystal clear azure sky above me. Pilots call that an undercast. I've felt his presence as I looked down at the vastness, beauty, and perfect symmetry of this majestic earth he created. I saw him in the faces of my children when they were born and heard him in their first cries.

There are several bird feeders in my back yard which can be seen from my kitchen window. We get a lot of songbirds. Occasionally, we spot a red-breasted gross beak or an oriole as they are migrating through. We love to watch the bluebirds, cardinals, blue jays, woodpeckers, titmice, ladder-back woodpeckers, and hummingbirds, not to mention the gold and purple house finch while they eat, play, and splash in the birdbath or perform courtship rituals.

One particular female cardinal has been dubbed "Queen Elizabeth." This breathtaking beautiful bird has a collar of white feathers. It reminds me of a ruffle that completely encircles her neck *(she reminds me more of Judge Judy than Queen Elizabeth)*. The ruffle is about one inch long and perhaps a half inch below her beak.

I see God every time I look out of my kitchen window and realize how much detail and how much variation there is in the design from individual to individual amongst even the smallest of creatures *(just for the record, I'm not calling the Queen of England or Judge Judy a birdbrain)*.

I can smell God in the flowers of the magnolia tree in my backyard and the air after a spring rain. I've felt his presence in the prayers of my friends when ill and the hugs from my family after a trying work day. God speaks to me in the powerful cheerful song of the tiny wren that wakens me in the morning; the gentle and lonesome, yet somehow comforting coo of the dove's cry; and the nearly imperceptible tiny high-pitched squeak of a ruby-throated hummingbird as I sat on my deck and watched the sunlight glint from his iridescent feathers while he hovered close enough to touch while drinking nectar from my feeder. I've tasted God in the saltiness of the air while walking on a beach, listening to powerful waves crash at my feet, and felt him in the wet sand between my toes.

The hymn written by Ms. Barbara Fowler Gaultney entitled "My Lord Is Near Me All the Time" comes to mind.[3] Ms. Gaultney wrote, and I've often sung, "I've seen it in the lightning, heard it in the thunder, and felt it in the rain. My Lord is near me all the time." Her inspiration for that hymn (according to the Baptist hymnal) comes from Psalm 139:7, "Where can I go from your Spirit? Where can I flee from your presence" (NIV)? If you doubt God's existence because you can't see feel hear or talk to him, either you're not looking diligently enough or you're looking in the wrong places.

---

[3] *Baptist Hymnal*, Published by Lifeway Worship, Nashville, TN, 2008.

> Ask and it will be given to you; seek and you
> will find; knock and the door will be opened to
> you. For everyone who asks receives; the one who
> seeks finds; and to the one who knocks, the door
> will be opened. (Matthew 7:7–8, NIV)

Do you remember the song "Looking for Love" made popular by Johnny Lee?[4] Johnny said he was looking for love in all the wrong places. If you look for God in the right places, you will find him.

The school shooting in Marshall County Kentucky happened not far from my home. The local news channel aired interviews with parents whose children attended the school. Every parent interview aired repeated words of a recurring theme. My first thoughts were *Oh my God* or *Thank God my son wasn't hurt* or *We were all praying*.

Who do you think they were they praying to? How many times have you heard a politician or a newscaster say our prayers are with them as they report on some horrific event? Let's make it personal. How many times have you told someone, "I'll be praying for you?" If you don't mean it, then don't say it! Stop reducing God's name to a meaningless platitude!

I recently saw a sign outside of a church which summarizes the idea with distinct clarity. The sign asks, "Is prayer your steering wheel or spare tire?" That sign is actually asking why there are so many part-time Christians who only call on the Almighty God when things go wrong.

How many times have you said, "God bless you" when somebody sneezes? How many times have you sent the text message "OMG?" How many times have you said "Oh my God" when something tragic happens or when you experience an unexpected pleasant surprise? Have you ever said, "I swear to God," "Oh my Gosh," or even worse, taken God's name in vain?

I was out eating dinner one evening. There was an elderly couple seated across from me at the restaurant. As they were getting up

---

[4] "Lookin' for Love," Artist Johnny Lee, Album Urban Cowboy, Written by Wanda Mallette, Bob Morrison, and Patti Ryan, Asylum Records, 1980.

and leaving, they walked past my table. He said something which couldn't be heard, and she replied, "Thank God he didn't." News flash, sports fans. That is taking God's name in vain. When someone uses God's name flippantly, it is physically painful to me. I grimaced upon hearing her comment.

Tell me if any of these expressions sound familiar to you. "That was a hell of a party;" "I just ate a hell of a meal;" "I've had a hell of a day;" "Let's get the hell out of Dodge;" "What the hell are you doing;" "What the hell are you talking about;" "How the hell did you do that;" "Where the hell are you going;" The _____ (fill in the blank with the name of your favorite sports team) are having a hell of a year." That one confuses me. Does it mean good or bad news? Now be honest with yourself. How many of these have you said without thinking about them? What you're really doing is using the word *hell* as an adjective.

Flippant minimization of the awfulness and the severe punishment that awaits unbelievers along with the eternity of hell won't change the inevitability of its existence. It is what it is. Have you noticed? No one ever says, "Where the heaven are you going? What the heaven do you mean? Or what the heaven did you say?" Why do you never hear "that scared the heaven out of me?" Thank you very much, but I'd rather not have the heaven scared out of me. Thank you, Pastor Larry. Your message was well-received.

If you are telling yourself God isn't real and you don't believe in him, then you're lying to yourself. If you genuinely believe heaven and hell aren't real, once again, you are lying to yourself. I tell you bluntly, straight up, without apologizing for my words and without pulling punches—you are full of it. That is nothing but hubris.

I challenge you to look up the definition of the word. You might find the meaning surprising. It doesn't work both ways. Stop telling yourself half-truths. Now would be a good time to start. The problem is that a half-truth is a whole lie. At the very least, you are telling yourself a lie by omission. A lie by omission is worse than a lie by intention.

Let's assume you start dating someone and the relationship looks promising, but you have some type of sexually transmitted disease. Perhaps you have a child from a former relationship or maybe served a little time for a mistake you made in your past. Would it be acceptable to not inform them? Would you want to be the uninformed party? That's a lie by omission.

Although I've not read it and don't know what it is about, I'll borrow the title from a book written by Judge Judith Sheindlin. The title speaks volumes and fits this discussion well: *Don't Pee on My Leg and Tell Me It's Raining.*[5] Stop lying to yourself. God is real and you know it.

If you are still adamant about it, if you still insist you don't believe in God, try this. Quit referring to him right now and do it cold turkey. Strike the words *heaven, God,* and *Jesus* from your vocabulary. My money says you can't do it, because God created you to praise him!

> Bring my sons from afar and my daughters
> from the ends of the earth, everyone who is called
> by my name, whom I created for my glory, whom
> I formed and made. (Isiah 43:7, NIV)

That isn't the half of it. God created everything for his Glory.

> Some of the Pharisees in the crowd said to
> Jesus, "Teacher, rebuke your disciples!" I tell you,
> he replied, "If they keep quiet, the stones will cry
> out." (Luke 19:40 NIV)

Why are there so many crosses on the side of the road? Pick any highway, take a drive, and take a look. Go into any cemetery and notice the grave markers you find there. Count the crosses you see on headstones. It seems the number of funerals I must attend increases exponentially with my age, and someone always says something like, "Thank God, at least they are in a better place." I've never heard any-

---

[5]   "Don't Pee on My Leg and Tell Me It's Raining," Judith Sheindlin, Harper Perennial, Harper Collins Publishers, New York, NY., Feb. 7, 1996.

one say, "Thank Satan, at least they are in a worse place." I seriously doubt you've ever heard anyone say that either.

The assumption is going to heaven is automatic. Sorry to burst your bubble, folks, but it just doesn't work that way. If you don't believe, you don't get a ticket on the glory-bound train. The greatest lie is the lie you tell yourself. My money says you can't strike the word *hell* from your vocabulary either.

Here is the problem. God expects to be your 100 percent. He expects to be everything to you. He expects your complete attention and uncompromising devotion. Gentlemen, if you were to tell your wives, "Honey, I love you. I will be faithful to you and I will be responsible. I will pay the bills, cut the grass every week, take care of you if you get sick, make sure your car is serviced when it needs to be, help with the laundry, housecleaning, and cooking. I will make sure everything at home is maintained and working properly. If the washer in the sink faucet leaks or if the toilet tank fill valve needs to be replaced, I'll take care of it *(I just replaced the toilet tank fill valve for the second time this week. The first one was faulty, and I didn't keep the receipt. Go figure).* You can count on me to take care of your every need and be everything a husband should be 364 days out of the year. But on one day of the year, I'm not going to come home because I'll be spending the night with another woman." What if you told her you'll only be gone on February 29th? After all, that's only one night every four years.

Do you think she would be happy with that? Do you think you could reasonably expect to stay married? My wife expects 100 percent devotion with no reservations, no compromise, and no exceptions. When I tell my wife I love her, the implication is she expects me to love her with my wallet, my time, my energy, my mind, my effort, my affection, my devotion, and your wives expect the same thing. She expects it all. All of it belongs to her.

In return, you should expect the same thing from her. If I'm not willing to give our relationship every fiber of myself, then she wants nothing to do with me. It's all or nothing. Before we married, she told me, "I don't share." Those feelings are justified. Why then would you think God is happy being second?

What if I told my wife, "I'll give all of myself to you every day, without fail, 24/7, 365 days a year, no matter what, but I don't like to talk? Don't expect me to discuss anything with you unless I want something or have a problem. Operate on the assumption no news is good news. If I've had a bad day at work, I'll fill you in. When my plans are to go to a movie with friends, I'll inform you. If I need something from the store, like deodorant or shampoo, I'll ask you. Otherwise, don't expect me to talk to you."

It seems unlikely that I'd be enjoying many anniversary dinners. That may sound ludicrous, but the way we often treat God isn't any different. How often do you really pray? Is it just when you're sick or want a new job? Is it only when you're worried about the children because they are out a little past curfew? God expects to hear from you every day. He loves you and wants you to talk to him. You can't have a relationship without communication. It just won't work.

Atheists don't inhabit foxholes, and I've spent time in a few of them. Do you really expect me to believe that, in times of trouble, you have never called on him? Once again, quit lying to yourself. He won't accept your calling on him only when you're having problems any more than your wife or husband will tolerate you talking only when a challenging situation presents itself. Be honest with yourself. Regardless, it is your choice to believe or disbelieve, but "As for me and my house, we will serve the Lord" (Joshua 24:15, NIV).

By now, you're likely in one of two camps. Either you're intrigued and want to find out more or you're about ready to give up and throw this book in the trash. You may be thinking, *What a waste of money. If I want to hear a sermon, I'll go to church.* Before you put the book down, let's try an exercise. I've given you the acronym LEDRSHHIP. I'll list each word in bold print with some space on the page.

Loyalty
Empathy
Duty
Respect
Selfless Service
Honor

Humility
Integrity
Personal Courage

Now go get a pencil, pen, magic-marker, highlighter, or a tube of lipstick. I don't care what you use; just get something you can write with. I'll wait. No, really, go get a pen. Do it. This is important. Obtain a writing implement of some type. Use eyeliner or a grease pencil. Anything will do. Don't read any further until you have done so.

Ready? Now you're prepared for the next step.

Think about somebody you really love. It might be a spouse, a parent, a child, or a friend. If they are sitting next to you, look at their face for a moment. Take some time and really look at it! If they aren't close by, then close your eyes for a moment and think about what they look like. Think about what they do for you, how important they are to you, what this person means to you. Pause a moment and really think about them.

Now imagine your life without them. Take some time and imagine how different your life would be if they were suddenly no longer a part of your world. It's scary, isn't it? Now for step three. If there is a word in the LEDRSHHIP list this person doesn't expect from you, circle it. It is highly improbable you circled even one of those words.

Now we're ready for the last step. Regardless of what you believe about Jesus, we both know you've heard about him. You might not believe he is who he claims to be, but you're familiar with the stories about miracles, the virgin birth, the cross, and resurrection. Knowing what you know about Jesus the man, not Jesus the Son of God, take one more look at the list. Circle every word in the list that Jesus the man exhibited. Yup, you circled every word, didn't you? I can't think of a better example of a leader than Jesus. Can you? If so, this book probably isn't for you.

Do you still want to put the book down? If so, don't throw it in the trash. You paid for it, so give it to someone instead. But please do me a favor first. Are you still the same person today that you were five years ago? Do you think the same way? Are the same things still important to you? Or have your priorities changed somewhat?

Wait five years and then start reading it again. If you get this far on your next attempt and still don't like it, then give this book to someone else. You probably need it more than the person you end up giving it to, but you will never realize that; so somebody else might as well get some use out of it.

Am I trying to get you to come to church? Read or believe in the Bible? Change the way you live, perhaps? Convert you? Not me! Nope! That isn't my job, but I do have a job to do. The Holy Spirit has charged me with a responsibility, which is to deliver his message. No, I'm not special. I don't have some divine gift of prophecy. I am far from being a saint or anything like that. The truth is I am often ashamed of myself and my behavior.

Please don't assume arrogance on my part either. What I speak of is not just my responsibility, far from it. It is the responsibility of every Christian. So what message are we discussing? Well, in short, it is a little something called Roman's Road. I promise to tell you all about it as you read through this manuscript, opinion paper, elongated diary, book, or whatever it becomes by the time it is finished. The last three words of the previous sentence were purposefully chosen for a specific reason. If you don't already know what that is, then see if you can figure it out.

Before you put this book down and decide to dismiss what I'm saying as the senseless and meaningless ramblings of one more inept, maniacal, religious quack, please keep in mind that there is much more than Christianity involved with these ideas. I'm attempting to clue you in to some very basic leadership characteristics which can drastically improve your life. We're discussing basic proven core building blocks which can change your future and enhance your success. If you say you're not a Christian and don't believe in God, I've got it. What I am saying is still meaningful. It can still help you.

However, if you discover that you have a heavy heart after reading this *(I earnestly pray you do)*, it isn't my fault. I didn't do it. Hand down the not guilty verdict right now! Of course, there are many things of which I am guilty, things in my past about which I'm terribly embarrassed of and shamed by. You already know that, but aren't you right there with me?

Let me warn you. This book is not all champagne, caviar *(not that I've ever tasted caviar)*, sunshine, and sweet-smelling fragrant rose petals. Some of what you are going to read here smells like what might come out of the southern end of a northern bound male bovine. I'll not reveal every terrible thing I have ever done, because I'm too ashamed, but you can expect complete honesty about what I do reveal. You will hear about the beautiful and the ugly on these pages, starting with some sincere heart-wrenching regrets.

Let me tell you what I most regret about my life. For this to make sense, you need to understand a little more about my childhood than I've already told you. I grew up with five siblings. In the order of birth, first came my oldest sister, Carolyn, the artist of the family and whose illustration graces the cover of this book, followed next by my sister, Jerry. I am the third child and first boy.

Robert came next. You've already met him; he jumped off of a roof with me. James was the fifth child, and he is the comedian of the family. He and I were visiting Carolyn recently, and she was showing us her latest painting which is stunning. James told her, "Sis, that is some serious paint by numbers." He inherited dad's ability to "spin a yarn."

Lastly, the sixth child, my youngest sister was born. She has requested to not be mentioned in this book, so I'll honor her request and not reveal her name or confidences.

Professionally, Mom was a school teacher but a stay-at-home mother while we were growing up. Mom and Dad were both devoted Christians and loved all of their children. They did things in their parental role with which I didn't agree, but what child agrees with everything their parents do?

While we were children, all of us accepted Jesus Christ as our Savior. There is nothing more important than that when parents reflect upon the accomplishments of their children. Dad baptized each of us and performed marriage ceremonies for Carolyn and Jerry. Together, my parents raised six children on the salary of a staff sergeant. I've no idea how they did that. I've experienced what it feels like to live on a staff sergeant's salary.

It is even more impressive that we never went without clean clothes, a warm coat when we needed it, a roof over our head, or food on the table. Our shoes were never too small and they never had holes in them. When they no longer fit, my shoes and my clothes became the property of Robert and eventually were passed down to James. There might have only been rice and beans on the table, perhaps with some cornbread, and I'm positive I ate a mountain of oatmeal over the years, but there was always something to eat *(for some strange reason, I no longer eat oatmeal)*. Somehow, the electricity, rent, and telephone bills were always paid. They may have been behind a few times *(several times, actually)*, but the utilities were never turned off.

We always had toys and gifts under the Christmas tree, and not a single one of us ever went without a birthday present. Were it not for Robert and Maggie Young, our grandparents, a.k.a. Nanny and Papa, that would likely not have been the case, but we didn't know that at the time; a child doesn't know why Santa Claus didn't stop by and visit but is keenly aware of his absence.

Dad took us fishing and hunting, taught us how to garden, taught us how to change the oil in a car, change a flat tire, and helped *(meaning we watched him a lot)* us build our pinewood derby cars for Cub Scouts. Somehow, our cars always looked better than our competitors, and even better, we always seemed to win our races.

Mom taught my sisters how to sew, cook, fix their hair, use makeup, and all the other things a girl needed to know *(don't ask me what that is; I'm not trying to be chauvinistic here, it's just that I'm not a girl and I grew up in the 60s when the world was much different)*. We took turns reading the Bible aloud every night before bedtime. It was exciting taking turns to read to everyone each night. We said grace and ate dinner together every evening as a family. That was an incredible accomplishment for a family of eight living on the pittance my father earned.

As the "First Lady" of the Church, Mom always had things to take care of, because the army tends to keep their soldiers rather busy *(that is another thing I learned from experience)*. Mom had committee meetings to attend, activities to coordinate, after-school programs, church members to visit. Then there was Sunday school, Sunday morning services, Sunday evening services, Wednesday night prayer meetings, vacation Bible school, and a myriad of other things she had to attend to. The list never seemed to end.

It often felt as if we were living in a fishbowl. We had to be the example of examples. We were expected to be the epitome of what a well-behaved child should be. We couldn't get our clothes dirty, couldn't curse, couldn't eat without saying grace, couldn't go out on a date, couldn't dance, couldn't go to the movies or stop at the store on Sunday, couldn't stay up past bedtime (10:00 p.m.) even on Friday or Saturday night, and couldn't watch the *Wonderful World of Disney*[6] because that would cause us to be late for Sunday evening service *(this, of course, was pre-VCR, much less a DVD or telephone answering machine. Do you remember the 8-track?).*

We couldn't this, couldn't that, couldn't, couldn't, couldn't—*Arrgh!* The problem is all of the "couldn'ts" turned me into a huge "wouldn't." The irony is that today, I cannot even begin to tell you how grateful I am and how many times I've been to my knees, thanking my creator for all of the "couldn'ts" I experienced in my childhood.

Your "couldn'ts" turned you into a "wouldn't?" Yes, I know what you're thinking. First of all, turning "couldn'ts" into "wouldn'ts" *(my spellchecker, grammar checker, and whoever I can talk to into editing this is probably really angry with me right now)* makes no sense grammatically; and secondly, what is this fruitcake even talking about? Is he nuts? Did he fall out of a coconut tree and conk his head really hard *(sorry, but I happen to like coconut and had to figure out a way to get the word in here somehow. Robert bet me that I couldn't do it. After all, coconut isn't a word that normally comes up in the average conversation. You lose, Robert)?*

---

[6] *Walt Disney's Wonderful World of Color*, TV series 9/24/1961 through 1969 broadcast by NBC original premiered in 1954 as Walt Disney's Disneyland, broadcast by ABC.

You are likely correct on both counts, but allow me to explain. It is highly probable that I'm nuts and conked my head at some point *(it isn't unusual for someone to tell me my head is as hard as a brick)*. As a child, I felt like religion was forced upon me. It isn't that I didn't believe. It's more like I reached the point where it wasn't fun anymore. It became tiresome and boring. It felt like I spent more time in church while growing up than in school. I joined the army at the age of eighteen. My primary reason was to get away from home. Basic training began September 16, 1974, three weeks after my eighteenth birthday.

The day I left home is the day I turned my back on my God. I wouldn't go to church, wouldn't read my Bible, wouldn't think about anyone except myself, wouldn't worry about the morality of my actions, wouldn't consider other people's feelings—wouldn't, wouldn't, wouldn't. Then I married a Jewish atheist *(What? Isn't that the absolute epitome of an oxymoron? I still don't understand how someone could claim that. It even puts the concept of military intelligence to shame. Military intelligence is spending a week outside in north Wisconsin on a field training exercise when the high temperature for the day is -9 in order to acclimate yourself to a desert environment)*. The marriage didn't last because it was doomed from the beginning.

> Be ye not unequally yoked together with unbelievers: for what fellowship hath righteousness with unrighteousness? And what communion hath light with darkness? (2 Corinthians 6:14)

I also chose her to become the mother of my two children. Now here comes the terrible tragedy. The thing in my life which I regret most is this: I wouldn't raise my children in a Christian home. I wouldn't insist on taking them to church. I wouldn't tell them about God. I wouldn't be the Christian father every child deserves to have. I wouldn't ask God for guidance as I made my decisions in life starting with one of the most important I could possibly make, that being who I chose to marry.

Now my children are grown and making their own way. I no longer have any influence on them, *and it hurts!* It never gets better. I pray and pray and pray and pray some more. Then I pray again.

My children don't believe in God. I sent them both a Bible for Christmas a few years ago. Not just any Bible, but a very nice study Bible—illustrated, red-letter edition, gold leaf pages, indexed, tabbed, great footnotes, their name embossed on the leather cover, Concordance, study index, daily reading suggestions, a nice Bible by all accounts. My daughter asked me why I sent it to her. *Man! That cut me to the core!* My children are not Christians, they are lost, *and it hurts!*

My daughter was living with her mother at the time. She moved and left her Bible, *and it hurts!* She said she didn't need it or want it, *and that hurt even more!* My children turned their back on God because I did, *and it hurts!* So I write these words to myself as much as I write them to you, and as I read them, *it hurts!* By the way, did I mention knowing that I'm responsible grieves me every day of my life? The pain never goes away and it never ends. *It hurts!*

If you are a Christian, please do me a favor. Stop reading right now and say a prayer for my children, Magen and Jarred. Pray that the Holy Spirit would move in them and convict them, that they would feel his presence, and that they would come to know the saving grace of our Lord Jesus Christ. Please pray for their salvation. If you are a Christian parent, you must know the anguish, the agony, the incredible sadness and guilt I feel—all courtesy of my wouldn'ts. If you are reading this and have not accepted Jesus as your savior, I pray for you, because you're who I am writing these words for. No, I am not trying to convert you. Let me repeat that, it is important—I am not trying to convert you. Like I said before, that isn't my job. My job is just to deliver the message. When you don't like the message, you don't shoot the messenger.

God is real.

Really real!

Spooky real!

The real reason I'm writing this is I want you to know how real God is. You may scoff at the thought, and it's your right. You might even be thinking to yourself something like, *Who has time for God? I'm too busy. It is impossible for me to fit God into the confusing equation of my life.*

The thing is, like it or not, He is already working in your life. It doesn't matter if you believe in him or not. Have you ever been in love *(or perhaps had a deep like)* with someone that didn't return your feelings? Most everyone has experienced a relationship like this. I'll bet that from time to time, you still think about them.

In my case, that would be Marilyn R. She was my first high school crush. She fell for my cousin. To make it worse, he was living with us at the time and knew I liked her *(isn't there supposed to be something like a guy code? What was up with that, Charles Wayne?)* My consolation is he didn't end up with her either, but she did go to the prom with me. Of course, that turned out to be an embarrassing fiasco because "it was against my religion to dance." Sorry, Marilyn.

Just because this person didn't return your feelings, did that stop you from wondering about them? Caring about them? Perhaps you still worry about them. You still likely want them to have their desires and be happy. Well, news flash, sports fans, God loves you. I want you to go back and read that sentence again. Okay, I know you didn't do it, no problem. I'll wait.

I'm still waiting. That is why you see the large blank space. Go back and read that sentence again. I'm patient, I'll wait again.

All right, let's continue. God loves you *(Ha! Got you. You read it again anyway! Sorry about being redundant; well, not really, because I'm trying to make a point here).* My point is a simple one. God *reeeeaaally* loves you. It doesn't matter if you believe in him or not. He still loves you. He still wants you to be happy. He still worries about you. He still cares about what happens to you.

Let me tell you something amazing, something which redefines the word *incredible*. Something that is unfathomable. God loves you so much that he works in your life when you don't want him to, even if you don't love him, even if you don't believe in him, even if you don't trust him, even when you turn your back on Him, and even when you ignore Him. He still wants you to be happy, because no matter what, he always has and always will love you. I found that out. I've experienced it. He has never broken a single promise He ever made. He never will.

He has made you some pretty big promises too. He is always there. He is always ready to help you, no matter how terrible or how wonderful your life may be at any particular moment. All I really want to accomplish is to convey what living as a Christian *(remember, if you have a problem with the word* Christian, *substitute it with the word* leader *here)* means to me. I want you to understand it from my perspective. More importantly, I want to remind myself of what being a Christian is about.

I have been a Christian since the age of eleven. I rededicated my life to the service of Jesus a little over ten years ago. Proverbs 22:6 says, "Train a child in the way he should go. When he is old, he will not turn away from it" (NIRV).

My life is proof of this verse. God's word is true. Every single bit of it. Choose to doubt if you desire. Did I mention that my job is only to deliver the message? Even though I often fall short of the mark, I've finally reached the point in my life where living each and every day as a Christian to the best of my ability has become my primary goal.

Telling you I'm a Christian isn't something stated with a callous, lackadaisical attitude. It isn't something claimed for popularity's sake, using a laisse faire attitude because everyone claims to be *(if you don't believe almost everyone claims to be a Christian, just ask your neighbor if they are)*. Give me a break already. Did you buy presents for your family this past Christmas? You are probably still working on paying off the credit cards you used. Did you get a present? Did you work that day? If you did, I'm sure you complained but didn't give back the overtime pay. Who do you think Christmas is about anyway? Just look at how the word is spelled. Yes, many claim to be Christians, but that doesn't mean they really are.

What about Easter? Did you buy an Easter basket for your children? Did you dye boiled eggs with them? Did you purchase a chocolate rabbit or a stuffed toy for them, perhaps new clothes? Have you been living in the woods, cut off from all civilization without access to a TV, cell phone, or newspaper for your entire life? Who are you trying to convince? Me or yourself?

Christmas isn't about camping out overnight on the sidewalk in front of your local electronics store on Thanksgiving so you can be first in the line in order to purchase a new flat screen TV at a discounted price. It isn't about racking up credit card debt that dwarfs the elevation of Mt. Fuji so you can get everyone in your family some overpriced trinket. That happiness is temporary at best. It usually lasts about as long as the wrapping paper. Easter isn't about boiled eggs or chocolate rabbits. I know it, and you know it. Let's get real here. We both know you have heard about God.

Claiming to be a Christian isn't something I say without careful thought and consideration. I don't claim to follow Jesus in order to be an instigator or make myself unpopular because someone else says they don't. It isn't something I say because it is popular. Being a Christian is much more than that to me. It is intrinsic to the very core of my being. It is not only what I am, it is who I am. Being a Christian is also quintessential to the LEDRSHHIP values of this manuscript. The two cannot be separated. If you can determine how to do that, shoot me an e-mail.

I came through life on the common road that almost everyone travels. I refer to the University of Hard Knocks. The curriculum at UHK teaches life isn't fair. It underscores that no matter how hard you try, some will have more and some will have less. Please don't misunderstand. I seek no sympathy, because my life is amazing. I am loved by my God, my wife, and my children.

Speaking of being loved by my wife, allow me to drift slightly off-course here. Gentlemen, let me tell you the secret to a happy marriage. You only need to remember and follow three very simple rules:

1) No matter what your wife says, respond with, "Yes, dear."
2) Never make your wife cry.

3) If you find that your wife is crying, ask her what she wants and then refer to rule #1.

Don't tell your wives you're in on this secret. This is how the three rules work. Perhaps your wife says she would like a new refrigerator or possibly a new range. Maybe she says she wants to go on a nice vacation. Say, "Yes, dear," and get her what she wants. If that means you need to work overtime, then do it.

Let's say she wants a new car or an entirely new kitchen remodel. Since you can't afford it, you might not remember rule #1. You might say, "I can't do that. Honey, I'm sorry, but we can't possibly afford that right now." Now she starts to cry, so you find yourself at rule #3. Ask what she wants. If she still wants a new car, get a second job and say, "Yes, dear."

Should three rules be too many for you to recall, let me give you an alternate "set of rules." They are easier to remember than the first set, because there are only two of them.

1. Your wife is always right, no exceptions.
2. Should there be any argument, discussion, or confusion— regardless of its nature or the reason for it—refer to rule #1.

The three rules *(or two, if you prefer)* contain a significant implication for LEDRSHHIP. If you want that next promotion or next pay raise, then no matter what your boss asks, say, "Yes, boss." Never disappoint your boss. Should you disappoint your boss, ask what he/she wants, and then say, "Yes, boss."

At my retirement party, one of the things my boss said about me was how grateful he had been to have me work for him, because no matter what he asked, he could depend on me to do it without question. That was truly a proud moment of my life. Jesus only needed the first rule to change the entire world. He always said, "Yes, Father."

I live in the greatest country on earth. I have a beautiful home that is paid for and comfortably furnished, I have minimal debt, I am healthy, and I eat well. Sometimes I eat too well because my wife is a wonderful cook, and my willpower leaves something to be desired *(my weight and the size of my belly both attest to this).* I have an excellent formal education which I worked hard to obtain. It has provided me with a feeling of accomplishment and the skills which allow me to provide a comfortable lifestyle for my family.

I finally was able to buy my first new Cadillac *(Sometimes I get to drive it, and I get to make the payment on it every month. That is likely the case for most married men).* My wife and I usually go on vacation twice a year, and I'm not talking about visiting relatives. That isn't a vacation. I have walked on the beach of both US coastlines.

But I've not visited the Louvre, Eiffel Tower, Vatican, Hawaii, or seen the French Riviera. I haven't gazed in wonder at the ceiling of the Sistine Chapel. It is extremely unlikely I'll ever have the opportunity to visit these landmarks, because I lack the financial ability. However, there is a key ring with an Eiffel Tower fob and a coffee mug in my office that says Hawaii on it.

These are souvenirs given to me by my students. They were able to travel to these places because of the training I was able to provide them. It really doesn't bother me that my eyes will never see these places. Of course, it would be nice to visit them, but they're not important to me. My final destination is a place called heaven. It makes Paris, Rome, Japan, Hawaii, the Hoover Dam, and the Grand Canyon—any place you can think of—look like a slum.

Here's the thing, though. Everything I have has all been a gift. They are gifts I worked hard to obtain but gifts nonetheless. Make no mistake here. God doesn't expect you to sit around all day with your hand held out. He helps those who help themselves. He expects you to work. In verse 10 of the third chapter of his second letter to the Thessalonian church, Paul phrased it like this: "We gave you a rule. We said anyone who will not work will not eat" (NIRV).

Don't get caught up in thinking merely about the physical aspect of work here either. Paul is also talking about the spiritual aspect of work.

As the ancient proverb says, "Give a man a fish and you feed him for a day; but teach him to fish, and you feed him for a lifetime."

James was Jesus's earthly brother. He grew up in the same house with him. Interestingly enough, James didn't believe Jesus was who he claimed to be either; at least, not at first. In Chapter 1 verse 17, James tells us, "Every good and perfect gift is from God. It comes down from the Father" (NIRV). That verse is displayed on a plaque in my kitchen for a reason. It's why when people ask me, "How are you?" my standard stock response, which never varies, sometimes to the chagrin of those who know me best *(particularly my pastor),* is, "Blessed by God and smart enough to know it." There are people in my church who are thinking about getting a T-shirt made with that printed on it.

Let me be honest, though. When I look around and see those who have accomplished more than I have—when I see someone who has a larger home, perhaps a newer car, maybe their children are more successful than mine, or a seemingly endless list of things I'd like to have—I sometimes begin to feel sorry for myself. At times, it is difficult to even remember the tenth commandment, much less obey it.

Exodus 20:17 (NIRV) says, "Do not long for anything that belongs to your neighbor. Do not long for your neighbor's house, wife, male or female servant, ox or donkey *(this could be interpreted in today's society as a car, I suppose, because I don't know very many people who ride a donkey to work, but the gas mileage would likely be pretty good).*" I have much to be grateful for, but it is difficult some-times for me to remember things are just things. It is difficult for me to remember that "whoever loves money never has money enough; whoever loves wealth is never satisfied with his income" (Ecclesiastes 5:10, NIV).

The day will come when we will all leave this earth. We won't take any of our things with us. Our days are numbered. Things will no longer matter. I think the best kept secret to finding happiness is not getting what you want but wanting what you have. In Philippians 4:11–12, Paul said, "I know what it is to be in need, and I know what it is to have plenty. I have learned the secret of being content in any and every situation, whether well fed or hungry, whether living in plenty or in want. I have learned to be content whatever the circum-stance" (NIV).

Henry David Thoreau once said, "The cost of a thing is the amount of what I call life, which is required to be exchanged for it, immediately or in the long run." I believe it is important to think about Mr. Thoreau's advice when we start thinking about things we might want. If I want a new car, I can go get one. Do I want a bigger house? That isn't a problem either. My credit rating is exceptional and I can buy anything I want *(the problem is paying for it)*.

It takes a long time for me to cut the lawn *(weeds are a more accurate description)* of my five-acre yard. I would like to have a tractor. It would be nice to spend more time enjoying my yard than working in it. The linoleum in my kitchen needs to be replaced. It is pitted beneath the refrigerator. There are scratches all over it. I could take money from savings and get a new floor right now if I want or make a down payment on a tractor, but then those funds would no longer be available. We might need them tomorrow for something more important.

The real question is, do I want to make the sacrifice of working longer hours or perhaps getting a second job to pay for whatever the "thing" is which I might be enamored by at the moment? I suppose it depends on how much we want the thing, whatever it might be.

I really enjoy being retired. It took a long time for me to get to that point in my life. It is really nice to know that the only time I have to set my alarm is to get up in time to make it to church or the occasional doctor's appointment, both of which seem to be the extent of my social life. I relish the increased amount of time I'm allowed to enjoy my family's company and the opportunity to sit on my deck watching the birds at my feeder every day. Being retired is everything it's cracked up to be and more.

Don't expect me to go get another job in order to have a tractor or new floor. I'll eventually get those things. My student loans will soon be paid off *(yes, you read that correctly; learning to fly is expensive)*. Then I'll be able to make payments on new flooring. My truck will soon be paid off as well. When it is, I'll be able to afford tractor payments. It's called patience. The tradeoff for having the things I want right now simply isn't worth the price of my time which they would require.

Yes, that was a very long introduction. That is why the title of this chapter is introduction and more. Let me make it up to you. Like this sentence, the next chapter is short. Be warned though, Chapter 5 makes up for it.

"L"

Loyalty

> Loyalty isn't grey. It's black and white. You're
> either loyal completely or not loyal at all.
>
> —Shamay

Let me begin this chapter with an open-ended question. Think of it as fodder for thought. What do you believe the difference is between loyalty and love? As you consider the answer to that question, consider this also. How many people pray for the purpose of giving thanks for what God has given them, to ask for forgiveness of sin, to ask God to help those in need, to shelter us from Satan, or for guidance and direction?

Compare the answer to this question: How many pray for the primary purpose of asking God for favors, more things, material possessions that don't matter, or to get them out of a problematic situation which is really just another way of asking for a favor? "I'm in trouble again, God. Can you help me out, please?" Shouldn't the focus of prayer be thankfulness, forgiveness, guidance, and being shown how you can do something to help those in need instead of asking for another useless trinket?

Consider these questions as you read this paraphrased story by Mark Horton. A man and his dog were walking along a road when he suddenly remembered dying and that the dog walking with him had been dead for several years. They came to a high, white marble wall. There was a beautiful arch glowing in the sunlight with a magnificent gate which looked like a giant pearl. The street leading to the gate was pure gold.

As they walked toward the gate, he saw a man sitting behind a desk next to it. He said, "Excuse me, please, where are we?"

"Heaven, sir," the man answered.

"Would you happen to have some water?" the traveler asked."

"Of course, sir, come in and I'll have some ice water brought up." He gestured, and the gate opened.

Pointing to his dog, he asked, "Can my friend come in too?"

"I'm sorry, sir, we don't accept pets."

The traveler turned back and went on his way with the dog. Soon the paved road gave way to gravel, then dirt, and then became progressively narrower, and eventually a narrow winding trail. Soon afterward, the traveler saw a rusty old gate which was open. The odd thing is there was no fence anywhere around. But a man was leaning against a tree by the gate. "Excuse me, please, do you have any water?"

"Yeah, sure, there's a pump over there." The man pointed to a place that couldn't be seen from outside the gate. "Come on in."

"How about my friend here?" the traveler asked.

"There's a bowl by the pump," answered the man.

The man and his dog went through the gate and saw an old-fashioned hand pump with a bowl beside it. The traveler filled the bowl, offered his dog a drink, and took one himself. Then the traveler and his dog walked back to the man by the tree.

"What do you call this place?" the traveler asked.

"Heaven," the man answered.

"That's confusing. The man down the road said that was heaven," the traveler replied.

"Oh, you mean the place with the gold streets and pearly gates? Nope, that's hell."

"Doesn't it make you mad for them to use your name like that?" asked the traveler.

"No! I can see how you might think that, but we're happy they screen out the folks who'll leave their best friends behind."

You may find the story strange, but the meaning is incredibly poignant. Joe Mehl said, "The only people I owe my loyalty to are those who have never made me question theirs." Loyalty is being faithful in allegiance to one's government, to a cause, country, group, or person.[7] I would add devoted to the definition. The difference between the real heaven and hell are most definite, but in Mr. Horton's story, you have to decide which is which. The answer in the story is debatable, and perhaps that is the point our author is attempting to make.

My interpretation of the story's moral is loyalty to the wrong cause is usually worse than being disloyal to the right one. Misplaced loyalty can be catastrophic and take you down a road that you just don't want to travel on. The difficulty with loyalty is you have to decide who or what you want to be loyal to.

I am loyal to my God, my family, my country, my friends, my employer—all in that order. The order of your loyalties may be different than mine are, and that is your decision to make. Regardless of how you prioritize them, nothing should ever trump your loyalty to God. He paid a terrible price for you, and your first loyalty should never be questionable. "You shall have no other Gods before me" (Exodus 20:3, NIV) is rather direct. In case you missed it, that isn't a request. Anything you place in front of your loyalty to God becomes an idol. It becomes a god.

Dependent on the circumstances, you might have to temporarily adjust the order of your remaining loyalties. Let me give you an example. I once managed a fast-food restaurant. James needed a job, so I hired him. He thought he was "in" with the boss and began to not show up for work. He wouldn't call to explain and wouldn't answer his phone when I called him. I couldn't determine the reason for the behavior. You will read a letter from him later in this book which explains it, so I won't "let the cat out of the bag."

---

[7] *The Merriam-Webster Dictionary*, Merriam-Webster Inc., Springfield MA., 1997.

The result was I had to fire him. It was heartbreaking for both of us. James was so angry that he didn't speak to me for several years. For a while, none of my siblings would either. Eventually, we all got beyond it. I had to place my loyalty for my employer in front of the loyalty I have for my brother, and I can't begin to explain how difficult that was.

Today, James and his wife each have their own businesses. They are financially successful and a positive influence on many lives. He attributes much of his success to the day his brother fired him.

Should you have the opportunity to discuss this with him, he'll tell you he learned one of the most valuable lessons of his life as a result. Eventually, he told me that because of that experience, he learned to do what is right regardless of circumstances, nothing in life is free, and hard work is worthwhile. My gift was the realization that sometimes you have to make hard choices, and when you make the difficult choice in good faith and for the right reasons, you'll be admired for standing by your principles. Expect a long rough road before you get there.

As a result of being loyal to the right cause, at the right time, you'll influence countless lives in ways you can't possibly imagine. If you will allow me to quote from Paul again, in 2 Corinthians 8:21, he says, "For we are taking pains to do what is right, not only in the eyes of the Lord but also in the eyes of man" (NIV).

When you are loyal to deserving causes, you needn't tell anyone. The content of your character will speak for you. Occasionally you will be fortunate enough to be blessed by seeing how your actions and influence have affected someone else. That happened for me with James, but it isn't the only time I've experienced it.

Just before I retired, a letter from one of my former students arrived. I had worked with her several years before but one student's face blends into the next one. I had completely forgotten her. After thirty years of teaching and seeing student after student come and go, you just can't remember them all. This young lady wrote to tell me she would be pursuing an advanced degree and to thank me for being a positive spiritual influence in her life. Something she said in her letter touched me. This is what she wrote:

As I have reflected over these few years of ministry, I wrestled with the idea of home. My home is in Chicago where I can walk out of my door and see Sears Tower watching over my city. Home was also SIUC for six years where I followed Jesus and encountered him as Father and friend. Home is parts of Michigan where I spent summers with God in worship, scripture, and community. Home is parts of St. Louis where I learned God's desire for reconciliation and design for culture and ethnicity.

In contrast, when I was in California last month to visit my new campus, I thought of myself as a foreigner in a new land. I became keenly aware of my midwestern roots and thought I would never fit in. Then I realized all of the other places I had been felt like home because of the transformational work God did in me while I was there. I now have peace and an eager expectation as I begin my new adventure, because I know that home is wherever God leads me.

This young lady understands loyalty. She understands nothing trumps loyalty to Jesus. I thank you, Victoria J. It was an honor and a joy to be your teacher. It was wonderful to hear from you.

Where are your loyalties? That is a decision you need to make. Don't leave your best friends behind, but choose your friendships *(or loyalties)* wisely. My job, family, home, yard, and church all keep me rather occupied. I am not unique in that aspect of my life, but here's the thing—anything we put in front of God becomes an idol. Yes, that is repetitive, but it is important. Anything we pledge our loyalties to, if God isn't first and foremost, becomes problematic. He is very clear about the issue.

Don't bow down and worship idols. I am the Lord your God, and I demand all your love.

If you reject me, I will punish your families for
three or four generations. (Exodus 20:2–4, NIV)

Yes, repetitive again, sorry; not really.

As a company commander, it was my responsibility to make
decisions about what I wanted my company to do. It was my First
Sergeant's responsibility to enforce those decisions. We often disagreed on which direction we needed to go and would discuss it
(some might say argue about it) behind closed doors. Sometimes my
ideas would prevail, and sometimes his would. When we opened the
door and walked out of the room, it didn't matter whose decision
it was. It became our decision, and we were both loyal to carrying
through whatever course of action we had decided on.

My First Sergeant once told me, "Sir, if you tell me to climb
up onto the roof and count the cars in the parking lot, I might
not understand why you want me to do that. I might ask you why.
Perhaps I might even suggest an alternative I believe is more logical.
The bottom line is that you are the boss. Once the final decision
is made, the only thing I'm going to care about is finding a ladder
which will get me to the roof." He was an exceptional leader and an
incredible First Sergeant.

We often disagreed behind closed doors but never failed to support each other in front of the troops. That is loyalty. Moms and
dads should never argue in front of the children. The boss and the
administration should never argue in front of the employees. My
boss should never denigrate his boss in my presence. Those actions
are the opposite of loyalty.

Abraham Lincoln said it this way: "A house divided against itself
cannot stand." There is no doubt that Abe was smart. What most
people miss is that Abe was quoting from Matthew 12:25. Jesus said
it first, and this is how he phrased it: "Every kingdom divided against
itself will be ruined, and every city or household divided against itself
will not stand" (NIV).

Jesus was speaking in a much different context, but that doesn't
deter from the same spiritual truth. Without loyalty, everything you

are attempting to accomplish simply falls apart. If it doesn't exist in your organization, find a way to create it.

We humans value loyalty, but not the way God does. We might feel bad about betraying a confidence, gossiping behind someone's back, or not keeping our word. It's not like we robbed a bank or shot someone, though. It isn't the worst thing we could do. For God, there is perhaps nothing worse than failing to keep his word. As a result, He expects us to put him first, no matter what. That means above your spouse, children, job, career—everything. You will never understand the blessings that will come your way for doing this until you learn to do it. Trust me, I'm still working on it, but I am trying.

Our church building is huge, but we are a small congregation. Zeigler, Illinois, is an old coal mining town. Unfortunately, the coal industry has been in a serious decline for decades. At one time, there were more than 500 members. Now we have less than 100. The church building was constructed, remodeled, and added to over a period of many years. We just celebrated our hundredth anniversary as a church, which is phenomenal considering we're a small church in a "one horse town."

The church grew (in terms of both members and facilities to accommodate them) as the town grew. The depression of the coal mining industry has had a devastating impact on Zeigler. Population has decreased, property values have plummeted, business after business has closed, community activities are nonexistent, and poverty abounds. We don't even have a post office anymore.

Here is the good news: We have a church visitation program. We have a summer lunch program to feed impoverished children, but we never send anyone away without a meal if they want to eat. You can't very well feed a child and send their parents away hungry. We give school supplies to children at the beginning of every school year and purchase two outfits of clothing for them, including shoes and undergarments, for anyone that asks and lives in the area. These efforts are greatly enhanced due to the generous annual donation we receive from the Carson Meyers Foundation. We have Vacation Bible School every summer and a food pantry, among other community outreach programs. We genuinely attempt to help our community in every way we can within the limitation of our resources. We try our best to help wherever we see an existing need. This is in spite of the demographic of our members, the vast majority of which are retirees living on limited fixed incomes.

We are successful in reaching the children of our community, but sadly, they grow up and leave us. There is nothing even close to the realm of a career opportunity which would attract them once they have obtained their educations. Our congregation is aging, and it is rare to see an adult visitor. This may sound similar to your church.

The good news is we are faithful. I want to say that another way. I truly believe our church family is genuine in our efforts to be loyal to God. We just put a new roof on the building today. It was a $25,000 project. It is a huge building. It may be a rarity, but we have the luxury of too much space in our building. That is a double-edged sword. $25,000 was a huge sum of money for a congregation with limited means.

We didn't have to borrow money, though. We didn't set up a GoFundMe page, and nobody made some huge monetary contribution in order to make it to possible. No one in our small church family has that financial capability. We established a special fund for the roof and slowly saved the money. More importantly, God provided the means for us to accomplish it.

> Seek first his kingdom and his righteousness
> and all these things will be given to you as well.
> (Matthew 6:33, NIV)

God knew the roof was leaking and needed to be replaced. We didn't have to tell him. I believe He provided the means, because we are loyal to him. God provides, but he expects you to put him first. Is your career more important? Is your family? What about your next promotion? Perhaps you're focused on school, work, or the degree you're pursuing. Maybe saving money for the down payment on your first house has become your major priority. Perhaps you are trying to maximize your bank account because retirement seems to be looming in the near future and the anticipated decrease of your earnings potential has become frightening.

These things are a priority, but they are all transitory. Are you loyal to him? He tells us to rely on him. He tells us to trust him.

> Trust in the Lord with all your heart and lean not on your own understanding; in all your ways acknowledge him, and he will make your paths straight. (Proverbs 3: 5–6, NIV)

Just like he knew we needed a roof, he also knows what your needs are. If He is your first loyalty, then all your needs will be provided for. He promises us that. He doesn't want us to worry about the physical necessities of life.

> Do not worry, saying, "What shall we eat?" or "What shall we drink?" or "What shall we wear?" for the pagans run after these things and your Heavenly Father knows that you need them. But seek first his kingdom and his righteousness, and all of these things will be given to you as well. Therefore, do not worry about tomorrow. (Matthew 6:31–34, NIV)

He is telling us to be loyal to him. If he isn't your first loyalty, if he isn't your first priority, then nothing is your priority.

Avoid blind loyalty, unless that blind loyalty is to Jesus. He expects that. Teaching students to fly airplanes involves an intense amount of one on one, hands-on interaction inside of an aircraft. While administering check rides, I regularly observed some common reoccurring errors. These were often attributable to a student's tendency to mimic the actions of their instructor, usually without question, and often without rational thought.

The instructor would teach their student what his instructor taught him, who learned it from his instructor, and so the chain continues. Sam Walter Foss was an American poet in the late nineteenth century. He observed numerous winding roads in the northeastern United States that originated from cow paths. This inspired him to write a poem. The following is an excerpt from "The Calf Path."[8] If you have the opportunity to read the entire poem, you'll find it thought-provoking and well-worth the investment of your time.

> And many men wound in and out.
> And dodged, and turned, and bent about,
> And uttered words of righteous wrath,
> Because 'twas such a crooked path.
> But still they followed, do not laugh
> The first migrations of that calf,
> And through this winding wood-way stalked
> Because he wobbled when he walked.

Be loyal, but think about your loyalties. We tend to discipline our children, think about our job performance in terms of, behave in our relationships according to, interact with our families because of, and perform a myriad of activities based on what we have experienced ourselves. When you work for someone, there are times when you have to just be quiet and do what you're told. A good leader understands there are valid reasons to question, on occasion, what we're doing and why we're doing it. The dilemma lies in knowing when or how to ask the questions.

Regardless of our profession, it is common for us to emulate the behavior of the flight instructor who emulated the behavior of his flight instructor who emulated the behavior of his flight instructor who emulated the behavior of his flight instructor…you get the idea. That is part of human nature, but consider this. Are you traveling through your life's journey following a calf path under the auspices of misplaced loyalty?

Be loyal first and foremost to Jesus. Remember the last part of Proverbs 3:6: "He will make your paths straight." Avoid the calf path. Take my word for it. It's well-worth the effort. As promised, a short chapter.

---

[8] "The Calf Path" Sam Walter Foss, 1893, approximately.

"E"

Empathy

Empathy depends not only on one's ability to identify someone else's emotions but also on one's capacity to put oneself in the other person's place and to experience an appropriate emotional response.
—Charles G. Morris, PhD

I am a Bible scholar. After having read this far, that statement should not come as a shock to your system, but please don't misunderstand me. I'm not claiming profound or exceptional biblical knowledge, as in *scholar,* the noun. My claim is an enjoyment of studying the Bible as in *scholar,* the verb. The more of the Bible I read, the more understanding I desire. The purity and truth of God's word is addictive. It is fun to read, but you have to invest some effort and energy to be able to make that statement. One thing which seems amazing to me is how often Jesus isn't the central character in many of the stories.

Let me explain by relating a story about five brothers and a doctor, all of whom had rather unusual names. The doctor was also an exceptional psychologist. He was also a bit of a nomad and made his living by traveling from town to town, practicing medicine, treating patients, and giving motivational speeches. His speeches were comprised of intelligent, well thought out and wise advice. As a result, he became something of a celebrity. People would come from miles around just to hear him speak, but the story isn't really about the doctor. Instead, the story is about the five brothers.

One of the brothers was named Apathy. Apathy was terribly sick and had been for a long time. He was so sick that he could no longer walk. He had not been able to get out of his bed for several years.

The second brother learned the famous doctor was coming to the local clinic where they lived. The second brother's name was Insistent. When Insistent learned the doctor was coming, he had a conversation with all of his brothers and suggested they take Apathy for a visit. Perhaps this famous doctor might be able to help.

All of them, except Apathy, thought it was a good idea. Apathy said, "I've already been to countless doctors, and nothing has helped. You know I don't like crowds. People laugh at me and it's embarrassing. Besides, what makes this doctor any better than the others? He's probably a quack. Your idea is pointless, and I don't want to go. I just don't care."

Insistent would not relent, though. Insistent was, well, insistent and convinced Apathy to visit the doctor while he would have the opportunity. Insistent would not be denied. He absolutely would not take no for an answer.

All of the brothers were poor. Not impoverished, really, they just didn't have any luxuries. They lived in a rural area, and the roads were terrible. Even if the roads had been passable, it would have done no good, because they couldn't afford a car or gasoline. Their only mode of transportation to the clinic was to put their sick brother on a stretcher and carry him.

I don't know if you have ever carried someone on a stretcher, but I can assure you it is physically demanding. It is a task which requires intense stamina. Even if they only had to go a mile, which would likely have been a short distance considering the circumstances, I can imagine the four brothers getting tired. I can imagine them wanting to turn back and give up.

Apathy was a big man. He was heavy. I can almost hear them complaining and wanting to go back home. This is where the third brother, named Consistent, becomes important to the story. The conversation writes itself.

Three of the brothers were complaining, and Apathy didn't care to begin with. After all, it wasn't even his idea. Consistent spoke up and told his brothers, "We will not quit. Apathy is our brother and needs to see the doctor, so we will persevere. We are going to take care of him."

When they finally arrived at the local clinic, the doctor was there; but there was also a huge crowd of people. The doctor was quite popular after all. The waiting area was standing room only with a long line of patients outside of the door, waiting to be seen. The third brother, named Proficient, came up with a plan. He told his brothers, "Listen, fellows we can't go through the door, the wall, or windows. Even if we could, there are so many patients waiting that the doctor will most likely leave before we get to see him. After all, he is only going to be in town for a few hours."

Proficient suggested they carry their sick brother to the roof, cut a hole in it, and lower the stretcher through the ceiling by ropes. They all agreed and proceeded to carry out the plan.

The fourth brother's name was Efficiency. Efficiency's friends had a nickname for him. Efficiency was sometimes called Urgency. Even though we haven't talked about him yet, Efficiency's role in the story is prominent throughout, not just at the end.

When Insistent came to all of them with his idea at the beginning, and once they all agreed to take Apathy to the doctor, I can hear Efficiency saying, "If we are going to do this, we have to hurry. Time is of the essence. We have to act right now. Our window of opportunity is limited. The doctor might not ever come back, and we won't get another chance (*does that sound like something you might hear your boss say at work?*)."

As fate would have it, the brothers got lucky. Apathy was lowered into the waiting room, right in front of Dr. Empathy. Dr. Empathy took one look at his patient and immediately knew what was wrong. Dr. Empathy told Apathy, "You need this new medicine that just became available. Apathy, what you are missing is Caring." Dr. Empathy gave Apathy a healthy dose of Caring, and Apathy soon began to feel much better. Eventually, Apathy was completely healed and was able to walk back home and join his brothers.

Apathy was so happy that he decided to change his name to Persistent, because he would not have gotten better unless all of his brothers had persisted.

If you have ever been to Sunday school, this story should sound familiar. If you want to read a slightly different version, consult the Gospel of Mark, chapter 2, verses 1 through 12. The names of the four men who carried the corners of the paraplegic man's bed that day are not recorded. We are told nothing about them. However, because of their actions, we can surmise much about them and their personality.

That is how my version of the story came about. The men who carried that stretcher humbled me. There is no question that Jesus performed a miracle when he healed the paralyzed man. I read that story a number of times over the years, but I kept missing the most important part. I just didn't see it. There is a second miracle in the story. Think of it as an "overlooked" miracle. Perhaps the reason we don't know much about the men who carried the stretcher is because it allows us to realize what the second miracle is and how significant the importance of it is.

The second miracle is the desire of friends to help friends, the desire of strangers to help strangers, the human trait of wanting to make someone else's life better when they suffer a loss or tragedy. We all possess the innate need to do something for someone else with no desire for reciprocity, the need to give of ourselves. This is a miracle God performed when he created mankind. It is uniquely human. Bugs, fish, dogs, cats, horses, cows, you name the species. Humans help others, even life-forms lower than themselves. Survival and reproduction are the two goals of other species. The overlooked miracle makes us different. The overlooked miracle is a significant part of LEDRSHHIP and Christianity.

I was not supposed to speak about God or Jesus where I worked. You may have been told the same thing. I was called in on the carpet a few times for doing so. I could hurt someone's feelings. If someone's beliefs were not the same as mine, they could resent it. They might complain. I refused to let that stop me. I did it anyway. I am proud to serve my Jesus in any way I can. As the expression goes, there is more than one way to skin a cat. I told the five brothers' story at my retirement party on my last day of work.

When my boss asked me if I would like to say a few words, I responded with the five brother's story. I embellished it with motions and voice inflections. I told this story, because it let me skin the cat using an alternate method. The characters teach us important life lessons, but there is something else to learn from the story. It also teaches us about success.

To perform my duties within the scope of both of my careers, I have had to be insistent about my expectations. If I don't articulate my expectations, then my subordinates and my students will not understand them, and it is unlikely they will be met. If I don't insist my students follow the proper checklists, then they won't. If I don't insist they follow the rules and proper protocols, they won't be safe. If I don't demand appropriate standards be adhered to, then they won't be.

If I am insistent about my expectations, but my actions are inconsistent with those expectations, I send a conflicting message. I send my subordinates and peers down a path which results in failure. If I want my students to act professionally in their mannerisms and conduct, then my actions must be consistent with that expectation. I have to be professional with my deportment, language, and appearance. I can't come to work wearing a shirt that needs to be ironed and complain that my student doesn't appear professional. If I don't follow procedures, they won't think procedures are important.

> How can you say to your brother, "Brother, let me take the speck out of your eye," when you yourself fail to see the plank in your own eye? You hypocrite, first take the plank out of your eye, and then you will see clearly to remove the speck from your brother's eye. (Luke 6:42, NIV)

If I choose to ignore a standard today and take the easy short-cut, the result is a new standard. I refuse to lower the standards. "Do as I say, not as I do" isn't an effective leadership technique. Did you ever work for someone like that? I know they probably never said those words aloud, but that doesn't mean they didn't subscribe to the philosophy. Are you sometimes the person who says *(by your actions)*, "Do as I say, not as I do?"

I have had to come up with a game plan and adjust it for the student who just doesn't get it the first time. I have had to adopt what I am doing and tailor my lesson in mid-delivery to meet the needs of my students. Information changes, improvements are made, and technology is constantly updated in my profession. This likely happens in yours as well. If I do not keep up, then I become an antiquated dinosaur *(my students already think I am a dinosaur)*. If I'm uninformed of new developments, methods, and procedures, then my proficiency will wane. It is impossible to be successful without an adaptable and proficient plan of action.

I've learned to be efficient at my duties. Because of that, my productivity for the last ten years of employment was consistently *(there's that word again)* within the top five of my peers in terms of course completion rates and check ride passes. Because of this attitude, my colleagues nominated and selected me as the teacher of the year during my last semester. It was an incredibly touching and humbling honor. It happened because I was insistent, consistent, proficient, efficient, and empathetic toward an awful lot of people.

For me, the implication of the brothers and the doctor is profound, but let's look at the moral of the story which is even more meaningful.

Sometimes people will nickname their vehicle. Let's assume you have named your car "Success." Insistence, consistence, proficiency, and efficiency are the wheels on your vehicle of success. If you have a flat tire, you have to repair it or you don't go anywhere. Empathy is the engine which drives your vehicle of success, caring is the steering wheel which controls your direction, and persistence is the fuel that goes into the gas tank. If you are unable to place yourself in the position of another, it is impossible to truly care for them *(Ever hear this one? Don't judge someone else until you walk a mile in their shoes)*.

As you drive your vehicle of success, you will occasionally have passengers who come along with you for the ride. Sometimes your passengers ride along for a relatively short distance. Sometimes it can be much farther, perhaps endless *(it can seem endless when your mother-in-law is riding along).*

Your passengers could be your family, friends, peers, boss, or the person in line in front of you at the grocery store. They tend to bring apathy along with them. If apathy gets into your car, tell him to get out. It's your car. Tell apathy he isn't welcome. He is the enemy of insistency, consistency, proficiency, efficiency, caring, and empathy. Apathy is heavy. The tires can't support his weight, and they will burst. They will wear out. Apathy ruins the gas mileage.

Instead of apathy, sometimes your passengers bring caring along with them instead. Caring is much better company. Welcome caring into your vehicle of success. He makes all the passengers feel good and is lightweight. He doesn't affect the gas mileage at all. If you get low on gas, he will most likely offer to chip in for fuel or perhaps buy you a cup of coffee at the next rest stop.

Insistence, consistence, proficiency, efficiency, persistence, caring, and empathy are invaluable tools to have in your quest for success, no matter your chosen career. Here is the real moral of the story, though, and it comes in the form of a question. Who is the sick brother? It is you, it is me, and it is everyone who reads the story. If you are not insistent, consistent, proficient, efficient, persistent, and empathetic, then you will become apathetic. When you cease to care, you become the sick brother. Your success in life is compromised. Your financial status, hygiene, job performance, personal relationships, health, and just about every parameter you can think of will suffer the consequences.

Are you drifting through life without applying the characteristics of insistence, consistence, proficiency, efficiency, persistence, caring, and empathy? Your own success comes from helping others, not from helping yourself. The brothers were insistent in their task, consistent and persistent with their actions, proficient with their plan, and urgent in their execution. The doctor and the brothers were all empathetic. The sick brother got well. I'm just saying.

Dad died at the age of forty-eight from heart failure. I can remember thinking he lived a long life. Now in my sixties, I realize how young he was. I would gladly give everything I own to hear dad preach just one more sermon. Mom passed away a little over ten years ago due to complications from diabetes. She was seventy-one. My first wife was eighteen when she died in an automobile accident. We had only been married for six months at the time, and before you ask, I wasn't driving. Courtesy of the US army, my living accommodations were located in Germany. She was out shopping with a friend and preparing for her trip to join me.

One of my students had just returned from his second deployment as a combat medic. His first tour was in Iraq and his second was in Afghanistan. Prior to entering military service, he asked me for advice. He wanted to know what to expect after enlisting and had numerous questions about basic training. I did my best to answer them. After being discharged, he decided to pull an unloaded weapon on a law enforcement officer. Unfortunately, the officer had no way of knowing the weapon wasn't loaded and he did what he had been trained to do. The coroner ruled the cause of death as suicide by cop. His family has requested that his name not be revealed because the situation is too personal and painful.

Let's call him Samson. Samson of the Bible had incredible strength (just like my student) but committed suicide (Judges 16:28–31) in order to defeat the Philistines who had tortured and imprisoned him. Samson, my student, had a six-month-old baby at the time he made that decision. Why did my Samson feel he couldn't take it anymore? Why did he resort to such a drastic and permanent solution for a temporary problem? Perhaps it was PTSD. Perhaps it was genetic or a case of anxiety. Maybe he was suffering from depression.

One day, Samson told me that as a youngster, he witnessed the violent murder of his father. Growing up without a dad to talk to could have made him angry. My belief is the Samson I knew was in a prison cell, which was just as real to him as the bars an inmate on death row might see, and that he was defeating his captors the only way he could. The why isn't important, and his family will never have the answer to many of their questions. The only certainty is the horrific outcome.

Two of my high school friends also committed suicide. I did not find out about it until years afterward. By that time, I had long since lost touch with them, but that hasn't altered my sense of loss.

Robert was babysitting his two-year-old grandson. His grandson was sitting on the table, and my brother was feeding him crawfish from a glass bowl. His grandson fell off of the table. He attempted to grab the bowl to keep from falling, but it slid and went to the floor with him. He landed on his chest and on top of the bowl which then shattered as it hit the floor. Robert and his wife rushed their grandson to the nearest hospital. A two-year-old does not have very much body mass. The child was taken by life flight to a children's hospital. He did not live.

No matter who you are, you never know when it is coming.

> But God said unto him, "You fool, this very
> night your life will be demanded from you. Then
> who will get what you have prepared for your-
> self?" (Luke 12:20, NIV)

There is no question that all of these are tragic and heartbreaking stories. We tend to think we have virtually unlimited time. We think we are young and life has just begun. I can tell you from experience that assumption is terribly inaccurate. Either you already have or you will bury a family member, and it will happen virtually instantaneously. I have no empirical data to support my claim and I have done no research to support what I'm saying here, but it seems to me that most people who die do so within an hour or two, at most, from the onset of whatever they succumb to. Every day is a gift, and we need to think of life from that perspective.

It isn't always something as final or as tragic as death. Jerry is a survivor of breast cancer. She has "recovered" from the disease but she is not the same. She can't do what she used to be able to do. It affects her daily routine and her outlook on life.

A young girl who comes to the Sunday school class which my wife and I teach had her house burn down. Nobody was hurt, but her family lost everything. The sadness in the face of that child is something I can't begin to explain. I cannot begin to imagine how that family feels.

A friend of mine from work, let's call him KN, is confined to a wheelchair. KN's son was in a minor traffic accident right in front of their home. I watched this boy grow up in our church and was there the day he was baptized. KN saw the accident happen, so he went out to check on his son and was struck by a car.

The woman who hit him was in her eighties with failing vision, so she had no insurance and no driver's license. She should not have been driving, and her family had told her so on numerous occasions, but they never took away her keys. KN has been living in constant pain for eight years and endured numerous painful surgeries which seem to have no end. Just like you never know when it will be your last day, you never know when your life will dramatically change.

Earlier, I said how much I regret turning my back on my God and my family, and I have attempted to rectify that to the best of my ability. These horrific stories have a great deal to do with the subject of empathy. Before you can appreciate that, you need to be informed about one more tragedy.

James was recently on his way to work traveling Interstate 20 just outside of Shreveport La. There was an accident blocking the highway in front of him and it was necessary for my brother to stop suddenly. He did and so did the vehicle behind him, but unfortunately the driver of that vehicle used my brother's truck for brakes. The vehicle which rear-ended my brother was an F250 that was trailering a second F250. The impact occurred at approximately 50mph. That is a huge amount of mass and the instantaneous deceleration *(the impact)* reminds me of Sir Isaac Newton's laws of motion, most notably the third one, which states for every action there is an equal and opposite reaction.

The equal and opposite reaction was that James spent several weeks in the hospital recovering from life threatening injuries which were aggravated by the fact he was already wearing a CPAP, followed up by the use of a new transportation mode for a while which he refers to as his two wheel steed *(aka., a wheel chair)* then twelve weeks of rehabilitation, and finally the use of a cane to walk with for the rest of his life, not to mention indescribable pain and the total destruction of his truck. PLEASE TURN OFF YOUR CELL PHONE WHEN YOU GET INTO YOUR VEHICLE!

My brother's accident, the young child whose house burned down, and KN have what you might call an odd common denominator. I was part of a church family when these tragedies occurred. When I experienced the others, I wasn't. When you suffer a tragedy—make no mistake about it, you will—there is a huge difference between having an empathetic family in your corner and not having one. Knowing someone is praying for you is incredibly comforting and helps with the feelings of loneliness.

In spite of prayer, God may not change things for you. He is God. Everything he does is for a reason, and we cannot possibly understand what his reasons are. Don't try; it's a pointless endeavor. Knowing someone cares enough about you to pray and suffer with you is monumental, especially when the circumstances don't change.

You never know what someone else is living through. No one knew about my feelings as I suffered through those tragic experiences, because I was too proud to ask for help. Nobody was able to be empathetic with me, because I refused to allow anyone to see my pain. Putting yourself in another's shoes doesn't only mean laughing with them. It means feeling what they feel, crying with them, and praying with them.

Sometimes we need to cry with our friends and need them to cry with us. That won't happen if you don't let them in. There is no shame in crying with a friend, because true friends understand the importance. Real friendship is being able to empathize with us. True leaders know how and when to ask the questions which allow them to be "let in." Don't be afraid to ask.

If dying on a cross for you doesn't convince you of Jesus's empathy, he made two statements while hanging there which might. The first is found in Luke 23:34. Jesus said, "Father, forgive them, for they do not know what they are doing" (NIV).

That is pretty straight forward. Let's personalize his words. Jesus said, "Gerald, I know you don't really get it. I feel the nails you are driving into my hands and my feet. The pain is unbearable. Gerald, I felt the lashes from the whip in your hands. When you spit in my face, Gerald, it was detestable. I heard the nasty insults and the awful things you said about me. I won't hold any of these things against you. I forgive you, Gerald, because you don't realize who I am or what you are doing. I understand why you have done these awful things to me (*don't forget to substitute your name for mine*)."

The second is found in John 19:26–27, "'Woman, here is your son!' and to the disciple, 'Here is your mother'" (NIV)! Jesus knew he wasn't going to be on earth much longer and wanted to make sure his mother would be taken care of. Women didn't work then. They were totally dependent on their husbands or their children for survival.

Jesus sees his mother. He loves her and knows she is watching him. He knows she is heartbroken; she will see him die. Let's surmise what he may have been thinking about in that moment. Perhaps he was remembering the way she had taken care of him, cooked his food, taught him to dress, mended His clothes, put a bandage on his knee when he fell and skinned it, comforted Him when he was sick, or any number of other things. Jesus is concerned about His earthly mother's needs, so he tells John, "Listen up here, my friend. You have to take up the slack here. I can't do it anymore, and you are the only one who can fill in. Take care of Mom for me."

It isn't easy to put yourself into someone else's shoes. Christians and leaders have a knack for it. It is an important part of who they are. Even in death, Jesus found a way to be empathetic. What a lesson for us all.

4

"D"
Duty

> To be conceited of doing one's duty is then a sign of how
> little one does it, and how little one sees what a contemptible
> thing it is not to do it. Could any but a low creature be
> conceited of not being contemptible? Until our duty becomes
> to us common as breathing, we are poor creatures.
>
> —George MacDonald,
> *The Wise Woman and Other Stories*[9]

Let me begin another chapter with an open-ended question. More thought fodder, if you will. Consider the difference between obligation and duty. Are they the same thing? Are they related? Does one have more importance or a higher priority for you than the other? Is one fueled internally, coming from the heart, while the other is externally forced upon you because it is defined by an operations manual a company policy? I'll answer the question or at least give you my version of the answer at the end of the chapter.

Our nation's flag was draped on the casket of my grandfather on my father's side. He served in WWI and died before I was born.

---

[9] George MacDonald, *The Wise Woman and Other Stories*, Wm. B. Eerdmans Publishing Co., Grand Rapids, MI, 2000.

I can't tell you much about my paternal grandfather, because my dad didn't talk about him, but I can tell you my grandfather knew about duty.

My father's casket was also draped by our flag. Dad served in the Korean conflict and in WW2. He retired after twenty-two years of active duty when he was placed on orders to go to Vietnam. Dad had an incredible sense of duty. He found a way to make things happen and took responsibility to support his family.

One day, my casket will be draped by that same flag, and since Jarred is a member of the United States Air Force Reserve, his will be as well. By my count, that is four generations from the same family.

A small cross hangs from a leather cord on the rearview mirror of my truck. It is made out of three nails *(do you see the significance here?)*. No matter what vehicle I own in the future, not just any cross, but that cross, will always hang from my rearview mirror. It was given to me by a young man named Chad M. Let me tell you about him.

Chad was a flight student placed on my schedule when he began to work on his flight instructor certificate. The first time we shook hands, I noticed he was missing the ring and pinky fingers from his right hand, yet he still had a grip like an iron vice (*I still grimace when I think about that first handshake*). I didn't really think about his missing fingers.

I'd been working with Chad about three weeks when he came into my office one day using crutches. That's when I realized he didn't have a right leg. Chad came to tell me that his prosthetic was bothering him, so he wouldn't be able to fly that day.

He could have called and told me he wasn't feeling well, and he would not have been questioned. Instead, he chose to come to the airport and tell me in person. It was physically painful for him to do so. That's when Chad told me he lost his leg and fingers while on a routine patrol in Iraq when his Humvee ran over an IED. Chad never let his injuries keep him from accomplishing his goals or sought sympathy because of them and, even with a prosthetic leg, was one of the best commercial pilots I've ever had the privilege of flying with.

SIUC students have the option of earning their multi-engine rating or flight instructor certificate. They can earn both certificates if they wish, and most students do, but at least one of these is required for graduation. Chad chose the flight instructor option, by far the most time-consuming and challenging, meaning if he did not finish, he would not earn his degree. Now fast-forward to the end of the semester. We finished the course three weeks ahead of schedule because he worked incredibly hard. All that remained was the check ride; a single test stood between Chad and his degree.

One week before we finished the course, Chad's father was diagnosed with terminal cancer. As I recall, the doctors expected him to live for about six months. The day after he found out about his dad, we had a lesson scheduled. He came in, completed it and ultimately the course, but made the decision to go home and help his father before taking the check ride. He was fully aware of the consequences of that decision.

Chad asked me to pray for his dad when he learned of the cancer, and we did on several occasions. When he decided to go home, Chad gave me the cross—which he made, by the way—and asked me to never stop praying for him. I haven't. Every time I get into my truck and see that cross, it reminds of my Savior, Chad, and the impact we all have on each other's lives by the way we live our own. Chad went home to be with his father and help his family because of a profound sense of duty.

Someone else who teaches an invaluable lesson about duty is Joseph. I'm sure you have heard the story before, but in the interest of brevity, I'll give you my "CliffsNotes" version:

Joseph was one of twelve and his father's favorite son. His brothers became terribly jealous, because their father favored him with gifts which they didn't receive, one of which was his "coat of many colors *(Do you remember the coat of many colors Dolly Parton sang about?*[10] *It's a great song, but not exactly the same story)*.

His brothers sold him into slavery, and Joseph became the slave of a wealthy high-ranking Egyptian named Potiphar. Joseph was honest, worked hard, and God blessed his efforts, which impressed

---

[10] Dolly Parton, "Coat of Many Colors." Title track on album "Coat of Many Colors," RCA Studio B, Nashville, TN, October 1, 1971.

Potiphar who eventually gave him the responsibility of managing his entire household.

Potiphar's wife thought Joseph was attractive. She attempted to seduce him one day as he was working in the house, but Joseph ran off. He refused to act immorally. As he was rushing out and trying to get away, Potiphar's wife grabbed at Joseph and caught his coat which came off. When Potiphar came home, his wife showed him the coat and accused Joseph of attempting to rape her. Potiphar felt betrayed, so Joseph was thrown into prison.

While he was in prison, the content of his character once again revealed itself. Joseph was eventually put in charge of all the prisoners and work details. Two of his fellow inmates had a dream, which Joseph was able to accurately interpret. The dream of one man revealed he would soon die, while the other man's dream revealed he would soon be released and return to the king's service.

After Joseph's friend was released, the king had a dream, but no one could tell him what it meant. Joseph's friend recommended the king ask Joseph to explain it. Joseph told the king his dream meant a severe famine and food shortage of seven years' duration would follow seven years of abundant harvests, and they needed to be prepared. The king put Joseph in charge of preparing for the famine and in charge of his army.

Joseph became second in command throughout the land of Egypt. He became deputy pharaoh, only answered to the king himself, and became quite wealthy. Three times, the content of Joseph's character (or his uncompromising loyalty within the performance of his duties) allowed him to rise from "rags to riches."

When the food became scarce, when the rains stopped falling, and when the fields stopped producing crops, people started to get a bit hungry. The famine wasn't just in Egypt where Joseph was now living as a powerful man. It was also in all of the neighboring countries, including where his brothers lived.

They were forced to purchase food from him, because there wasn't anywhere else to buy it. Joseph could have been vindictive, but he chose to be kind and feed them. He chose to love them. He brought them and their families to Egypt to live there with him and gave them everything they could possibly need or want.

Joseph gave them land, houses, clothes, and livestock. You name it, he gave it to them. It wasn't just land, but the best land. It wasn't just houses, but the best houses in the best places to live. It wasn't just food. It was the choicest food.

Joseph believed that even though his brothers acted evilly toward him, God had planned everything for a reason. He understood that where he was and that everything which happened to him was part of a plan much larger than himself, and he put his personal feelings aside. He refused to allow his feelings to influence his actions, to keep him from the performance of his duty.

Even though the book of Romans wouldn't be written until centuries later, it was just as true in Joseph's time as it is today.

> And we know that in all things God works for the good of those who love him, who have been called according to his plan. (Romans 8:28, NIV)

I can't count the number of times that verse has helped me cope with a difficult situation.

Joseph was coming to check on his brother's welfare at the request of his father. Joseph's envious brothers thanked him for doing his duty by selling him into slavery.

Joseph had the duty to do his best work for Potiphar. He may have been a slave, but he wanted for nothing. Potiphar had put him in charge of his house. Joseph gave his duties everything he had and became successful as a result. He also had the duty to behave in an honorable way, to behave with integrity. Potiphar's wife was throwing herself at him, and Joseph could have taken his pleasure, but instead, he chose to perform his duty in an honorable way. He was "thanked" with a prison cell.

While in prison, Joseph rose to a level of success envied by his fellow inmates, because he understood duty had nothing to do with circumstance. Duty is about doing your best, no matter the task, no matter the situation. Joseph understood duty meant honesty.

Because of his honesty with his fellow prisoners, he was awarded his freedom. While he was working for the king, his understanding of duty, his refusal to compromise his character and values, resulted in him gaining great wealth and power.

Even with his wealth, fame, and power, Joseph never lost sight of the duty he had to his family. Even though his brothers didn't deserve it, he treated them with dignity, love, and respect. Lastly, but most importantly, he understood his duty to act in a Godly manner.

The events of Joseph's life are like a chain. You've heard the expression that a chain is only as strong as the weakest link. If Joseph had failed to perform his duty at any point, then one of the links in the chain would have broken and the end of the story would have been much different. The outcome would have changed.

The lessons Joseph teaches us about duty are important for two reasons. The first is Joseph's life is recorded with great detail in the Bible. If it is in God's word, it is important, and if it is recorded in detail, it must be really important. Secondly, it's not only detailed and in the Bible, it is in Genesis, which is the very first book in the Bible. Joseph did not know God had a reason for bringing his brothers and their families to Egypt.

Let's take a seat in our time machine and travel about 400 years forward. The Bible now talks about someone else with just as much detail. Does the name Moses ring any bells? God used Moses to lead all of Jacob's descendants to the promised land. Let's take a look at the lineage of Moses. Jacob was known as the father of the Israelites, because each of his twelve sons represented one of the Israelite tribes.

We're going to take a short detour before scrolling in on Moses and his lineage but the diversion is important. It's also important to understand who Moses is and how he fits into the picture of duty. If you really want to understand what the Bible tells us, you have to personalize it. You can't grasp the significance of biblical stories unless you place yourself in them. I'll give you a few examples, starting with what is arguably perhaps the most well-known verse of the Bible.

> For God so loved the world that he gave his
> only begotten Son, that whosoever believeth in
> him should not perish but have ever lasting life.
> (John 3:16, KJV)

There are twenty-six words in that incredible sentence filled with so much hope and promise. Nineteen of them are one-syllable words. Max Lucado wrote an entire book about this single verse entitled *3:16 The Numbers of Hope*. Mr. Lucado tells us, "If you know nothing of the Bible, start here. If you know everything in the Bible, return here. The heart of the human problem is the heart of the human, and God's treatment is prescribed in John 3:16." He then summarizes the verse with eight words: "God loves, God gave, we believe, we live."[11]

Let me rephrase John 3:16 for you. God loved Gerald Thornhill *(don't forget to substitute your name for mine)* so much that one day, he decided to have a conversation with his Son and ask him to do something. God said, "Hey, Jesus, listen up for a second. I know we have it pretty good here at home, but there is this guy named Gerald Thornhill, and I'm a little worried about him. He won't be born for more than 2,000 years, but this is the plan.

"I want you to leave our palace and go to a destitute country. When you get there, you'll have to live a humble life as a poor man. I've made arrangements for your lodging, food, and clothing, but you're only going to have the absolute bare necessities. You won't be respected, and nobody is going to believe who you are.

"Now here comes the tough part, Jesus. I want you to be tortured, and then you will eventually die from a terribly horrific, indescribably cruel death. Now, Jesus, the reason I want you to do this is because I really love Gerald Thornhill, and when he is finally born, I want him to have the choice of believing or not believing what you did for him. If he does, then he can come live with us."

---

[11] Max Lucado, "3:16 The Numbers of Hope," Thomas Nelson Publishing, Nashville, TN., 2007.

Now here is the great part. Jesus said, "Sure thing, Dad, no problem."

Let me paraphrase 3:16 in a more personal way similar to the way Mr. Lucado did. Remember to substitute your name for mine. God loves Gerald. God gave Gerald an incredible gift. Gerald believes it. Gerald gets to live.

Let me paraphrase a few more verses for you. God did not send Jesus to earth to condemn Gerald Thornhill. God sent Jesus to earth to save Gerald Thornhill (John 3:17). "Gerald Thornhill, if you've never done anything wrong then it's okay for you to complain about someone else (John 8:7). Gerald Thornhill, I want you to be a witness for me where you live in Zeigler, and then in Carbondale, where you work, and then in St. Louis when you are on vacation while you are waiting to catch your plane, and then in San Francisco. Gerald, the bottom line is I want you to tell people about me wherever you go (Acts 1:8). Gerald, don't let any unwholesome talk come out of your mouth. Only say what is helpful for building others up according to their needs (Ephesians 4:29). Gerald, your attitude should be the same as that of Christ Jesus (Philippians 2:5)."

You get the idea. Now put yourself into the place of the Israelites, and let's personalize it. I am Gerald Thornhill and an Israelite. If you are part of the human race, if not literally, then at least figuratively, you're an Israelite.

> I will make them one nation in the land,
> on the mountains of Israel. There will be one
> king over all of them and they will never again
> be two nations or be divided into two kingdoms.
> (Ezekiel 37:22, NIV)

I grew up as slave working terrible hours under horrible conditions (*Hold the phone!* Before you say I'm not a slave, consider this. Do you have a job? Do you answer to a boss in order to make your living? Does the money in your bank account—*or maybe the lack thereof*—determine where you can go on vacation and how long can you stay? Does your salary dictate the size of your house, the car you drive, or the neighborhood you can afford to you live in? You determine your own salary, right? No? You don't? Somebody else does? *Shock!* You are a slave, my friend, and an Israelite as well!).

My parents and my grandparents were slaves too. Along comes this guy named Moses, and suddenly, strange horrible things started happening. First, the Nile River turned into blood and there was no water to drink. All the fish died, everything stank, and the odor was terrible. It permeated my house, my clothes, everything. I can't get away from it, and it's nauseating.

Then the frogs started coming. They are all over the place; they're in my bedroom, on my bed, in my closet, on my kitchen table, in the cupboard where I keep my food, and I can't walk without stepping on them. If that weren't bad enough, the constant croaking is deafening!

Then came the flies; you wouldn't believe how many flies! Just like the frogs, they got into everything; and the constant biting and their incessant buzzing is maddening.

Next, hordes of wild animals came from everywhere and destroyed anything that hadn't already been decimated. I can't even explain what happened after that; it defies logic. All the livestock everywhere suddenly just died. Chickens, cows, oxen, donkeys, pigs, sheep, everything—they just died for no understandable or apparent reason. No explanation, and you wouldn't believe the stench.

Then everybody got these huge boils all over our skin, so painful. That was followed up by an awful hailstorm. The hailstones were huge, and they killed anybody who was outside. Then we got hordes of insatiable locusts. If it hadn't already been destroyed, the locusts ate it or destroyed it. Nobody can buy food anymore, because there isn't any food left to buy. Even if there was, I don't have any money to buy it with, because I'm a slave. So I'm starving, my children are crying, they're scared, hungry, and thirsty. I feel helpless.

After all of that, it got dark in the middle of the day. Imagine the darkest night you've ever seen. It was twice that—dark all day and all night long. You couldn't see anything.

Then this Moses guy speaks up and says, "Hey, everybody! Listen up for a minute! I've got some important news. I'm going to take you away from all this. You will have plenty to eat and your own land. You're not going to be a slave anymore."

Now that is welcome news, but the proof is in the pudding. I must admit, though, anything is better than this. So off all of us go, following this Moses guy. We've survived all these plagues, only to get to the Red Sea and realize that Pharaoh's army is in hot pursuit. The army is behind us and the sea is in front of us. We have nowhere to go; we're trapped. They want to bring us back and make us slaves again or maybe kill most of us.

You wouldn't believe what happened next. I saw it with my own eyes and I still hardly believe it. Moses held out his cane over the sea, the wind blew the water up on both sides, and we walked over the seabed, on dry ground, with a wall of water on each side. Once we were across, Moses held out his cane again. The water rushed back in and drowned the entire Egyptian army.

But now here we all are in the middle of the dessert. The army isn't chasing us and there are no plagues anymore, but that doesn't do anything about how hungry or thirsty everyone is. This desert heat is unbearable, and the sand gets into everything, so I begin to complain.

Bread falls out of the sky. All I have to do is go pick some of it up off the ground every morning. I get tired of eating just bread, though, so I complain once more. All of a sudden, quail are everywhere. All I have to do is go pick them up off the ground, just like the bread. I can eat all of the quail I want.

I'm still thirsty, because there isn't any water, so Moses hits a big rock with his cane, and water comes running out. Moses takes care of everything I complain about, but he keeps telling me it is God who is solving all of my problems. Who is this God anyway? Does he really exist? I can't see Him. I can't hear him (sound familiar?).

We finally get to this "promised land" Moses has been telling us about. It doesn't take us very long, and everyone thinks it is a good idea if we send a few scouts to check things out; let them look things over and see what we're getting into. They come back forty days later and give us a discouraging report. The scouts tell us the people there are giants; they're mean, and all the cities have huge impenetrable walls. They'll kill us if we come into their country, and everyone is scared.

Nobody trusts this God that Moses keeps talking about, least of all me (sound familiar, again?). I complain the loudest. Moses tells us that since we don't have any faith, we're going to spend one year wandering around this forsaken desert for each day the scouts were gone. That means I am going to die without ever seeing this promised land. My diet will be bread and quail for the next forty years. *Aw, yuck!* You've got to be kidding me! What is this, a cruel April Fool's joke?

Now let's personalize the story and get to the nugget of truth. The constant complaints aren't just complaints. They represent our dissatisfaction with our personal circumstances, our unwillingness to look for the good things which have happened to us, our focus on the sorrow instead of the joy that God showers on us every day.

I once lived in an apartment, and my next-door neighbor had a pet rattlesnake which he kept in an aquarium. He was lonely and depressed one afternoon, so he thought it would be a good idea to take the snake out and play with it. He put the snake on his bed and lay down with it and, of course, the snake bit him.

My neighbor created a serious problem for himself, because he was focused on his problems; he was focused on complaining. We cannot function if we concentrate on negativity. The results are devastating, and there is a good chance we might be bitten by a snake. It is easier to get rid of the snake. Better still, never adopt the snake in the first place, and if you do, by all means don't lie down and play with it. Just in case you missed the inference, we aren't really discussing snakes.

The promised land isn't simply a mythical "land flowing with milk and honey." The promised land represents heaven. There aren't any snakes in the promised land, because the promised land also represents a successful life. It is the reward for serving God and performing your duty in the manner he wants. We get to the promised land by serving God the way he wants us to. The promised land represents heaven, because it represents being in God's presence.

How often do you complain? Are you playing with a snake? I won't speak for God, but I'm pretty sure he gets rather tired of constantly hearing it. Do you get tired of hearing your children complain when you're doing the best you can for them? Let's personalize one more verse, this time from Philippians 2:14: "Gerald, do everything without complaining or arguing, so that you may become blameless and pure, a child of God without fault."

Let's get in our time machine again and go backwards this time. We'll get back to Moses's lineage (eventually) and why that is so important. Jacob's grandfather was Abraham and merits much more than an honorable mention when it comes to this idea of duty. Abraham gets pretty good billing in Genesis also.

If LEDRSHHIP represented the five categories on the Hollywood walk of fame *(motion pictures, television, radio, recording, and live performance/theater)*, Abraham would have a star for each.

Speaking of stars, "He (meaning God) took him (meaning Abraham) outside and said, 'Look up at the sky and count the stars, if indeed you can count them." Then he said, 'So shall your offspring be'" (Genesis 15:5, NIV).

Let me rephrase that a bit. God told Abraham to look up at the sky, and don't make the mistake of glossing over the first two words "God told." It means God spoke to Abraham personally, directly. He doesn't do that very often, and the audience he selects is extremely limited.

Abraham and his wife, Sarai, took God at his word. They waited and waited and waited but didn't have any children. If you've waited for a child and been unable to conceive, you're familiar with the agony they felt. Finally, when Abraham was ninety-nine and his wife was ninety, their first son, Isaac, was born. Take another look at their ages. I got that right. Abraham was ninety-nine, and Sarai was ninety. Imagine how happy they must have been; imagine the joy of their experience.

Then God really threw Abraham for a loop. God wanted to know the true nature of Abraham's character. He was going to find out if Abraham would do his duty. He was going to find out if Abraham was for real or if he was just all talk. God was not playing around and pulled out all the stops. He put the pedal to the metal and went all out. (Genesis 22:1, NIV) "Sometime later, God tested

Abraham." *Wow!* I mean *wow! God* tested Abraham! What a way to start a verse! Do you grasp the significance?

We don't know exactly how old Isaac was when God tested Abraham, but let's assume he was perhaps ten. You can read the whole story in the twenty-second chapter of Genesis, but this is what God did. God said to Abraham, "Look, I know I promised you children, and now you have a son. You were 100 years old when he was born, so now you are 110. Your wife is 100, and it is unlikely she will have any more children. Here's the plan, Abraham. I need you to prove that you love me. Take your son and sacrifice him. Build an altar, put Isaac on it, kill him, and then burn up his body."

Now I don't know about you, but if I was Abraham, I would be saying, "*What? Huh?*"

Hey, God! What's up with this? Are you kidding around here or what? I would be screaming out my reaction. It would probably be something like, "*No way, God, are you nuts?*" My reaction would not be a calm one either.

That wasn't Abraham's choice at all. Abraham's reaction was, "Okay, God, you got it. Whatever you want, I'll do it." Abraham chose compliance. It was a reaction of completing his duty, no matter what that duty happened to be. It's a great story, Genesis chapter 22.

I don't believe God had the intention of letting Abraham kill Isaac, but it's certain God wanted to know if Abraham would do what he was told. My feelings are Abraham trusted God enough to believe his son would be brought back to life after he killed him. We don't know what Abraham thought, because we aren't told. We do know that Abraham trusted God implicitly. Abraham understood duty to God.

Thank you for being patient. We've finally gotten back to the significance of Moses's lineage. Isaac grows up and has children, one of whom is Jacob. Jacob is given the name Israel, because he is the father of the Israelites. Jacob is also the father of Joseph, as in "coat of many colors" fame.

Moses comes from the same family line. Without Abraham's obedience and adherence to duty, there is no Jacob, which means there is no Joseph, the Israelites never go to Egypt, and there is no exodus from Egypt because Moses is never born.

Now take a wild guess who else is part of the same family tree. Can you say Mary and Joseph, (a different Joseph this time) as in the earthly parents of Jesus himself? If Abraham fails to perform his duty, the Ten Commandments don't exist, there is no promised land, and most of the countries on this planet have much different laws than the ones which currently exist. Abraham definitely understood what the word *duty* meant. Aren't you grateful he did?

Let's not forget about Isaac's understanding of the concept either. He doesn't exactly get top billing in the story, but don't let that fool you about the significance of his role. His dad says, "Hey, Isaac, here's the plan. You carry this wood up the mountain for us. We're going to stack it onto a great big pile. Then I want you to lie down on top of it. Now, son, after that, I'm going to tie you up so you can't move and use this knife. I'll stab you to death with it, set the wood on fire, and burn you up."

Get this. Isaac said, "Okay, Dad, not a problem. Glad to do it." I'm rather confident my children would not have been that accommodating.

Risk management is a critical skill employed by many industries. Aviators spend most of their working hours with risk management at the forefront of their thoughts. It was a normal part of my world due to the danger which was a daily part of both of my professions. At first thought, risk management seems to be a simple common sense concept, but I challenge you to define it. I'm not sure I have a good definition, but let me explain it this way.

Let's say you are driving home from work and decide to drive at 100 miles per hour. Admittedly, that would not be an intelligent decision, but nobody is going to tell you not to drive at that speed. Sure, you would be violating the speed limit, breaking the law, and would likely go to jail should you pass a police officer, but nobody is going to tell you that you can't do it. There are some inherent dangers that go along with making that decision.

For example, you could negotiate a blind curve or hill and run over an obstruction in the roadway. Perhaps it is a board with a pro-

truding nail. As a result, your tire is punctured by the nail and rup-
tures. Because of the bursting tire combined with the high rate of
speed, you lose control of your vehicle which then ends up in a ditch
and is totaled. Perhaps you live and perhaps you don't.

Let's assume you live but are now in the hospital with several
surgeries to endure, not to mention rehabilitation and learning to
walk on crutches or perhaps having to use a wheelchair for the rest
of your life. In addition, you have to replace your totaled vehicle,
assuming your injuries don't prevent you from driving.

As you mull this over, you conclude these outcomes are not
acceptable. You don't want to be disabled, you don't want to incur the
expense of replacing your vehicle, and you don't want to suffer the
financial loss which would result from being unable to work while
you're in rehabilitation. You decide to do something about it. You
impose a restriction on yourself and drive at the posted speed limit.

The risk is the obstruction in the roadway. Your chances of
encountering the obstruction may be minimal, but you can't do anything about that risk. You can't eliminate, minimize, or control it. You
don't know where the obstruction is or if it will be there. Someone
else might run over the board before you arrive. The risk exists. Every
time you get in your vehicle and go somewhere, you accept it. Risk
management is how you react to its existence.

Driving at a safe speed is the management part of the equation.
When you come around the same blind curve and run over the same
obstruction, the outcome is now much different. You still end up
with a flat tire but are able to control the vehicle. You are able to
maneuver to the side of the road and change the tire. Perhaps you
are late for dinner, and maybe you get your shirt dirty or possibly
ruin it as you're changing the tire. You decide that buying a new
shirt and missing dinner is an acceptable outcome. Living the rest of
your life with a disability which could have been prevented, higher
insurance premiums, paying the deductible for repairing your totaled
vehicle, or perhaps dying prematurely is an outcome you decide is
unacceptable.

Actions have consequences. I used a technique with my children as they were growing up. If they wanted to do something which

they knew I wouldn't approve of, my stock response was, "Go ahead. You know what the consequences will be." I learned that technique from Carolyn. I think it is interesting that Carolyn's daughter uses the same technique with her children. The first time I heard my niece say, "Go ahead, you know what the consequences will be" brought a huge smile to my face. You can learn much from risk management techniques.

Think of duty as being similar to risk management. Nobody makes you perform your duties. If you don't like your job, working conditions, colleagues, hours, or salary, then fine, it's your decision. Many are the people dissatisfied with their current employment situation and who feel devalued or unappreciated. The question becomes, "What do I do about it?" I can complain, leave early, or lie by calling in sick when I'm not. I can berate the boss and complain about him to my coworkers behind his back or even shirk my responsibilities.

Employment termination may be the consequence for that behavior. If I decide being fired is not an acceptable outcome and subsequently choose to perform my duties in an honorable way, then perhaps I may receive a promotion, greater job satisfaction, and be happier. There is always the option of searching for other employment. As long as my boss keeps paying me, as long as I continue to spend my salary, my duty is to stop complaining and do what is asked of me.

Duty defined is ethical, legal, or moral accountability. The word comes from the French word *deu* meaning that which is owed. If you realize you have some kind of a duty, you must also recognize you have an obligation to repay your debt.

The philosopher Cicero[12] suggests we incur duties because of four reasons. These are the result of being human, our place in life, our character, and our moral code. Duty then becomes a self-imposed concept. It becomes a personal commitment. When you recognize a duty, you must commit yourself to fulfilling it, regardless of your own self-interests or desires.

---

[12] Marcus Tullius Cicero, *Cicero, On Duties*, 44 BC

Jesus proved he understands duty by two things he said on the cross. In Matthew 27:46 (NIV), Jesus shouts out, "My God, My God, why have you forsaken me?"

Let's paraphrase that. "God, I've done what you wanted! I did my duty! I did what was right. I did what I had to do, what you asked me, but now you've abandoned Me. I don't understand why you've turned away from me."

Moments before he died in John 19:30 (NIV), Jesus said, "It is finished!" (*Do you remember that I said earlier those three words were chosen for a specific reason?*)

Let's paraphrase that as well. "I've done what you wanted! I did my duty! I did what was right. I did what I had to do."

Joseph, Isaac, Moses, and Abraham all understood duty. Chad understands duty. Jesus most assuredly understands the concept of duty. He did his duty at a tremendous cost. He didn't have to, but he did it, because he loves you. What about you?

All right, here is my answer to the question "What is the difference between obligation and duty?" I think duty is a matter of the heart. It is an internal desire born of love and that someone who is dutiful fulfills their obligations out of that sense of love. What's your opinion?

"R"
Respect

It does not matter how long you are spending on the
Earth, how much money you have gathered, or how much
attention you have received. It is the amount of positive
vibration you have radiated in life that matters.

—Amit Ray, PhD[13]

Duty and respect are intertwined. They are not separable, because
if you are being dutiful, it is out of a profound sense of respect to
something or someone. Consequently, this chapter on respect may
sound like a continuance of the chapter on duty. In many respects
(pun intended), it is, but the two concepts have distinct differences.
This is unusual for an author to do but allow me to summarize this
chapter before we begin. Lack of respect is far more noticeable than
its presence.

No matter how you attempt to justify it, taking a knee when
our national anthem is played is an insult to my son, my father, my
grandfather, Chad, me, and everyone else who has ever donned the
uniform of any organization, military or otherwise, in service to this

---

[13] Amit Ray, PhD, *Meditation: Insights and Inspirations*, Inner Light Publishers,
2010.

great country. It is an affront to all citizens who are profoundly patriotic to this nation.

Keeping your hat on or not standing when you see our flag pass by during a parade is just as insulting. I would rather you spit in my face. Let me quote the words which begin the fourth verse of our national anthem. "Thus be it ever when free men shall stand between their loved homes and war's desolation."[14] And while we are on the subject of insults, it's Merry *Christ*mas, not Happy Holidays.

Such individuals are clearly not PC. Don't misinterpret me. We're not discussing political correctness, but rather Patriotic Correctness. You are free to protest whatever you like and should if it is your desire; however, never disrespect the United States flag and what it stands for. This country, like every other country, has made mistakes. But unlike other countries, it evolves and atones for them. We protect people in distant lands from unjust actions of other nations. You'll not find a more giving country or one with as much willingness to help others in all of history as the United States of America. We also tolerate far more undeserved abuse than we deserve.

There is no doubt we have some serious problems in this country. Some things need to be changed immediately if not sooner. Things like gender and racial discrimination, biased courts, sexual harassment, pay inequality, political corruption, phone scams, mass shootings in our churches and schools, theaters, at our concerts, unfair educational opportunities, unemployment, rampant drug abuse resulting in theft, homicides, and…the list appears endless.

However, we have a lot of wonderful things here as well, things other countries envy; things like virtually unlimited resources and space, the incredible generosity and spirit of the American people, exceptional health care, outstanding secondary educational opportunities. But most importantly, we have the right to do anything we want as long as it doesn't interfere with someone else. Why do you think third world nations hate us so much? Could it be they are envious of what this nation offers? For all the complaints you hear,

---

[14] Francis Scott Key, "The Star-Spangled Banner," Chesapeake Bay MD, VA, 9/13/1814.

why do so many people try to immigrate here, even illegally and at the risk of life in the process?

Let me answer that question for you. It is very simple. I've been to other places; this is the greatest nation on earth.

Protest your cause *du jour* if you wish. That is your right, and more power to you. Depending on what you're protesting about, you could find me standing next to you and championing the cause. Even if I disagree with you, it doesn't matter. I've been shot at while I was protecting your right to disagree with me. It was my duty. I was glad, proud, and happy to be allowed to protect your freedom of choice, but how dare anyone—particularly an out of touch with reality, pampered celebrity—dishonor the thousands of men and women who have sacrificed so much so that you can enjoy the fruits of this nation. If you don't like this country, leave it; nobody is forcing you to stay.

If you choose to live here, if you enjoy the right to choose your career, your relationships, where or if you attend college, where and when you go on vacation, where you live, or what car you buy, then you have a duty to support this country, its principles, its values, and respect the thousands of men and women who have made it possible. You have a duty to respect it. You have a duty to show up for jury duty without complaining, a duty to vote in every election you can, and a duty to speak up against Cadet Bone Spurs when he does something incredibly stupid[15] *(Thank you for doing your duty in so many ways, Senator Duckworth. Your comment is much too humorous to exclude).*

Poverty, discrimination, racial bias, hunger, wall-building, isolation of children, and unequal educational opportunities, which we seemingly ignore in this country, are an egregious unforgivable sin against humanity. They are an embarrassment to the wealthiest country on Earth. These challenges will not be rectified with trite platitudes and self-serving meaningless political slogans. The only

---

[15] Tammy Duckworth, Sen., IL (D) "We don't live in a dictatorship or a monarchy. I swore an oath in the military—and in the Senate—to preserve, protect, and defend the Constitution of the United States, not to mindlessly cater to the whims of Cadet Bone Spurs and clap when he demands I clap," 2/6/2018.

discernible difference these tactics make is a new incumbent's name on the ballot during some future election.

The military taught me that when you bring a problem to a superior officer, be prepared to bring a solution with it. It was not uncommon for my commander to ask me, "What do you propose we do?" There is a real way to solve the disgrace this country experiences because of these blights on society, but it doesn't happen because some two-bit clown with an axe to grind kneels during a song. You're not going to like it, but the answer is simple. Ready? Here it comes. *Put God first!* Start with prayer.

> If my people who are called by my name will humble themselves, and pray and seek My face, and turn from their wicked ways, then I will hear from heaven, and will forgive their sin and heal their land. (2 Chronicles 7:14, NIV)

We previously discussed some of the problems our country faces. Though they constitute a seemingly endless list, the three simple words you just read—put God first—would solve all of them. Let me give you an example.

Arguably, some of the most horrific news stories we hear, and which seem to report on ever increasing numbers of the dead are about mass shootings. They occur in our churches, schools, restaurants, businesses, and theaters.

Here is a thought. If children were attending church as they grew up, if their parents were teaching them to worship the Creator and follow Christian tenets, if they were not allowed to play violent video games which desensitize them toward violence, then instead of blasting away at innocent people they have never met from the anonymity of a hotel room, darkness of a movie theater, nightclub, or the solitude of a church sanctuary, they would be in a church somewhere, on their knees, praying and thanking God that he has allowed them to live a fortunate life. We have allowed the pendulum of political correctness to swing so far that the result has been the successful removal of God from our culture and country. If God was even a remote concept in the lives of these terrorists *(translation: idiots)*, the thought of a mass killing spree would never enter their minds. More and more violence is the only possible result of the dismissal of God from our collective lives.

Before we leave the subject of *putting God first*, listen up, parents. Church isn't a babysitting service so you can enjoy a couple of free hours every week. I know you use it for that, because I'm the one teaching their Sunday school class. The only time I see your shadow, much less you cross the threshold of the building, is when we feed you a meal after the service, give you something like clothes and school supplies for your children, or you need to ask for food from the food pantry or want money to pay your electric bill. Where do you think the funding which provides these things comes from?

Let me answer. The lion's share comes from the pockets of senior citizens living on fixed incomes that have worked hard and scrimped their entire lives. We are grateful for the ability to provide these things. We will continue to do so as long as we are able. We'll cheerfully continue to contribute our time, resources, energy, and hard-earned money to make these things available for you when you're in need. That is what being a Christian means. That is what loving Jesus means. But at the very least, a simple "thank you" would be a nice gesture.

If you need these resources, please don't hesitate to ask; but if you don't need them, don't ask. You are depriving others who are actually in dire straits. I give of myself because I want to, but stop expecting me to do it. Check your sense of entitlement at the door and stop bad mouthing me when I can't help.

It doesn't do any good to ship your children off to church or Sunday school if you can't be bothered to attend with them and live by Christian tenets yourself. Do you really believe your children don't see your example? Numerous are the words which have brought me to tears while penning this manuscript. It has been a painful process. If you haven't realized it yet, my heart is on these pages.

This morning, our church saw one of the most heartbreaking events I have ever witnessed, and trust me, I've seen many. A young man in his early twenties and a young teenage girl were baptized at the beginning of the service. Their families came to watch and sat on the front pew as well they should have. We had never seen these people before. We went out of our way to welcome them to our church, introduce ourselves, engage them in conversation, and make them feel comfortable. Immediately after the baptisms, they got up, walked down the center aisle, and left the building during the middle of the service.

I seriously doubt they gave any consideration to how ashamed, how demeaning it was, or how saddened the baptismal candidates must have felt. You must set the example. Do you really believe your children aren't watching you? At the very least, stay for the entire service when your son or daughter chooses to make a commitment to live their life for Jesus.

I have to wonder if they will leave their child's college graduation as soon as their son's name is called and he walks across the stage. What about leaving the softball game immediately after their daughter has her first at bat? Would somebody please explain the difference to me? LEDRSHHIP doesn't mean living your life with a sense of entitlement and showing up for the sole purpose of receiving. LEDRSHHIP means leading by example. LEDRSHHIP means showing up and staying for the entire game. Church, it isn't just for kids. It never was.

I rarely agree with President Trump. If asked to be a character witness for the man, my summation would likely be that there is a good probability for a starving feral female cat in heat to be embarrassed by his lack of moral turpitude. The way he treats women is despicable, but he is dead right on this one point—I think NFL player Mr. Tota Lee Outatuch, a.k.a. Mr. Phullup O'Krapola, a.k.a. Mr. Justa N. Udernut, a.k.a. Mr. Whas A. Mattau, a.k.a. Mr. R. U. Krazee...far too many aliases to list, but you get the idea—should be tried for treason. I've altered his name to protect the guilty, but we all know who I'm talking about *(in case you are doubtful, his initials might be C. K.).*[16] By the way, the penalty a soldier could potentially face for treason during a time of war is death.

---

[16] Donald Trump, 45th POTUS, "The NFL owners should fire any players who protest during the national anthem." 9/23/2017.

I'll not demean anyone within the confines of these pages for two reasons. I'll admit I'm guilty of being judgmental, but at least I try not to be. The most important reason is pretty simple. In Matthew 7:1–2 (NIV), Jesus tells me, "Do not judge or you will be judged for with the same judgment you pronounce, you will be judged; and with the measure you use, it will be measured to you." When I point my finger at you, three fingers are pointing straight toward me. Dad used to tell me that, but I'm sure the expression did not originate from him. The second reason is because if I accuse somebody of something, I could potentially face a lawsuit for slander.

However, I'm well within my rights to articulate what I think. It's called freedom of speech and is part of the first amendment of the US Constitution. I wore a uniform for a long time protecting that right for you. You're welcome. Prepare yourself, though. It's a double-edged sword which means I get to exercise my First Amendment rights too, and that is precisely what is about to occur.

I don't think Mr. Spoil D. Chicken has the courage to be a soldier. He doesn't come close. His behavior reeks of cowardice as does anyone else's who chooses to kneel with him. I applaud Vice President Pence for leaving the Colts football game after the national anthem protest on October 8, 2017, and this is why.

I didn't want to spend a year on top of a mountain in Germany, but I did it. Let me tell you from experience, it gets really cold on mountaintops in Germany, particularly in the middle of January. I didn't want to sleep on the desert sand in Iraq, 6,000 miles from home in 140-degree heat the day my son graduated from high school, but I did it. Let me tell you from experience, the Iraq desert gets rather warm, particularly when you're sleeping in a tent during the month of August. Let me promise you something, though. If you are dutiful, you will be respected. People may not like you, but they will respect you.

I don't respect anyone who refuses to stand for our flag or national anthem and I value my respect much more than my popularity. Let me say it another way. I don't respect anyone who refuses to perform their duty as a citizen of this country. If you have a problem with how I feel about that, you have a problem with it. We'll have to agree to disagree, but you will not change my mind.

Have you noticed how much advertising the NFL has been doing since this silliness began? Have you thought about why they are spending millions of dollars to convince you to watch a ridiculous game?

The answer is quite simple—they are losing money; or perhaps more appropriately phrased, not making as much as they once did. The seemingly endless revenue stream which the NFL has grown accustomed to and shown little appreciation for is drastically waning. There is a new "game" on. Just go online. Take a look at how much attendance at NFL games has decreased, how TV viewing has changed, and how NFL merchandise sales have plummeted since Mr. Childish Brat felt the need to "show his solidarity."

As a result, players are now going to be fined for taking a knee during our national anthem, but so what? How much will the fine be? Will it be $1,000 dollars? Perhaps $5,000? Or maybe even $10,000? $10,000 to an NFL player is likely comparable to about $1 to me.

Don't get me wrong. I love to watch a good football game, but I didn't watch Super Bowl 52 or any other NFL game since this temper tantrum reminiscent of a two-year-old began. I refuse to support—in any way—any person, group, or organization which demeans and degrades our flag. My personal wish is for the NFL to be forced into bankruptcy court and no amount of hypocritical advertising about how much they appreciate service members will change my mind unless they fix this and apologize. The fine doesn't make any difference. The apology comes first, and I haven't heard one yet. Have you?

Is it just me? When a single ticket to a football game *(I'm talking Super Bowl prices here),* so high up in the nosebleed section it takes high-powered binoculars to tell what color the grass is *(should you be lucky enough to be able to buy one),* costs more money than I make in a month, it seems a bit out of balance. When that same ticket is sold on a secondary market for double the amount of the printed face value *(which equates to 16 percent of what I earn in a year),* it is far beyond out of balance.

If my wife and I were to attend the game, it would amount to four months of my annual salary *(and that is gross income, prior to taxes, insurance retirement, etc.)*, not including hotel and food, which would be exorbitant, and airline tickets to get there. It is extortion, greed, and wrong. *Unconscionable* would be a better word. When the player who receives millions of dollars every year to play in that game is cheered for burning the flag, I find it a difficult and bitter pill to swallow *(No, C. K., you didn't burn my flag, but as far as I am concerned you might as well have. That is precisely what your actions indicate—a willingness to do so)*. That flag is the symbol of this great nation. Your protest for "solidarity *(no matter who is doing the protesting)*," goes way too far, because our flag is much bigger than your protest.

Get real, Naperquack *(or whoever chooses to kneel with you)*. The irony, apparently lost on you, your anthem-kneeling compatriots, and the NFL *(perhaps because either you refuse to listen or perhaps because you're not smart enough to understand me)*, is that for many hardworking American citizens whose respect you have completely alienated, you have now become a symbol for the antithesis of your protest. You now represent a lack of "solidarity."

I speak to anyone in the NFL who might happen to actually care. Let me tell you how to fix this problem. Do your duty, Buckwheat[17] *(Thank you, Little Rascals. Am I telling on my age with that one or what?)* Apologize and earn back my respect. Until then, don't expect me to watch. Mr. C. K., even if you were to come to my house, give me a ticket on the player's bench to the next Super Bowl game, invite me to be your personal guest, buy my dinner after the game at any restaurant I wanted to go to, put me up in a suite at the Ritz Carlton, and offer to fly me to the game on your private jet, I wouldn't even consider attending. I realize I am only one person, but I am one person and I can make a difference. "One person with courage is a majority."[18] *(Wouldn't it be awesome if every owner of every*

---

[17] "The Little Rascals," Metro-Goldwyn-Mayer Television 1929-1938 syndication from "Our Gang Comedies," Hal Roach Studios, 1922-1938.

[18] John C. Maxwell, "The 21 Indispensable Qualities of a Leader," Maxwell Motivation, Inc., Nashville, TN., 1999.

NFL team were to receive a copy of this book from several season ticket holders requesting that they read this chapter? It's just a suggestion folks!)

Listen closely, Mr. Brad E. Feller. The only possession you have obtained to date, which is more impressive than your ego, is your sense of entitlement. It isn't my right to judge you or point fingers, but perhaps you should read the tenth chapter of Mark's Gospel beginning with verse 17. This is when Jesus tells the story of a rich man that wanted to go to heaven when he died. Pay particular attention to verse 25 where Jesus explained to his disciples what he told him. Allow me to quote it for you.

> It is easier for a camel to go through the eye
> of a needle than for someone who is rich to enter
> the kingdom of God. (NIV)

He may have been speaking directly to you. Lamborghinis and large houses are not impressive possessions. Living your life to glorify Jesus is impressive. You can't do that when you are thinking about yourself.

Does anyone really believe your voice is being heard as you kneel during the national anthem *(it's being heard all right, but not in the manner you wanted)*? Do you believe it's acceptable to remain seated or leave a hat on your head when your flag passes by in a parade? If you think you're not harming anyone by your actions, then ask Chad about them. Ask Senator Tammy Duckworth. I've not met the woman, but I'm sure she would agree with my opinion and would be willing to give everything she owns if she could stand when those beautiful poignant and sentimental words are sung. Ask Mr. Bob Kalsu, eighth-round selection by the Buffalo Bills in the 1968 NFL draft. Oh, sorry, you can't ask him. He was killed in Vietnam in July of 1970!

Perhaps you could ask Pat Tillman instead. Oh, sorry, you can't ask him either. You remember him, don't you? He left the NFL in the aftermath of the attack on the World Trade Center. He was killed in Afghanistan protecting your flag!

Can you tell? The NFL has most assuredly, most definitely lost my respect. That's the thing about respect. You earn it by honesty, valuing others' opinions and not undermining someone's core values when you disagree with them. Kneeling for the national anthem undermines America's core values. It denigrates and insults anyone who has ever worn a uniform for this country in any capacity. Respect is not flag desecration based upon some self-aggrandizing shortsighted erroneous premise, pursued without thought and without considering the consequences of your actions. For those of you who choose to kneel with this blithering idiot, keep in mind that blindly following the actions of a self-serving clown doesn't result in earning respect either. I'm sure she wasn't the originator of the expression, but my grandmother once told me, "When you lie down with a dog, expect to wake up with fleas."

It isn't always easy to recognize respect when you observe it. One gains or loses it with every interaction they have with someone. Respect is much more easily destroyed than garnered. James respects me. He has been on the receiving end of my making a difficult choice for the right reasons *(I'm referring to the day I fired him)*.

While it isn't always easy to recognize respect, there are glaring indications of its absence. If the NFL isn't enough to convince you, then let me give you a few more examples.

When did it become normal for our society to use profanity on a regular basis? When did it become acceptable for a man to wear a hat indoors, much less into a church building? When was the last time you addressed a supervisor who is younger than you are as "Sir" or "Ma'am?" Who gave you permission to throw trash out of your car window and into my yard? I really don't enjoy picking up your garbage. Do you really save any significant amount of time by leaving your shopping cart in the middle of the parking lot where the wind will blow it into the side of my vehicle and damage it, instead of returning it to the corral where it belongs? Or better yet, back inside the store? Considering the size of many people I see, you could probably use the exercise.

Gentlemen, this one is specifically for you. When did we stop pulling out a chair for our lady when she is sitting down or forget how to open a door for her? Youngsters, this is your question. Why do you remain seated on a bus while an older person is forced to stand? There are many more questions to ask, but you should have the idea.

You might surmise these examples of poor behavior merely represent bad manners, and the point is not without merit. My counterargument would be good manners are an outward manifestation of and born out of respect. You say manners, I say respect or the lack thereof. Either way, we need more of it. Keep in mind the basic premise of this chapter. Respect is difficult to recognize, but its lack is far more noticeable.

Lack of manners (a.k.a. lack of respect) can cost you. Today, a man came inside our church to eat lunch while wearing a cap. Our food program is for children. This man seemed to have lost sight of that picture. He walked in the door, expecting to be taken care of. While we don't want anyone in our community to be hungry and are more than willing to provide a meal for him, we can't allow ourselves to lose sight of the fact that this is a ministry for impoverished children. Our resources are limited, and they are our priority.

One of the workers was very courteous to him. I heard her ask, "Sir, we are trying to teach our children manners. Would you please remove your hat?"

He replied in an angry manner, "No. I am an ex-Navy Seal, and you can't tell me what to do!"

We subsequently refused to serve him. He left hungry, because he lacked the respect to follow a simple rule. How much of life do we miss out on because we don't even try to follow God's simple rules? How much do we forfeit because we refuse to abide by the principles of LEDRSHHIP? I know the Navy wouldn't have allowed him to wear a hat inside, and I know the Navy taught him about rules. God has taught all of us something about following rules. When we refuse to obey them, sometimes the consequence will be hunger. In case you missed the inference, we aren't talking about hats or missing a meal every now and then.

Respect is realizing that even though someone may have a different point of view, have more money, less money, look different, live in a different city, have different beliefs, make their living differently, work for you, is your boss, or dresses differently...it makes no difference. Respect is mostly about being willing to listen to others and value them, regardless of what your opinion about them is.

Sometimes we learn what to do by seeing others do what they shouldn't. We've all had bosses, friends, or perhaps family members who micromanage, constantly criticize, or demand the unreasonable. When I wore a uniform, I had just such a commander. It was frustrating to work for him, but nevertheless, he taught me a valuable lesson.

Prior to taking my first command, I asked, "Sir, what does it take to become a successful commander?"

He told me to do two simple things. First, always be better than your best soldier, and secondly, never make the same mistake twice. He was really saying never accept less than my personal best, whatever that happens to be, realize you are going to make mistakes, learn from them, and always use the opportunity to improve.

I also realized you can learn from anyone, even if you don't really enjoy their company. Paul, in Colossians 3:23 (NIV) agrees. "Whatever you do, work at it with all your heart, as working for the Lord, not for human masters." He reminds us of this in 1 Corinthians 10:31. "Whether you eat or drink, or whatever you do, do it all for the glory of God" (NIV).

While deployed in Iraq, I served as the Executive Officer (XO) of a US Army Postal Company, meaning I was second in command. The average work day was sixteen to eighteen hours long, and during the last year I was there, my company, consisting of less than fifty personnel, processed a little over three million pounds of mail, all sorted by hand. Yes, you read that number correctly. No machines of any type were used, and every single package that any soldier on base wanted to mail home was gone through item by item in order to ensure no customs or military laws were violated. That is a monumental and seemingly insurmountable task.

My company was also tasked with additional base responsibilities such as guard duty, perimeter defense, trash detail, convoy security, etc., which often resulted in as much as 25 percent of my personnel being absent for various details. It was an incredibly difficult and challenging time.

It was my job, among other things, to coordinate company activities and provide my commander with information; in short, to make sure things ran smoothly. Being constantly busy would be classified as an extreme understatement. The same micromanaging commander who told me to always be better than my best man, and never make the same mistake twice, was my commander in Iraq. I won't judge him; it isn't my right.

From my perspective, though, he never seemed to do much except sit in his office and complain when things weren't going exactly the way he felt they should. If it were just me who felt the same way, I'd take that into account and not mention it, but it seemed most everyone felt the same way. I did my best to discourage any negativity and gossip, but most of the troops still talked about him in a disgruntled manner. The consensus was they believed he failed to provide the guidance he should have and didn't fulfill the responsibilities of a company commander.

One morning, he asked me to type a memorandum which he needed to send up the chain of command regarding a report he had been asked about. This particular day was filled with constant interruptions, each of which demanded my immediate attention. I dealt with each situation as it arose, and every time I came back to the office, he would ask me if I had finished his memorandum. Each time, I would reply, "Still working on it, sir." It was finally completed around 6:00 p.m. that evening. Right about the time I was ready to print his document, he asked me if I was finished. I happily replied, "Yes, sir!"

The military no longer uses computer flash drives, because they are capable of storing vast amounts of information and are easily compromised or stolen. At the time we were still using them, my commander had the habit of calling them memory sticks. He handed me his thumb drive and said, "Here. Stick it for me."

Had I given it any thought, I would not have responded in the manner I did. I didn't bat an eye and I never looked up from my computer screen. What I said was, "Where do you want me to stick it, sir?" The entire staff was in the office, and I can't begin to tell you how much they laughed. Perhaps it wasn't as funny as everyone thought. Perhaps what made it seem funny was the tension we were facing every minute of every day, coupled with the insanely long work hours and the added pressure of being shot at regularly.

I sent this story to the "Humor in Uniform" section of *Reader's Digest*, but they chose to not publish it. I'm betting that since this story is now in a best-selling book, they regret that decision *(I'm being optimistic here; most people love that about me).* My commander went into his office, slammed the door, and not one word was ever said again about that memorandum. He never asked me to print it for him. He never used it. I still don't know how he rectified the situation or what he reported to his upper chain of command.

Six months after our return from Iraq, I received a package in my mail. It was from one of the soldiers who served with me. Inside was my picture. Above my picture, in bold print, were the words "Quote of the Deployment." Over my picture were the words, "Where do you want me to stick it, sir?"

I did not respect this man, because he didn't earn it. It seems he went out of his way to destroy it instead. That didn't prevent me from learning about respect from him or, more specifically, what the lack of it means. I did respect his rank. He was my boss. I was and always will be a US Army soldier. Even though I have now retired, once a soldier, always a soldier. That means something, starting with respecting a superior officer or at the very least, respecting their rank. You will never find me guilty of denigrating my uniform or my country. Sometimes the most meaningful lessons can also be amusing.

My wife is an amazing woman. I believe God paid extra special attention to his work the day He created her. We both have children from a previous marriage, but we both refuse to differentiate between them. We both think of and refer to all three of them as ours. I've no doubt that God smiled at me the day I was blessed by meeting her.

She will likely be annoyed that I'm writing about her, because she is a private person. On numerous occasions, she has heard me tell her that I got the best end of the bargain. I tell her this, because

I believe it. If you ask her, she'll tell you I'm mistaken and a biased reporter. We all have our faults.

The point is my wife loves me for who I am, faults included. She accepts them with a gentle grace. When I've disappointed her, she lets me know why and then forgives me. Most importantly, she trusts and believes in me. Let me say that another way. She respects me.

Christians (leaders if you prefer) need to let others know when they are disappointed with them, but never in a way which undermines someone's self-worth or core values. That isn't respect. Christians (leaders) need to render praise and give rewards when due. Christians and worthwhile leaders need to believe and trust the people they come into contact with. This concept can be summarized with a single word—forgiveness.

Jesus had something to say about the subject. You'll find these words in Matthew 18:21–22: "Peter came to Jesus and asked, 'Lord, how many times shall I forgive my brother or sister who sins against me? Up to seven times?' Jesus answered, "I tell you, not seven times, but seventy times seven" (NIV).

When I was about to become a father, I sought parenting advice from my mother. I asked her, "What was the most difficult thing you ever had to do as a parent?"

She said it was learning to let her children make mistakes. She was telling me we need to let those we love stumble when it's time for them to learn a hard lesson, but always be ready to catch them. Let them stumble, but don't let them fall. The challenge lies in knowing when to let them slip and when to reach out. Hebrews 12:11 (NIV) sums it up this way. "No discipline seems pleasant at the time, but painful. Later on, however, it produces a harvest of righteousness and peace for those who have been trained by it."

If I want a piece of toast, I can cut down a tree, rub two sticks together, build a fire, and then place bread over the flames. The method requires intense effort but will accomplish the goal. It is just as effective to put a piece of bread in my electric toaster and push the button. The results are identical. Let me give you the pilot's version of the same concept. If I am on a heading of north and want to turn to the east, it is a 90-degree right turn. I could also turn to the east by turning 270 degrees to the left. The result is identical; my heading would still be east. The left turn takes longer and could be more dangerous *(a good pilot would never do that, because they would never alter heading by more than 180 degrees at a time)*.

To make my next point, we're going the really long way around the turn. Let's make a 350-degree turn to the right, resulting in a 10-degree left heading change. We're going to use a dull axe and chop down a tree to build a fire because we want a piece of toast. I'll let you know when we stop turning.

I am grateful, thankful for, and understand the need to discipline children, but there is a limitation. So far, I've painted a somewhat normal picture of my parents. There is no doubt in my mind that my siblings and I were loved by my parents. They did some pretty amazing things in spite of some incredible challenges.

As I promised earlier, this book it isn't all rose petals. I sent a copy of this manuscript while it was still in the very early stages of development to each of my brothers and sisters. Since they were all going to be mentioned, I wanted them to have an idea of how the project was developing. It was nothing but an outline and a few of the stories you have read thus far. Carolyn read it and sent me a text message which said, "I don't think we had the same parents. I wish I'd known the ones you describe."

I called her and explained I just hadn't included any of the awful things yet. Believe me when I say there were some pretty terrible things.

During that conversation, she told me she had recently been looking through pictures of us when we were children when she saw an old family photograph. She noticed she was eight at the time, and she was smiling. I asked her why that was important.

She answered "Because in every picture taken after that, I never smiled." She also said that lately, she's had several conversations with that eight-year-old girl, trying to figure out what happened to her.

My parents believed in physical punishment and had no compunction about distributing it with generous liberality and great frequency. Their justification came from a single verse of scripture.

> Whoever spares the rod hates their children,
> but the one who loves their children is careful to
> discipline then. (Proverbs 13:24, NIV)

I've been told scripture contradicts itself. That is simply not true. My response to that statement is scripture must be interpreted with scripture. Let me interpret your favorite verse, Mom and Dad.

> Woe to those who call evil good and good
> evil, who put darkness for light and light for
> darkness, who put bitter for sweet and sweet for
> bitter. (Isaiah 5:20, NIV)

Even better, how about this one?

> Fathers, don't stir up anger in your children,
> but bring them up in the training and instruction
> of the Lord. (Ephesians 6:4)

Mom and dad most assuredly "stirred up anger" in the hearts of us all.

There is no gift more precious than a child, nothing is sweeter or more innocent than a child, nothing is better than a child, and nothing will bring more joy or light to your life than a child will. Yes, children must be disciplined when they misbehave. Boundaries must be established along with consequences for deviations, but physical violence is not required to accomplish that goal.

I'll admit to having raised my voice and speaking more sternly than I should have on more occasions than necessary, but I never struck any of my children. There just isn't a justifiable reason to resort to hitting a child physically under the auspices of discipline. Each of our children has graduated college, and they are moral people. They all have jobs doing things they enjoy. None of them are burdened with student loan debt, and they are productive members of society.

We are proud of them. Physical violence perpetuated against their own child is just about one of the most evil things human beings can do. By today's standards, my parents would have unquestionably been considered guilty of child abuse.

I don't want to drag my mother and father through the mud, but it is necessary for me to discuss some of the most memorable disciplinary tactics they employed. No child should ever endure events like the ones I'm about to describe. If my siblings and I can survive childhood and eventually aspire to a productive life, anyone can, regardless of their circumstances.

> So do not fear, for I am with you; do not be dismayed, for I am your God. I will strengthen you and help you; I will uphold you with my righteous right hand. (Isaiah 41:10, NIV)

All right, here comes the bad stuff. Don't say you weren't warned. Robert and I got into a disagreement one afternoon; about what, I no longer recall. It isn't important. I began chasing him around the yard with a jack handle, attempting to convince him I was right and he was wrong by swinging the jack handle at him to emphasize my point. I believe I was about six or seven at the time, and he is two years younger than I *(I do remember that he was running really fast; I can't say I blame him, because as I recall, I did make a connection once or twice)*. Gratefully, no major damage was done, and Robert still loves me, but he did receive a few bruises on his back as a result of the incident which have long ago healed *(he should have run just a little bit faster; sorry, Robert)*.

Dad got home and proceeded to "give me a whipping," which was always with a belt and always left marks, usually from about mid-calf up to my shoulders. He would whip me for a while and then stop.

Robert was forced to watch. Each time Dad stopped, he would tell me to look at my brother and then ask, "Now isn't that pretty?" in such a manner that he sounded sarcastic. One thing I learned very quickly was never argue with Dad. Based on the way he asked the question, I thought he wanted me to respond by answering yes, so I did. Then it would start all over again.

Each whipping lasted about five minutes and seemed like an eternity. When I finally realized he wanted me to say no, the whipping stopped. I don't know how many times the process was repeated, but it was enough that I had welts *(a lot of welts)* and lost blood.

I'll tell you more about my first job when we get to the chapter on "I," Integrity. For now, I'll say sometimes it got boring sitting around the barbershop if we weren't busy. One day, I thought I'd take the Monopoly game to work and asked Mom if it would be all right. She said I could lose some of the pieces to the game, so she didn't think it was good idea. She didn't tell me I couldn't take the game, so of course I took it. I wasn't attempting to defy or disobey her. I interpreted her response much different than the manner she intended.

That night at dinner, Dad asked me why I took the Monopoly game to work when Mom had told me not to. I answered that Mom hadn't told me I couldn't but had said she didn't think it was a good idea because I might lose some of the pieces, so I was very careful not to. I was sitting next to Dad at the table, and Jerry was sitting next to me. Dad hit me so hard that I lost my balance as my chair rocked backwards. I attempted to prevent myself from falling and reached for Jerry's chair, which was a pointless endeavor. We both ended up in a heap on the floor. I have not played the game of Monopoly since.

Carolyn is seven years older than I. I cannot possibly remember how many times she told Mom or Dad she did something, accepted responsibility for some rule infraction or childhood accident, in order to deflect punishment from the rest of us. She protected all of us, because Dad could have a vile temper, and she knew where that road went. Children play and things get broken as a consequence, things like the glass French doors when you just happen to slam them *(I wouldn't know anything about that now, would I?)*.

On two occasions, Dad was reduced in military rank which meant a decrease of disposable family income. I'm not precisely sure of the circumstances involved. To the best of my understanding, the first time was for writing personal checks that were returned because of non-sufficient funds, and the second was because he got into a physical altercation with a superior officer who asked him, "How are your kids?"

Apparently, Dad took offense to the use of the word *kids*. His justification was *kids* are the progeny of goats. Somehow, losing his rank was Carolyn's fault. Nope, it doesn't make sense to me either.

James and I were reminiscing recently. Dad was stationed in Italy for a while, and we took a weekend trip to Venice. Yes, the city with the gondolas and canals. I remember the trip, and so did he, but James was perhaps three years old at the time, so his perspective was different than mine. James told me he remembered being scared the entire time, because he thought he forgot to turn the water off in the bathtub. He thought he was going to be in trouble. He thought he was going to get a whipping. Make no mistake either. My parents didn't call it a spanking. They called it a whipping, and for good reason.

Charles Wayne *(yes, the same cousin who stole my first high school crush)* and I would sneak out at night after Mom and Dad went to sleep. Robert would come with us sometimes, but not often. I still don't know if that was because he was smarter or because he was younger than we were. We would hitchhike into town and go to the drive-in movie, go bowling, or try to get someone to buy us cheap wine because we were underage *(do they still make Boone's Farm Apple Wine?)*.

One night, Charles Wayne and I were picked up by two young men not much older than us. The police stopped them while we were in the car, and all of us were asked for our names. After Charles and I gave our names, the police officers gave the driver a warning and let him go but also followed us. A little later, we arrived where we were going, so Charles and I got out of the vehicle. After the two young men drove off, we watched with something between horror and amazement as the same police officers who had been following us pulled them over a second time and placed them in handcuffs.

Dad was an auxiliary volunteer sheriff at the time. He knew most of the police officers in town by name. When the young men were pulled over the first time, the officer recognized Charles Wayne's and my name, which is why he let the driver go. What we didn't know yet was these young men had just burglarized a drugstore. The trunk of their vehicle was filled with stolen medication and merchandise.

The next night, Dad got a phone call from the state police. Of course, our secret about sneaking out at night was no longer a secret. Dad took each of us out into the front yard separately where the neighbors could watch. The discipline he provided was with his fist. I'm talking about eye-blackening, teeth-loosening, and nose-breaking, full-on, as hard as he could swing closed fist.

Charles Wayne and I were perhaps fifteen or sixteen at the time. Dad kept taunting us and begging us to swing at him. I refused to do so. I was not about to hit my father. Eventually, he got tired and quit. Charles Wayne got the brunt of it, because he was first. The only thing I learned from the experience was don't get caught if you do something wrong, and fear my dad. Somehow, I doubt that is what he was attempting to teach me.

If you kick your dog every time you see him, the dog will learn to avoid you. If you beat your dog, don't expect to play with or pet him, because he will learn to fear you. I never snuck out again, though, so perhaps you could argue my father's method was effective. Sadly, and not surprisingly, I'm not the only one of us who experienced similar events.

* * * * *

Carolyn's story:

Dad was pastoring a small rural church, and we were living in the parsonage. The church owned eight cows, and part of his job included caring for them. That really meant it was Jerry's and my responsibility. There were four houses, each was in the middle of what you might call a block. The four corners which formed the block were approximately a mile apart from each other and the roads were made of gravel. I am not sure how old I was at the time, but I think Robert was about one, which means Gerald would have been three. I call him Butch, but I'm the only one who can call him that. It was his childhood nickname. I would have been ten or eleven, and Jerry about eight or nine.

I don't remember when Sis and I had to start doing the cooking and cleaning, but we were really young. I can remember standing on a kitchen chair to wash dishes and to iron towels, sheets, and underwear. Why did I have to iron pillowcases? Why did I have to iron handkerchiefs? There is no other way to say it. I felt like a slave doing whatever Mom told us to do so she could do who knows what.

Sometimes, the cows would get out. When they did, Jerry and I would have to go find them and herd them back into the fence. One day, a stray dog showed up about a week before we were scheduled to leave for an extended visit with Nanny and Papa. Dad didn't like the dog and wanted to get rid of him but agreed to let him stay until we left.

I named him Rover. We left a large bowl of food and a large bowl of water for him on the front porch. When we came home, Rover was barely able to walk, but he was still there guarding the house. Apparently, Rover rationed his food and ate just enough to stay alive while waiting for us to come back. Dad was impressed by that and agreed to let me keep the dog.

Jerry and I liked it when the cows got out, because we had a reason to be out of the house. Rover would go along with us, and the longer we were outside, the better. It got us out of doing meaningless chores. I taught Rover to turn the cows just before they would go inside the gate, which meant we would have to walk around the four-mile block again to get them back in the pasture.

One afternoon, Jerry and I were outside playing, but we were also taking care of Butch. Rover was lying on the ground. Butch was running and jumped over Rover but accidently clipped him with the toe of his boot. Rover snapped at him and bit his leg, so I had to tell Dad, and he got angry. You didn't take a dog to the vet in those days for heartworm, rabies shots, or neutering. You just kept the dog until the dog died.

Since the bite pierced the skin, we had to keep Rover to make sure he didn't have rabies. A week later, Dad said he was going to kill the dog. I begged Dad to let me find a home for him. Dad gave me one week. I asked all my friends at school and everyone at church, but I couldn't find anyone to take him.

One Sunday afternoon, people from church came over after the service. The cows got out, so Jerry and I went outside to round them up. Right about the time the cows got back to the gate, Rover turned them. Dad saw it and told Mom to get his gun. I knew what was coming, and I stood next to Rover. We were standing in the corner between the front steps and the porch, and Rover was trembling as he looked up at me. I was crying and I begged, "Daddy, please don't kill my dog."

He yelled at me and told me to go inside. I think if I hadn't, he would have shot the dog while I was standing next to him. As soon as I closed the door, the gun went off. I stood up to dad two times in my life. This was the first time. I didn't speak to him for a month. The second time was after I got married and left home.

Dad lost his pastor's job with the church soon after he shot Rover, so we had to move from the parsonage. I don't know exactly why that happened, but I know members of the congregation were at the house when he killed my dog. Somehow, it was my fault that dad lost his job. Go figure.

* * * * *

Before we get to Jerry's story I have to interrupt for a moment. I reached my 60th birthday before really understanding everything that happened with Rover. I was a child when dad shot Rover and as a child this is what I knew. I was running and jumped over the dog. The dog bit me. Dad shot the dog. For the vast majority of my life I thought dad killed Rover because of what I did. You can't imagine the guilt I felt over the years because of this. Only recently was the situation clarified in my mind when Carolyn and I sat down over coffee one afternoon and were able to discuss it. The information I had was limited. Is the information you have about Jesus limited? Let me tell you how to take care of that problem. Talk to him like I finally talked to Carolyn. Let me tell you the best place to start. It's called prayer. It's called church. It's called The Holy Bible, aka., God's Word. Until you talk to him, you will not understand him. Until you talk to him you are living your life with limited information.

Speaking of talking to your siblings, one morning I went to visit Jerry. She was crocheting and is the only one in the family who does. I asked her who taught her how to crochet. This was her answer.

Jerry's story:

I was eight or nine, and I had a lump in the back of my throat for a long time that wouldn't go away. Nothing got rid of it. Mom and Dad kept telling me nothing was wrong, but they finally took me to the doctor anyway. The doctor diagnosed me with depression and put me on Meprobamate. When we got home, I got the crap beat out of me. They threw my medication in the toilet and flushed it.

I remember Dad kicking me around and around the living room floor. I was trying to avoid a kick, and Dad missed, so he slapped me really hard. He hit me so hard that I flew over the ottoman. It wasn't long after that when I realized with my child's understanding if I were to live, I had to get away.

I arranged to spend the night with a different friend every day for a week. On the first night I was going to be gone, my friend's mother was teaching me to crochet. I didn't learn much, though, because Dad came and jerked me out of her house. I could never play with my friend anymore. When I got home, I got beat again. The army found out about my diagnosis and my running away. Mom and Dad shunned me for a long time as a result. My only escape was studying and reading.

I did well in school, but it was because I learned to excel in order to be accepted and loved. I only recently realized that my pattern of conflict avoidance and allowing myself to be taken advantage of started then. I always knew I hid in books but didn't know why. Maybe now I'll not be afraid anymore. Mental work is hard.

* * * * *

All right, it's me again. What follows is a letter from James, but it's necessary for me to give you a short background prior to reading it. Several years ago, Robert and James got into a disagreement about something. I don't know what it was about, and they have yet to put it behind them. Eventually, they will. They are adults, intelligent men, brothers, and love each other. They'll figure it out, and it is their business.

In order to accomplish that end, and as a means of explanation, James wrote a letter, then sent a copy to each of us. When I read his letter, I told him he should be the one writing a book. In the interest of brevity, his letter is slightly edited. *Condensed* is probably a more accurate word. I've chosen to interject some comments in italics for explanatory purposes. *Now to his letter.*

* * * * *

Hey, y'all, it's Jim,

The downside to letters is the conversation contained therein is generally from one perspective, and then the following correspondence or the lack of it in some situations usually stems from the original piece. One must also know while writing it that it might not be received in the same spirit as it's written in and be willing to assume the risk involved. I am willing *(Have you ever written an e-mail to a coworker and had it misinterpreted?).*

I've been working on this letter for two months, and I'm still not finished. I would like to be so I can send you my sentiments, but writing this takes an open-minded self-examination and a willingness to share, in complete honesty with you, a few things I've learned about myself. So if for no other reason, please read on just to see what I might say.

I hope this letter comes across to you as intended, which is to let you know that as family, you and your families are important to me. I wanted to take a few moments and reintroduce myself to each of you as I'm not the same person you may think you know me to be.

Perhaps right this very moment, you're thinking *If you weren't, you wouldn't have to say so*. Maybe you're thinking reading this is just wasted time. If you think so, it probably is, and you shouldn't.

For anyone curious enough to follow me this far, I thank you and want you to know I regret not knowing each of you better years ago when it might have mattered. I can't change what happened any more than you can put the moon in your pocket, but I can learn from it.

I will always be sorrowful for wasting so much time resulting in lost relationships with each of you. I've been working on me for some time now. I've learned it's okay to inspect, correct, protect, and respect myself, and I do.

So now in regard for all of our ancestors and all future generations spawned from them, I'm taking the steps I see as necessary to find a way which will make it possible to prevent further or permanent estrangement from those of you to which I am, but please be mindful of this. While I would like things to be better between us, I will not compromise "me" in order to find your favor.

For the sake of strengthening family ties, it seems apparent to me to first admit the simple truth that there's not one among the six of us from a personal perspective that can honestly say we really "know" each other. The only thing our brains allow us to do is remember the personal relationships we had at one time as they were then, and when doing so, our emotions begin fighting for leadership of our actions.

Mankind: The only animal "ever" created; capable of reason over response.

Emotion: A disease distorting the capability of reason; "It has no cure, but it can be controlled."

The "silver dollar question" is, do you want that which may be difficult but possibly self-rewarding? Or do you feel your energy would be better spent in other areas of your life? No one will ever have the right to make you choose or have the right to condemn that choice.

I don't think anyone really knows when our family began to disintegrate. I believe it was when that brown and white GMC pickup truck—towing a blue *(because we painted it)* homemade plywood trailer along with the company of a Chevrolet Impala towing a U-Haul trailer, both "loaded to the gills"—made a one-way trip to Alexandria, LA, bringing with them the eight of us, but leaving many treasures there to be tended to by others *(James is referring to a family move from Gold Beach, Oregon. Many of the toys belonged to the six of us children and would now likely be valuable collectors' items now. Some of these were actually pawned for gas money during the trip. I remember helping Dad build the trailer on a small mobile home frame).* I understand why that decision was made and I support it. Dad played the only hand he had available, and along that line, I feel bad for him.

Gerald, doing what you had to do was not easy, and I've forgiven myself. I'm remorseful still today for leaving you out on a limb like that. It's just not something family should do, and I thank you for forgiving me. First, though, with your permission, I would like to address the "chicken

116

shack" situation *(Sorry to keep bringing this up, but he's referring to the day I fired him)*.

When I got to Lafayette, I had just left Houston where I left a three-person (family included) roommate type situation that had lasted for nineteen months. We were young, and it took about a year to get set up, but we established a home (rental, but it was ours), bought a nice car with equal shares invested, and established a functioning fairly enjoyable home environment with solid relationships. It took commitment and work.

Eventually, the time came for the next chapter of our lives to be written. It was drastic and immediate, but my choice. I really had no idea what I was going to do or what I "wanted" to do but had no doubt I would find help if I could find you, and I needed help. I quickly came to admit I had simply traded locations and players only to still be in the same place.

That was the beginning of my spiral. It had nothing to do with anger or embarrassment that we seldom communicated after I left your place. I was foolishly and selfishly involved in my own world, and you deserved better.

Speaking of deserving better, I don't remember how long I stayed with her, but I stayed with Carolyn for a while in Bunkie, and something happened I'll never forget. That winter recorded a minus 20-degree wind chill with snow, ice, and frozen pipes plentiful. It was during this extremely cold winter one night when the totally unexpected occurred.

I became involved in helping fight a fire that took out a furniture store along with several buildings on Main Street. The water from the hoses froze on the ground, so we were walking, standing, and working on ice while fighting a fire! From that experience, I gained the utmost respect for what firefighters go through and developed an even deeper fondness for England Air Force Base. It was their ladder-truck, fire-fighting equipment, and manpower which became the "cavalry to the rescue" for the town of Bunkie, LA.

"Good deeds seldom go unpunished," of course, and with ruined, wet clothes, socks, and shoes, I attempted to hitchhike, meaning I walked from Bunkie to Carolyn's which was about seven miles with snow patches and ice for company. That wasn't the first time doing the right thing got me in a bind.

Robert, do you remember my getting back late to the church group during our trip to Six Flags over Dallas? I was offered and should have accepted the excuse for tardiness from one of the attending EMTS, but in the moment, I thought, *Screw them if they don't believe me.* That was a big mistake.

I befriended two children from an orphanage that day and spent most of the afternoon with them. This happened when I rode the Cyclone with a boy slightly younger than I. He had a panic attack, so I went to the infirmary with him. He begged me not to leave him there as he was separated from his group and scared which, of course, made me late getting back to the church bus.

Boy, oh boy! Did that one bite me in the ass! I was accused by the youth minister of having sex with a prostitute and not caring about anyone but myself.

He told me I'd never amount to anything with this type of behavior, and not one single person believed me. Even worse, Robert, you said, "Even if I did believe you, I still couldn't say anything to anybody." I suppose not Robert. I mean, why get your wife mad at you because of me? She didn't like me anyway, right?

I admit it would not have been easy to believe me, because along with other nonsensical things I'm guilty of, I rightfully garnered my moniker of a f—k-up years ago, but there are two things to consider. The first is from then, and until I die, my story has never changed nor will it, no matter how many times I have repeated it. The second is the person I am today is willing to "own it" if it's mine.

Gerald, maybe in your book, you could write about how both of our "parents" taught each of us a lot about what not to teach your children to do. I know we all lived through our own versions of hell on earth while living "under their roof." I'm also aware that I know very little of what each of you endured, but I'm equally aware neither of you could know much of mine either, unless I take you there.

I'm simply stating facts here and in no way seek sympathy. I've been diagnosed with clinical depression and ADHD with OCD tendencies for which I take medication.

I leave myself notes on dry-erase boards, on my truck dashboard, and on my calendar. I take shopping lists and pens to stores. I work hard each day to control it, and I forgive myself for my mistakes.

I mention this, because it seems like "my father" didn't want a child with a "label" or "on medication," so help was not sought. Instead, he labeled me as "lazy," because I didn't finish things like schoolwork or couldn't remember where I put things like my shoes. I was constantly getting into trouble because of it, and never once did he think about how unjust that was.

Gerald, you mentioned going fishing but failed to mention pleasure and companionship was not the reason behind it. Instead, it was about filling a freezer, and all else be damned. Not that this incident was intentional on anyone's part. I suppose I knew all along "why" I was the one sent back for worms the day I almost drowned, but just recently, my suspicion was confirmed.

* * * * *

Okay, this is me now. We'll get back to James' letter in a few minutes, but I need to go rather far off-script to explain what he meant by going back for worms, because it is so important. As you have likely ascertained on your own, it is unlikely anybody would refer to my brother as a man of few words. I have often been told to stop bloviating. James could give me a run for my money. However, to say he is a master of understatement is a monumental discredit. His simple statement about going back for worms represents, perhaps, the most significant single event that happened to any of us during our childhood.

Dad, Robert, James, and I went fishing. We went to a popular spot where we often caught our limit. After parking in the lot and to get to our spot, it was necessary to walk down a path next to a narrow river which emptied into a small lake. The river was approximately fifteen feet across and ten to twelve feet deep. The initial path on one side of the river progressively narrowed and eventually ended. A log was lying across the river, forming a makeshift bridge to where the pathway continued on the other side. We walked across the log and continued down the path to our fishing spot at the lake.

After we had been fishing for a while, it became evident we would soon run out of bait. James was sent back to the car for a bucket of worms. He saw no one on the path while completing his bait-retrieval errand, and the only vehicle in the parking lot was Dad's car. About two-thirds of the way across the log on his way back to our fishing spot, James slipped. He lost his footing and fell into the river. He yelled for help but was too far away for us to hear him or the splash when he hit the water.

I want you to do something before you read any further. Find a private—and I emphasize the word *quiet*—place. If you do this in your house and your family is present, you might want to warn them first. I don't recommend a public venue either. A crowded airport, movie theater, or a shopping mall may not be the best place to do this. Yell out the word *help* as loudly as you can. You will discover that afterward, you are completely void of air. The next thing you will do is breathe in.

Now imagine you are an eight-year-old boy with nobody around in a fast-moving river and you don't know how to swim. Your boots have filled with water and come off of your feet. The only thing you have to hold onto is a bucket of dirt with worms in it. You are underwater and you can't breathe. The first thing you will do is panic. Then you will take a breath, instantly filling your lungs with water in the process. Then you are going to start coughing.

As he began to fall from the log, James noticed two men seemed to suddenly appear on the bank he was attempting to reach and they were fishing with cane poles. One of them held out his pole and screamed, "Grab the pole, grab the pole, grab the pole!" The fact that my brother is alive today is proof that he did indeed grab the pole.

Notice he said grab the pole three times. Three is arguably one of the most powerful numbers in scripture. How many days did Jesus lie in the tomb? Oh, that's right, it was three. How many times was Jesus tempted by Satan? Oh, that's right, it was three, and it's recorded in three different gospels. How many times did the Apostle Peter deny knowing Christ? Oh, that's right, once again, three. How many times did Jesus ask Peter if he loved Him? Care to guess? I'll bet the number is three.

After being pulled back to the shore, the men were suddenly gone. They simply vanished! James never saw them again. Dad, Robert, and I never saw them at all, nor did we hear them screaming at our brother. All four of us walked down that path and crossed the same log together twice. James crossed it two more times by himself, a total of four times.

After the incident, we went home, because James was shoeless and our bait was gone. James believes the two men who rescued him were angels, and I agree. James, have you read any of the books in the series entitled *Chicken Soup for the Soul?*[19] This story would fit perfectly. It's just a suggestion, James.

Let's summarize this. Two men suddenly appear in the perfect spot, allowing them to rescue my brother; they use what is perhaps the most powerful number in the Bible in the process, then suddenly disappear and leave not one shred of evidence of their presence.

You may be skeptical of the account. You might believe James made the whole thing up. Perhaps he imagined it. You could argue with me and say, "Gerald, by your own admission, you never saw your brother's benefactors," then follow that up by telling me, "The existence of guardian angels is a load of dung!" Your pessimism would be understandable, but I was there, and let me assure you that my brother doesn't lie. We grew up together and faced some horrific situations.

There is a problem if you believe James' story. Believing in angels means you also have to acknowledge a belief in a God who could create them. That's only the beginning, though. It also means an acknowledgment of heaven, hell, Satan, and demons as well. You can't argue both ways; it's all or nothing. You have to take the whole package.

It's the same thing with the Bible. No picking and choosing just to argue a particular point of view. If you acknowledge belief in all of them, it means admitting to yourself that you could end up living in hell for a very long time. No one wants to admit that possibility,

---

[19] *Chicken Soup for the Soul*, "Angels and Miracles," Amy Newmark, Chicken Soup for the Soul LLC., 2016, Distributed by Simon & Shuster.

so they lie to themselves about it, but lying about something doesn't change its existence. Yes, it's a trite expression, but nonetheless very true. At the end of the day, it is what it is. Stop lying to yourself, my friend. There is a future in it, but it isn't pleasant.

Sorry for the diversion. Let's get back to James' letter.

* * * * *

There were times when Dad would have rather not taken me, just like there were days when he didn't want me underfoot when he was working on a car and had little to zero patience or tolerance for my boyish presence. Case in point: Do either of you remember me getting hit flat-handed in the middle of my back and being knocked through a barbed wire fence on one of our fishing trips *(Yes, James, I remember that)*? Our "father" was holding the top strand of wire up with his hand while holding the lower strands down with his foot, creating a space to cross through. As I hurriedly went through, I accidently caught the rod and reels with my ankle.

How about the afternoon he hit me so hard, he knocked me out the screen door and onto the porch because of the way I was eating fish? I was being careful and knew what I was doing, even if he didn't. When I got up, he told me, "Now you'll eat fish the right way."

I ask you now, was this tough love or a total lack of patience? Can you remember how I was "lying" if I disagreed with something? Or worse, gave a different version of something that happened than what he imagined? I can still remember several examples of this and will likely never forget them.

I wonder, was it the same way for all of us? Were we all considered to be lying when we weren't and then threatened with a beating if we didn't "change our story" or "shut up?" There is something else I find myself curious about. Was it just me or did he always, and with each of us, seem to look for things to fuss about that in the grand scheme of things meant nothing at all? If with each of us, I can't help but wonder why anyone would do to someone else something so unfair and something they themselves must have detested.

Gerald, I know you can remember the stupid and harsh beating I took for "sweeping the dishes," because you apologized to me for it when we last saw each other. I told you then and I'm telling you now that one person alone was responsible for that, and it's not you.

Robert, this one's for you: All of those times he forced us to "duke it out." I didn't want to hit you and would have rather taken another butt-whipping from him rather than do so. Just in case you've been thinking it was because I was scared, I wasn't. I was just never angry enough to hit you. Something else you should consider is the fact that even when it made no sense to do so, you've had a long history of "correcting me."

I have even less respect for our "mother" than I do for him. There's not enough patience combined within each of us or enough space for me to make a list, but right up there at the top is "manipulative." Gerald, you mentioned not knowing how our parents managed. Let me remind you. Love offerings from churches on Sunday, he would "visit," vegetable gardens we would work long hours in while we were children, budget shopping resulting in clothes that made us look like dorks, hand-me-downs, garage sales, thrift stores, and home remedies.

Speaking of the latter, for a period of six months or so and no matter how hard I fought, cried, screamed, and begged them not to, our parents forced me to accept hydrogen peroxide being poured into my ears in order to clean them. Our father, of course, knew I was "faking" and would use either intimidation, physically force me to lie down, and even hit me to get me to cooperate. So about every two weeks, we would go through this same ordeal, and I would always end up losing. Submit or get in trouble and be forced to submit anyway. Not much of a choice I say.

Finally! I'm going to get some relief, but with a catch: They made a doctor's appointment for me with an ENT, but before the day arrived, our "father" made sure—absolutely sure—I understood that if nothing was actually wrong with me, my ass was grass and he was going to be the lawnmower. He made sure I understood this way more than once. Each time he did so, he further reinforced his lack of trust in me, and not only to me, but to anyone that may have heard him.

There is a term called "soft tissue" which means unprotected flesh. What was the diagnosis? I had a ruptured eardrum. Where was all of this peroxide going that they were pouring into my ear? It was going into my inner ear which, to say the very least, hurt like a son of a bitch! The best way I've been able to describe what this felt like would be to imagine a small drill bit digging into your brain.

I've yet to find anyone who can actually understand what my parents put me through with just this one continuous saga of being expected to lay down and willingly submit to such pain or attempt to fight a grown man I already knew could and would kick my ass and, after that, still be forcefully detained, and through restraint, accept the situation. Is it really that hard to understand how physically and psychologically damaging that was to a nine-year-old boy?

This was my "*parents*" doing this to me.

I was taught by my "mother and father" something no child should ever have to learn—submit and take the abuse or try to fight and make it worse. I carried this lesson with me for a long time, but it never served me well. Did they "love" us? They were not able to "love" us enough to be patient or find a way to reach us on an individual basis; but yes, I believe they loved us as much as they could. It wasn't nearly enough. I was taught my word meant nothing, my opinions only mattered if they were my parents' opinions, whippings with coat hangers, electric cords, shoes, boards, green switches on bare legs, leather belts and hands were imminent and could be administered for any reason—even for telling the truth.

Now I'm almost certain this "rings the big brass bell" for each of us, but here's my point. I ask you, why repeat it? Either vocally or physically, I'm hoping you'll be honest with yourself and answer four simple questions:

(1) Is it more important to appear to be correct than it is to do the right thing?
(2) Is it possible I would rather alienate others than apologize to them?

(3) Is it possible I have clouded someone else's judgement because of my own misgivings?

(4) Do I care enough about myself or others that when I find myself lacking, I am willing to make things right?

This has been a letter of explanation and this is my summation. While strength may come in numbers, I would much rather carry my own load and walk alone than among others and carry their load as well.

Jim Thornhill

Why should a child have to bear the responsibility of taking a whipping in order to keep their siblings from enduring one? How can a child be responsible for her parents' actions? Why should a sixty-year-old man refuse to play a simple board game due to a traumatic childhood experience? Why should a child be scared of their parents? What possesses a man to hit a child with his fist? How can a man look into the eyes of his crying daughter and then shoot her dog? How can a man repeatedly kick his daughter?

I made many mistakes with my children, but I never hit them. As far as I know, they never feared me. When Dad was angry, a common expression he used was, "I will stomp a mudhole in your back and walk it dry." I never thought he meant the phrase literally, but I most assuredly feared my father. Another top ten recording was, "I will beat you till you piss yourself and then beat you again for pissing yourself."

Respect cannot be earned by instilling fear. If you doubt the validity of that sentence, read *The Prince* by Machiavelli.[20] Perhaps Dad was bipolar. Perhaps he suffered from PTSD. I can't ask him for answers to these questions, and even if it was possible, the responses would not matter. The damage has been done. I believe the whole

---

[20] Niccolo Machiavelli, *The Prince*, 1513.

point Machiavelli was trying to make is you can force someone to obey you but you will never be able to force someone to respect you.

I'll not compare my parents to David and Louise Turpin, but there are some eerie similarities in the hypocritical way they allegedly lived and the way my parents raised us. The Turpin's presented a public persona of Christian people who were involved in their church. Their neighbors thought everything about them was normal. Based on the news reports I have seen, the family appeared to be—from the outside looking in, at least—well-adjusted in every respect.

My parents could not have been more involved in church. We could not have been held in higher regard by our community. The Turpin's allegedly held their children hostage. While my parents did not hold us hostage in our home, what we were allowed to do out of our home was severely restricted. Like the Turpin's, the image my parents displayed in public was not always reflective of what happened in our home. What is seen on the outside of a man is rarely what exists on the inside. A Chinese proverb says, "Outside noisy, inside empty." We were often noisy as a family on the outside, yet empty on the inside. Are you noisy on the outside and empty on the inside?

We finally got here. The tree has been cut down, the fire is burning, and the bread is toasting. We've turned 350 degrees to the right and changed heading by 10 degrees to the left. Here comes the point.

I have no doubt that Mom and Dad loved each of us, but I can't see where they had any respect for us. The result is I don't respect them either. You cannot respect someone when your interactions with them are questionable and the use of fear becomes the primary means of motivation. When you don't respect someone, they will not respect you.

I love my parents. I'm grateful for the life lessons they taught me. I've reconciled with and come to the conclusion they honestly believed they were doing what they thought was right. I'm sure many of the things they did to us were a product of their own upbringing. I have reconciled with that fact as well. I'm proud to be their son and attempt to honor them. Sadly, I'm also ashamed to admit I am their son. Yes, this sounds contradictory.

Allow me to explain. It is ironic that two plaques hang on Carolyn's living room wall. I remember the day Dad brought them home. They are family crests. Mom's maiden name is Young. The family motto on the Young crest is "Prudence excels strength." The family motto on the Thornhill crest is "Conquer or die." That contradiction epitomizes my childhood. Can anyone recommend a good psychiatrist?

I appreciate the sacrifices my parents made. It must have been challenging at best to raise six children with their limited financial resources. Their sound advice has proven to be invaluable on countless occasions. Please understand I do not speak here for any of my siblings. As much as it pains me to see these words on paper, I also have to say that after becoming an adult and analyzing my childhood from the perspective of the rearview mirror, my respect for them is nonexistent. How sad.

It is possible to like or even love somebody while simultaneously not respecting them. They are separate emotions. It is just as possible to be a supervisor and not be respected by your subordinates. If you want respect, you have to earn it. Respect does not automatically happen because of the position you have or your relationship with somebody.

It's a terrible thing to admit that one doesn't respect their parents, but in my case, it is the absolute unvarnished truth. As you might deduce, it was extremely painful for me to write these words; worse yet, it's indescribably horrific for me to see them in print and read them. That doesn't alter reality. If you feed chili laden with beans to your family for dinner, expect flatulence as a byproduct. In case you missed the inference, we're not discussing a buildup of pressure in your intestinal tract.

Today was Father's Day, and this morning's sermon brought me to tears. As he closed his message, the preacher described a Norman Rockwell painting where a little boy was trying to walk in his father's footsteps. He then asked some questions. I will paraphrase what he said, because I can't remember exactly how it was phrased.

Fathers, your children are going to follow in your footsteps. They are going to learn from your example. Will they pray? Will they become loving husbands or wives? Will they go to church? Will they learn to love the Lord? Will they become examples for their own children and teach them as Christian fathers? If they don't do these things, it will be because you failed them.

So what was it that brought me to tears? Let me remind you of something you read earlier regarding Magen and Jarred. They were not raised in the church. The fault rests squarely on my shoulders. The hymn for the altar call was "Trust and Obey." After hearing my pastor's words, it took every ounce of my energy to sing that song. Before I began to direct that song. I seriously considered asking my wife to substitute for me. Her voice is much prettier than mine anyway. After hearing the sermon. I knew it would take every fiber of my being to not cry like a baby in front of the entire congregation.

After the service was over. I went downstairs to the church basement. away from all prying eyes. I fell on my knees and burst into tears. I am crying as I write these words. I have been brought to tears several times as I have proofread this paragraph. My wife was unaware, but eventually, I'll tell her about it.

Sometimes I don't respect myself, particularly when it comes to remembering my past. Do you want to be a great leader? Do you really want to learn what LEDRSHHIP is all about? Let me tell you how to do it. *Put God first!* Don't believe in God? Just remember this: Your peers and your subordinates are going to follow your example. Earn their respect. More importantly, earn your own respect.

When I tell someone I respect them, they are not lightly spoken words, carelessly uttered without due consideration. If I tell you I respect you, it means something. Conversely, when I say I don't respect someone, it represents about the greatest insult I can think of. Who do I most respect? That one is too easy. It is my Jesus.

I hope my children respect me. I hope my siblings respect me. I hope my subordinates, my friends, my students, and my supervisor all respect me. I hope my parents respect me, and yes, I will see them again, even though they have departed this world. I hope I have earned the respect of all these people because of, and by being, the person I am. Perhaps one day, most of them will tell me they do.

Consider as you read this, do the people you interact with respect you? They will never tell you one way or the other, but if they don't, you will most assuredly realize it. It is up to you to earn that respect. It doesn't matter how much somebody may love you; their respect is quite another matter. Once you destroy it, you will never regain it. My ultimate desire is to earn the respect of God as well as any man can. I will know I have accomplished that when I hear Him say, "Well done, good and faithful servant" (Matthew 25:21, NIV)!

I have forgiven my parents and come to terms with the abuse experienced at their hands but cannot forget the suffering. It is part of what has made me become the man I am. I've heard it said forgiving also means forgetting but vehemently disagree with the idea. I'll agree with you that forgiving means reconciliation. Reconciliation is a willingness to get beyond what has happened and no longer dwell on and cease to harbor animosity because of it. LEDRSHHIP means reconciliation. I would like to forget the abusive details of my childhood more than you would like to win the lottery. They are unpleasant to say the least.

If what you have heard about my parents so far hasn't brought tears to your eyes, then you simply aren't human. There isn't any other way to put it. There is a reason for my revealing the horrible things which happened to me and to my siblings. It isn't therapy, but I must admit, putting these words on paper has been somewhat therapeutic.

This is why I did it. There is an incredible difference between God's forgiveness and human forgiveness. There is no comparison. When God forgives, he also chooses to forget. Do you still remember your first phone number? I was blessed with a gift of remembering numbers, which is sometimes a curse. It seems like it took forever for me to forget the Vehicle Identification Number (VIN) of my first new car, and yes, it did have a factory installed 8-track tape player in it.

Even though they have yet to apologize to America for their actions, I have forgiven the NFL for their childish protest of our national anthem, but I haven't forgotten their protest or watched a football game since then either. Forgiving from the human perspective doesn't always mean forgetting. It is not in our nature to forget when we have been hurt. Forgiving is not reconciliation.

I am extremely grateful for God's choice of forgetfulness. His choosing to forget goes far beyond reconciliation.

> Praise the Lord, O my soul, and forget not all his benefits who forgives all your sins and heals all your diseases, who redeems your life from the pit and crowns you with love and compassion… He will not always accuse, nor will he harbor his anger forever; He does not treat us as our sins deserve or repay us according to our iniquities. For as high as the Heavens are above the earth, so great is his love for those who fear him; as far as the east is from the west, so far has he removed our transgressions from us. (Psalm 103 2–12, NIV)

I want to forgive like God does, but I can't do that. Forgiveness earns respect from the forgiven.

Jesus had something to tell us about respect as He hung on the cross. It is difficult to know precisely the order of the seven statements he made hanging there, because neither of the four Gospel writers records all of them. Logic dictates this was the last of his seven statements. Although there are some LEDRSHHIP crossovers in each of His statements, I believe the last one is more about respect than anything else.

You might argue Jesus's last statement from the cross is about trust. I would agree with you on that point, but then I would also argue that trust is the inward result of ultimate respect.

> It was now about noon, and darkness came over the whole land until three in the afternoon, for the sun stopped shining. And the curtain of

the temple was torn in two. Jesus called out with
a loud voice, "Father, into your hands I commit
my spirit." When he had said this, he breathed
his last. (Luke 23:44–46, NIV)

How is it possible to have greater respect for someone than to
trust them with your spirit? God expects and demands your respect.

You will never become a good leader until you learn to earn
the respect of everyone you encounter. You will never understand
LEDRSHHIP until you earn your own respect either.

"S"

Selfless Service

Only a life lived for others is a life worthwhile.

—Albert Einstein[21]

I believe I can get whatever I want in life if I help enough other people get what they want. Let's say I want a new (fill in the blank) but I can't afford it. Here's a thought: My soldiers needed to pass their Army Physical Training Test (APFT). I ran with them, encouraged, and coached them. They needed to qualify with their weapons. I conducted classes where they were taught firing techniques. Then we went to the firing range where I made sure someone was able to spot for them while encouraging them. They needed to go to their military occupational schools so they could be promoted. I enrolled them in their courses, studied with, and quizzed them.

Sometimes they would tell me their employer wouldn't let them off to attend schools. That wasn't going to deter me from helping the members in my command. I phoned their supervisors and explained the importance. If that didn't work, I would make an unannounced personal visit while wearing my uniform.

---

[21] Albert Einstein, *Albert Einstein Quotes*, Create Space Independent Publishing, 2016.

Eventually, commanders get new assignments. When the time came for me to relinquish my second command, my company had the highest combat readiness rating in the brigade. That rating did not belong to me but to every soldier who was part of that company, and I made sure they knew it. My reward was a promotion which meant more money in my pocket, but the story doesn't stop there. Those efforts continue to benefit me financially, even today, because my monthly military retirement is more than it would have otherwise been.

The idea of selfless service is a sound biblical principle. John Maxwell said it like this: The first mark of servanthood is the ability to put others ahead of yourself and your personal desires. It is more than putting your agenda on hold. It means *intentionally* being aware of your people's needs, being available to help them, and to accept their desires as important.[22]

The most amazing lesson in the Bible I can think of about serving others comes from Jesus himself. It was just before the Passover festival. This story is in John's Gospel, Chapter 13:1–5. "Jesus knew that the hour had come for him to leave this world and go to the Father. Having loved his own who were in the world, he loved them to the end. The evening meal was in progress, and the devil had already prompted Judas, the son of Simon Iscariot, to betray Jesus. Jesus knew that the Father had put all things under his power, and that he had come from God and was returning to God; so he got up from the meal, took off His outer clothing, and wrapped a towel around his waist. After that, he poured water into a basin and began to wash his disciples' feet, drying them with the towel that was wrapped around him" (NIV).

Let's analyze those five verses and paint a mental picture of what actually happened. The first player in the story is the Creator of the universe, God incarnate (a.k.a. Jesus) who had the power to simply speak Earth into existence. Jesus, the one and only Jesus (a.k.a. God) drops to his knees and looks into the eyes of a man that he created.

---

[22] John C. Maxwell, *The 21 Indispensable Qualities of a Leader*, Maxwell Motivation, Inc., Nashville, TN, 1999.

He knows this man is going to betray him for a few worthless trinkets. Now, take a breath, wait for it… He washes his feet! I mean, *wow!* How much more humble can you be? We're talking about the example of all examples!

Humor me and read the whole story. It continues all the way through verse 17. Surprisingly, even though he is a major player, Judas isn't talked about much. The primary focus of our story is on Peter. You will have to figure out why Peter is such an important part of this story on your own. Judas is a major player, not because he betrays Jesus, but because without him, there is no lesson in service. In case you missed the point, Jesus washed his feet. Jesus washed Judas' feet! *Jesus!* If you really want something to think about, ask yourself this question: Why did he do that? Keep in mind that feet in those days of sandals—which were the primary mode of transportation, unpaved streets, and earthen floors—were not a wholesome sight. I'm pretty sure we are talking about some rather nasty feet here. Let's not lose sight of this fact either. In case you missed the inference, we aren't really talking about washing somebody's grungy feet either.

If Jesus can set that kind of an example of selfless service for us, what does it say to you? Selfless service means help others. In Matthew 22:39, Jesus said it pretty simply. "Love your neighbor as yourself" (NIV). That one verse pretty much wraps selfless service up in a Christmas package with a bright shiny ribbon and puts a bow on it, but keep that verse in mind. We'll come back to it later.

In chapter 3, "E" Empathy, I reminded you of the story Mark told us in the second chapter of his gospel about the paralytic man whom Jesus healed. We looked at the personal characteristics of the paralytic man's friends. What those men did is inspiring, and I'm awestruck by their efforts, but let's add more to it.

If you've spent any significant amount of time studying Mark's gospel, you might have arrived at the same conclusion as me. Mark tells us some amazing stories. He also informs us about incredible miracles, some rather intense philosophy, and the list goes on. What is not readily apparent is he uses his stories as tools in order to concentrate on one central overarching theme.

It isn't spelled out for you; you really have to read and think about what he is saying before you can understand where Mark is taking us. Let me assure you, it is well-worth the effort. Mark's philosophy centers around one resounding principle—selfless service. For me, the key verse in Mark's Gospel is chapter 10, verse 45. Mark quotes Jesus when he says, "Even the Son of Man did not come to be served, but to serve, and to give his life as a ransom for many" (NIV).

If I were tasked with summarizing and reducing Mark's Gospel to one sentence, it would certainly be a monumental undertaking and challenging to say the very least. That sentence would likely be something along the lines of, "Help others and put their needs above your own." A shorter version might be, "Love others more than yourself." Take a look at Matthew 22:35–40 (NIV):

"One of them, an expert in the law, tested him with this question: Teacher, which is the greatest commandment in the law? Jesus replied: Love the Lord your God with all your heart and with all your soul and with all your mind. This is the first and greatest commandment. And the second is like it. Love your neighbor as yourself. All the law and the prophets hang on these two commandments."

Perhaps you've heard the "Golden Rule"—treat people the way you want to be treated. I prefer the Platinum Rule. If you really want to be a great Christian (or leader), treat people better than you want to be treated.

A seven-year-old boy attended our church and the Sunday school class we teach. I will only use his first name, Matthew. We watched Matthew grow up and become a fine young Christian man. One evening, as I was watching the local newscast, Matthew suddenly became front and center stage. He was the lead story on the 6:00 p.m. evening newscast.

Matthew had been accused of committing a felony crime. To this day, nobody in our church believes he is guilty of what he was accused. I know him well; I observed Matthew interacting with his brothers as he grew and matured. Matthew accepted a plea and confessed to a lesser crime in order to avoid trial and receive a reduced sentence. I'm confident he was covering for someone. Everyone at church believes they know who the guilty party is, but I'll not reveal her name.

Matthew hasn't confirmed our thoughts. We have chosen to not ask him, because it isn't important to either of us. My Christian love for Matthew is unconditional, as he is, and it isn't any of my business unless he decides to reveal any additional information. He has now been released on probation after serving his sentence.

Matthew is very musically talented. At the time of his incarceration, he was becoming known, locally beginning to attract large audiences. We attempt to invite him to dinner in our home on a regular basis. *(Matthew, we still keep diet vanilla Coca Cola in the cupboard for you even though you haven't been over for a while. Do you know how hard it is to find diet vanilla coke?)* On a recent visit, he told me that while in prison, he occupied himself by conducting Bible study groups. As a result of those efforts, several inmates came to believe in Christ.

Matthew lives by the principle outlined in the twenty-ninth chapter of Jeremiah. No doubt you have likely heard the expression, "Make the best of your situation regardless of the circumstances." Like many colloquialisms, it isn't just an expression but instead is rooted in scripture.

The Jews had been taken into captivity by King Nebuchadnezzar and exiled from Jerusalem into Babylon. God gave the prophet Jeremiah a message to pass along to them. God advised them to build houses, plant gardens, marry, have children, increase in number, and seek peace. In Verse 11 (NIV), he tells them the reason for these instructions. "'For I know the plans I have for you,' declares the Lord, 'plans to prosper you and not to harm you, plans to give you a hope and a future.'" Matthew spent his time in prison well. He served others by making a difference in the lives of his fellow inmates.

One evening, over dinner conversation, Matthew told me he had an epiphany during his incarceration. He realized it really didn't matter if five or 5,000 people were coming to hear him perform. The only thing which really mattered to him was whether or not he was serving Christ in the manner Christ desires. He told us that he wouldn't have come to that realization were it not for him being in prison. That level of insight is quite refreshing, particularly coming from a young man in his early twenties.

Our church youth group regularly attends a Christian summer camp which we financially support. We let them use the fellowship hall to conduct one of their fund-raisers, which is an annual spaghetti dinner. It is advertised all over town with banners and flyers. Donations are requested for the meal but not required. Most of Zeigler's population looks forward to it all year long.

Our church members contribute the food, but the youth group is responsible for cooking, setting tables, rolling silverware, washing dishes, wiping tables, vacuuming the floor, cleaning up, making drinks, and waiting on everyone who comes to eat. They are the ones who receive the money, and if they want to attend, we require them to work for it. If they don't help, they don't go.

Matthew contributed his time this year to assist the youth group. I watched him work incredibly hard, knowing fully well he would not attend the summer camp because he was too old. I saw him busing tables, bringing orders, cleaning the floor, filling drinks, and mopping up spills. I was at the donation collection table.

Matthew has a full-time dangerous job working at a sawmill earning $300 a week prior to taxes with no benefits. He pays child support, his living expenses, rent, utilities, car insurance, etc., just like everyone else. Matthew gave me a $20 donation for a plate of spaghetti that got cold before he could eat it.

When he gave me the money, I told him he reminded me of the widow Jesus spoke about in Mark 12:41–44 who contributed two small copper coins to the offering *(read it; it's a humbling story)*. Matthew said he had to do what was right. He leads by example; he lives a life of selfless service.

I like to think I've lived a life of serving people. I was there to help and had already made a generous contribution. Matthew's attitude of service made mine look pale by comparison. He humbled me, not because of the amount of the contribution. The amount wasn't important, it was the generosity of his sacrifice.

Let's say I am a screenwriter writing a movie script about selfless service. This is the gist of the story I'd tell:

Setting: Late-60s, rural Mississippi, mid-winter.

Primary character: Mr. Smith, Caucasian adult male, early thirties.

Action: Mr. Smith is driving to work early on a Sunday morning. It is terribly cold, and light snow covers the ground *(it doesn't snow very much in Mississippi)*. He hears a loud bang and realizes he has a flat tire, so he pulls onto the side of the road to change it. As Mr. Smith is changing the tire, two men stop behind him and offer to help but, unfortunately, their offer isn't sincere.

When Mr. Smith isn't looking, one of the men strikes Mr. Smith over the head from behind with a tire iron, giving him a concussion and causing him to lose consciousness. Then they rob Mr. Smith, taking his wallet, watch, clothes, wedding ring, and vehicle.

Soon a police officer comes by and notices Mr. Smith lying on the side of the road. He has to be at work early that day. The policeman was in trouble with his sergeant the day before because he had been late on several occasions. The policeman drives past Mr. Smith without assisting and leaves him there.

Next, a local preacher drives by on his way to church. He needs to unlock the doors, turn on the heat, start the coffee, and work on his sermon. The preacher sees Mr. Smith and drives past him as well, leaving him lying on the side of the road, just as the police officer did. The preacher is in a hurry and has important things to do.

A young African-American family (we will call them the Joneses) drives by next. They have two children in the backseat. Mr. Jones is a science teacher at Jackson State University, and Mrs. Jones is a teacher at the local elementary school. They are on winter break and going home for Christmas to see their parents. The trunk of their vehicle is filled with luggage and Christmas presents for their children.

They notice Mr. Smith lying on the road, bleeding and obviously needing help. They stop to assist. They get a blanket from the trunk, wrap him in it, and help him into the car. They drive to the next town and see a Holiday Inn. Mr. Jones goes in the office to inquire about a room but is told there are no vacancies in spite of the sign outside the building indicating the contrary. Being a smart

African-American man in racially bigoted America living in the south during the sixties, Mr. Jones quickly realizes why he is told there are no vacancies at the hotel.

Mr. Jones tells the desk clerk the room isn't for him, it's for Mr. Smith. Mr. Jones pays for a one-week stay and leaves Mr. Smith in the care of the hotelier. He also leaves some extra cash and asks that a doctor be called to take care of Mr. Smith first thing on Monday morning. Mr. Jones promises to stop on his way home and settle any outstanding bills Mr. Smith might have accrued.

I know you have heard this story before, using a slightly different cast of characters. It is the story of the Good Samaritan. The Good Samaritan is a parable Jesus told in the tenth chapter of Luke, verses 30 through 37. A parable is a seemingly unrelated story that parallels a spiritual truth.

Jesus spoke and taught with parables. He had to disguise his intent because the religious leaders of the day were looking for an excuse to kill him. Using parables allowed him to make his point without directly insulting those who wished to harm him. He used parables sort of like a secret code.

Jesus was calling the priests and Levites who were the religious leaders of the day out when he told this story. He was telling them, "You are the very people who should be helping others, yet you are not." The Samaritan had every reason to hate the Jewish man. The one person who would be least expected to help did precisely that. He chose to help. Samaritans would not even travel through Jewish territory. They would walk for miles just to avoid it. Instead, the very person who had the most to fear and the most to lose acted mercifully.

The Good Samaritan shows us the epitome of selfless service. Selfless service is helping someone else, regardless of your feelings about them and regardless of the personal cost or consequences you might face for the effort.

Are you the policeman, the preacher, or the Jones's living in racially biased America during the 1960's in my version of the Good Samaritan? Let me answer that question for you with a resounding and emphatic YES shouted from a megaphone at full volume. Expect me to be blunt. I'm calling you out. Yes, you are the policeman, the fireman, the first responder, the Soldier, the preacher or any other title you care to substitute. If you just read that story then I'm speaking directly to you. When you notice that somebody needs help, you are the very person who should step up and help them. Regardless of who you are, it is your responsibility to help someone should they require your assistance.

In a nutshell, serving others comes down to love taking action. If you will pardon the colloquialism, it means putting your money where your mouth is. I love my wife. I love her totally, absolutely, and completely. It means everything I have is hers, and her needs come before mine. If the laundry needs to be done, if the dishes need to be washed, if the floor needs to be vacuumed, or the house needs to be cleaned, then those responsibilities come before what I might want to do. It means my wallet, my time, my energy, my effort, and my body all belong to her. The action I choose to take is whatever it takes to make her happy. I serve her because of my love for her. My love takes the action of making her priorities my priorities.

I know this is a short chapter, but it is pretty difficult to improve on the way Jesus said things. Dare I use the word *impossible*?

7

"H"

Honor

Honor isn't about making the right choices. It's
about dealing with the consequences.

—Midori Koto

*H*onor is a noun, meaning honesty and fairness in one's beliefs or actions. It is also a verb, meaning to regard with great respect.

Richard Flanagan's *The Narrow Road to the Deep North*[23] tells the tale of Australian POWs building the Burma railway under brutal conditions during WWII. One of the prisoners suffered a horrendous beating from the Japanese guards. His fellow prisoners were forced to stand at attention and watch. That night, the injured prisoner fell into the camp latrine and drowned. After the war, some of his buddies were out for a night of drinking and revelry when they came upon Nikitaris' fish shop.

They remembered how their friend used to talk about how much he loved to take his girlfriend there, and someday, he wanted to return to set the fish free. Remembering their friend, the soldiers broke the window and let the fish go in the harbor. Remorse set in,

---

[23] Richard Flanagan, *The Narrow Road to the Deep North,*" Penguin Random House LLC, New York City, NY, September 23, 2013.

143

so the next day, they came back to pay for the damages. When they explained themselves to Mr. Nikitaris, something amazing happened.

First, Mr. Nikitaris refused their money, then he fed them, gave them wine to drink, and pastries for dessert that his daughter had made. The soldiers soon realized the old man had lost his son in the war as well.

The story is an example of a profound sense of honor—honor about brothers-in-arms who were honoring the memory of their friend, an old man who was honoring their loss, a group of wounded men honoring his loss, and all of them finding solace in the meaning of their mutual sufferings. It's a book well-worth reading.

You're probably thinking you wouldn't ever be in a situation like the one author Flanagan describes, and it is highly probable you are correct in that assumption. It is an extreme example. It isn't the situation which is important but your reaction to it which matters.

Consider this, though. You have been, you know someone who has, you will witness, or you'll find yourself in a situation similar to this next one, because events similar to it happen every day. The main difference is someone noticed it.

Recently at the Hopkins, Minnesota, Dairy Queen, a blind customer pulled out some money to pay for his order and accidently dropped a $20 bill.[24] The customer behind him quickly picked it up and put the money in her pocket. Joey Prusak was behind the counter and witnessed the event. He asked the second customer to return the money. She refused. Prusak expelled her from the restaurant and gave the blind man a twenty-dollar bill from his own pocket. Then he went back to work.

"I was just doing what I thought was right. I did it without even thinking about it. Ninety-nine people out of 100 would have done the same thing," Prusak told the Associated Press.

Joey, my apologies, but with great sadness, I must burst your bubble. Unfortunately, from my vantage point at least, the world in which we live isn't nearly as idealistic as you seem to believe, my young friend. Even though your behavior should be normal in our

---

[24] ABC News, September 20, 2013.

society, sir, I sadly believe you are the exception. You are an honorable man, and that is a rarity.

A nineteen-year-old fast-food worker teaches all of us about honor by proving it isn't only what we do, but how we do it. There is a cost to honorable behavior. Ask Joey. It cost him $20, but the great thing is that the story didn't end there.

The next customer in line noticed someone did the right thing; someone finally acted honorably. He spoke up about the situation, and Joey has become famous for doing what everyone should do. He has been offered numerous jobs and received two interesting phone calls. One was from John Gainor, Dairy Queen CEO, and the other was from billionaire Warren Buffett whose company owns Dairy Queen. Mr. Buffett also invited Joey to the next shareholder's meeting as a special guest of Mr. Gainor where he was rewarded with a trip to the 2014 Daytona 500. He was also invited to be a guest on *The Queen Latifah Show*.

Instead of costing him, in Joey's case, honorable behavior was intrinsically rewarded. That doesn't always happen. It isn't my desire to negate his actions in any way. I'd like to think my children would have acted the same way had they been standing behind that counter. Joey said what he did was normal; so why then was he so richly rewarded for his behavior? It's because an honorable person is a rarity.

I did a number of odd-jobs to work my way through college. At one point, I was fortunate enough to sell tickets for an event at which the late motivational speakers and authors Dr. Norman Vincent Peale along with Mr. Zig Ziglar were both speaking. I say fortunate, because I got to hear them both speak and had the opportunity to meet them after the program. They were both impressive men who added immeasurably to this world. It was an incredible experience to talk with them. My personal belief is Mr. Ziglar's best book is *See You at the Top*.[25] I strongly recommend it.

Mr. Ziglar has some rather colorful quotations, one of which is, "We all need a checkup from the neck up to avoid our stinkin' thinkin';" but my personal favorite is, "It is character that gets us

---

[25] Zig Ziglar, "See You at the Top," October 24, 1975.

out of bed, commitment that moves us to action, and discipline that enables us to follow through."

I believe Mr. Ziglar is telling us honor represents the content of our character. If you're an honorable person, you understand. It was an incredible experience to shake hands with Mr. Ziglar and Dr. Peale, because they are honorable men.

The article which follows, "Playing Catch Up," was initially published in the January 2017 edition of *Aircraft Owners and Pilots Association Flight Training* magazine (AOPA). It is reprinted with permission from AOPA in its entirety. I'm not certain where the story about who kicked the dog, a part of the article, came from. You'll understand that comment after you read it. It's also possible that a cat was kicked instead of a dog. The story sounds suspiciously similar to the kind of story Mr. Ziglar would tell. Good stories are like that. You tend to remember them and the lesson they teach, but not necessarily the origin.

Before reporting me to the ASPCA, please be assured it isn't my habit to kick tiny defenseless animals. My apologies in advance if you're not a pilot, because it is written for them and is slightly technical in nature. I'll let you know my reason for including it after you read it, but let me give you a hint before you begin. It has a little something to do with honor, particularly the first and last paragraphs.

Playing Catch Up

Years ago, I read a troubling story. A man had a rough day at work. When he got home, he took it out on his wife. She in turn yelled at their son who then went out to play. The boy was upset and he kicked the family dog. The point of the story is, who really kicked the dog? The implied lesson is, "Don't let someone else kick your dog." Well, guess what? I let the dean at my college kick my dog.

I work at a FAA Part 141 flight school located in the Midwest and have been employed here for 20 years. I am an assistant chief flight instructor with more than 5,000 flight hours. Like other institutions, our university is feeling the crunch of an uncertain economic environment. The dean of our college gets pressure from above him in the university food chain. He is a results-driven man. He puts pressure on the chief flight instructor to make sure our students complete their flight courses quickly. The chief, in turn, puts pressure on me.

I had a full calendar. Several students were assigned to me for progress checks. In addition, my personal students were behind schedule. Although he never said a word to me about it, I could feel my boss breathing down my neck. I was determined to catch up, no matter what (Do you see some hazardous attitudes developing here?).

I was conducting a progress check for an instrument flight student. She was wearing Foggles and could not see outside. I take full responsibility for these events. Upon departure from My Home Airport (MHA) the sky was clear with scattered clouds at 2,500 feet reported at the Airport Next Door (AND). There is an AND in Anderson, South Carolina—and before you ask, these events did not transpire there.

As the flight progressed, the scattered layer became broken. Ten miles southwest of AND, level at 3,000 feet, I requested from AND tower direct DUUMM—as far as I know, DUUMM isn't an initial approach fix anywhere, just the way I was acting—VOR 2 approach straight in. AND's tower replied Unable, opposite direction IFR traffic, ILS 20. I then requested direct AND VOR (located on the field) followed by the VOR 20 approach. AND tower approved because we were above the opposite direction traffic. We were also above the clouds, visibility greater than 10. Were we really 1,000 feet above? I told myself we were, but if an examiner had been onboard, I doubt he would have agreed.

Proceeding toward the VOR, I saw a hole in the clouds. I had the student descend below them to 2,000 feet, continue toward the VOR, and expect the VOR 20 approach; I requested altitude modification for the practice approach. Tower approved.

We descended through the hole, and I told myself we were clear by 2,000 feet horizontally, but once again, I doubt an examiner would have agreed. The bases appeared to be at 2,500 feet. We were now below cloud level at 2,000. After crossing over the VOR, we flew outbound on the 010 radial. Tower requested that we report the procedure turn outbound and stated clouds broken 1,600. We were at 2,000 and below the clouds, but 500 feet below? Who was I trying to fool?

As the student began the procedure turn outbound, IFR traffic reported it was climbing to 2,500 feet because we were 1.5 miles directly in front of them. AND tower approved. What frightens me is I never saw the other traffic. I never saw it! We continued the procedure turn, subsequently completed our approach, the IFR traffic reestablished glideslope, and both aircraft landed without incident. MHA, exactly 11.3 nautical miles from AND, was reporting clear the entire time.

I endangered everyone on board both aircraft because I was determined to complete my task. Nothing was going to get in my way. As an instructor with more than 20 years' experience, my attitude was inexcusable. FAR 91.155 is there for a reason. How many times have I told one of my students there is always a better day to fly, don't take unnecessary risks?

Yet, being fully aware of the regulations, the situation, and the potential for a catastrophic outcome, taking a foolish chance is precisely what I did. If the FAA decided to take certificate action against me, it would have been deserved. There is nothing the FAA could do to me that would come close to the punishment I have already put myself through as I reflect upon how stupid I feel and ashamed I am of my actions. It won't happen again. Sorry, Dean, you don't get to kick my dog twice.

The End (No, not the book, just the article).

* * * * *

So what does my article about flight training have to do with honor (*yes, my article; I wrote it*)? A great deal, actually. To answer the question, reread the first and the last paragraphs. It's very simple. I committed an egregious error in judgment, and people could have died. I admitted it and was prepared for the consequences. It wasn't intentional; it was simply a bad choice, and we all make them. Choices have consequences. I accepted the responsibility for making a terribly reckless one and acknowledged it in writing and in a national publication. The reason I chose to submit my article was so others could learn from my mistake.

That admission and my lapse in judgment, without question, had the potential to end my aviation career. While that concerned me, by comparison, it pales in my mind to the realization of just how serious the outcome could have been. The closure rate of two aircraft hurtling toward each other at 100 knots each is 200 knots per hour. We were 1.5 nautical miles apart. Let me rephrase that. Everyone on board both aircraft was twenty-seven seconds from never kissing their spouse hello again, twenty-seven seconds from never looking into the eyes of their children again, twenty-seven seconds from never having a chance to apologize for the thing they regretted doing, twenty-seven seconds from never coming home again—twenty-seven seconds from being dead.

With more than thirty years' experience as a pilot, I had no idea how eminent a catastrophic event was at the time. My instincts of how close we were to an inflight collision failed me. I don't know the name of the pilot who was flying the other aircraft, but I'll tell you, he is an honorable man. He is honorable because he reacted without malice or anger. He reacted with respect for me and the tower controller, with an understanding of the situation. He simply did what needed to be done.

His concern wasn't about righting a wrong, making a report, or getting his pound of flesh. The man just did his job, and all of us lived to fly another day because of his honorable actions. In spite of the personal consequences you might face, honor means accepting responsibility for your shortcomings and doing something about them. That is what ensures a different outcome the next time.

Upon reading my article, Robert told me it must have taken great courage for me to send it out for publication. He then asked me why I didn't keep silent about the situation and avoid calling attention to a potentially career-ending mistake. It was much more than courage, Robert. Let me explain.

It was a matter of *loyalty* to my industry and to me. It was a reminder to all pilots that we are human and prone to error. It was reinforcement to myself that each of us needs to show *empathy* toward our fellow aviators when they inevitably experience a lapse in sound judgement. It was a matter of *duty* to keep my fellow aviators safe by reminding them how quickly those mistakes can happen and how dire the consequences can be. It was a sign of *respect* for the pilot of the other aircraft who took a dangerous situation in stride, then did his job well and thanklessly. It was a matter of *serving* the industry which I have been privileged to be a part of for so many years along with my fellow airmen. It was a matter of *honor*. Three paragraphs have already been devoted to that. It was a matter of *humility*, admitting that even with all my experience, I risked innocent lives. It was a matter of *integrity*, doing the right thing because it was the right thing to do.

My point is without *honor*, LEDRSHHIP does not exist. Robert, perhaps there was a small amount of *personal courage* involved. In case you missed the inference, we're not really discussing aviators.

8

"H"

Humility

Do nothing out of selfish ambition or vain conceit.
Rather, in humility, value others above yourselves.
—Philippians 2:3, NIV

It was a struggle to decide which chapter to place this next story in.
It could be used equally well to discuss humility or honor; perhaps,
more appropriately phrased, the lack of both. I decided on humility, and the truth is it almost came down to a coin flip. I've always
thought humility and pride represent opposite ends of the same spectrum. The analogy of a coin comes to mind.

It's been said there are three sides to an issue. There is your
side, my side, and the right side, similar to the two sides and edge of
a coin. Think of this story as the edge of a coin if one side of it was
honor and the other one was humility.

It is often difficult to do the right thing, especially when you
don't feel like it, especially if you've done the wrong thing in the first
place *(I hear your thoughts. Is this another coconut story? What is wrong
with this guy?)*. Before we go very far with this, let me first say I'm
in the wrong here, but you were promised honesty. What we never
know is how God might use your effort, how he might use your
humility, and how that can impact those around you. He can do that

even when you've done the wrong thing. God has a plan for everything. *Everything!* Let me tell you about my pride and what it cost me; or more accurately, how expensive my lack of humility became.

There were two men that worked with me for several years, and both have the same first name which I'll not reveal. No doubt, you have met multiple Bob's or Jim's in your life *(that was a shameless and cheap way of giving a shout out to my brothers)*. It isn't my intention to embarrass or insult either of my former colleagues nor do I wish to confuse my readers. To simplify things, we'll modify their names and refer to my former colleagues as Saul and Paul, both of whom have now retired. There is a specific reason for my choice of names, which you may have already ascertained.

During a staff meeting one morning, Saul had a bur under his saddle. He took it upon himself to point out how unfair things seemed to be. He felt it necessary to point out that some of us were not living up to our responsibilities and carrying our fair share of the load. He included me in that group. To make it worse, Saul put it in writing, including facts and figures. It embarrassed me, and my reaction was rash. Saul wounded my pride. Later that day, I fired off a detestable e-mail telling him what I thought about his inconsiderate actions. How dare he call me out in public like that!

The problem is I forgot about something. "Do not repay evil with evil or insult with insult. On the contrary, repay evil with blessing" (1 Peter 3:9, NIV). I remembered the verse well enough because I'd memorized it as a child but gave it no thought as my e-mail was drafted. What I'd forgotten was these words aren't a suggestion, but a command, and easily comprehendible. Everyone is aware of the Ten Commandments, but God gives us many more than the famous ten.

In my defense, I was not the only one angered by his actions but was the only one who chose to react. Everyone else kept their feelings to themselves, but not me. I decided to articulate my anger, to do something about it. Unfortunately, I said some very hateful things in that e-mail. My detestable behavior wasn't bad enough though. I wanted vindication, revenge, to regain my pride.

My Uncle Bill once told me, "Never argue with an idiot, because nobody will know which one of you is crazy." I should have listened to his advice. Proverbs 26:4 parrots my uncle's words. "Do not answer a fool according to his folly, or you will be just like him" (NIV).

I no longer remember what Saul said but most certainly remember my anger and the need to make sure everyone was aware of those feelings. What would be a better way for me to accomplish that than include the entire staff on the copy line of my e-mail to Saul? The horrible thing about an e-mail like that is once you press the send key, there's no going back; your actions can't be undone.

Upon reflection, I sent another e-mail to Saul and apologized for my behavior. I humbled myself in that letter of apology. I not only told him how wrong I'd been, but also how right he was. Since Saul had been publicly humiliated by my action, it was only fair the entire staff receive a copy of the apology also. It was necessary for me to swallow my pride and publicly humiliate myself as a result of my insensitivity. It was the right thing do.

Saul accepted my apology, but things were never the same between us. Prior to this, he was at least minimally cordial and occasionally just downright friendly. He once lent me a copy of "My American Journey"[26] by retired General Colin Powell because he knew I wanted to read it. Afterward we spent some time discussing it. We would have the occasional and typical work-type conversations which I'm sure you have engaged in with your peers from time to time.

After my scathing e-mail and subsequent apology, things became dramatically different. Saul would answer when I would tell him good morning, but his reply was always curt. Since then, he was never the first to tell me good morning should we pass each other in the hallway. Should I tell him good afternoon later during the course of the day, he would simply ignore me. He often pretended to not hear my attempts to engage him in conversation.

Let's just say there was no friendship. We both learned to live with the situation by keeping a distance between ourselves, but it was never my choice. It was his. Saul has forgiven me, but he hasn't forgotten; I'm sure he never will.

---

[26] Colin Powell, "My American Journey," May 14, 2003.

Even though I've been forgiven by Saul, we have not reconciled. Again, that was never my choice. I genuinely attempted to reconcile with Saul. I "made every effort to live in peace" with Saul "and to be holy; without holiness, no one will see the Lord" (Hebrews 12:14, NIV). Forgiveness and reconciliation are two very different things. When Saul retired, he had not gotten past his anger, and in all likelihood, probably still hasn't. Instead of anger, a word which might more appropriately describe Saul's feelings toward me might be *livid*.

Saul has every human right to be but upset, but here is the problem. Jesus's own brother gave us all some advice about that. James 1:20 (NIV) tells us, "Human anger does not produce the righteousness that God desires." Forgiveness isn't for the other guy. Forgiveness—and more importantly, reconciliation—is for you.

Forgiveness is just the first step. You must learn how to let go of the anger, to get beyond it, to reconcile. Without question, I deserve the cold shoulder Saul gave me for so many years before he retired. What about him, though? Does Saul deserve the cold shoulder he gave himself? Does he deserve to be miserable because he refuses reconciliation? Do you know anyone like him? And more to the point, are you occasionally Saul?

Let's fast forward five years later. By this time, I'd forgotten how my apology had been phrased but not the reason for it. It is difficult to forget a mistake when you are constantly reminded of it on a daily basis, but this is only the beginning of the story.

One afternoon, Paul approached me and asked me if we could talk for a few minutes. Then he gave me a copy of the apology I'd made to Saul five years earlier. Paul told me he kept it because my words had touched him. My apology to Saul influenced Paul, and he began going back to church. He then told me he could tell I was a Christian man and thanked me for making a difference in his life. God uses you, even in the worst of circumstances. He uses your mistakes to teach you and your lapse in judgment to influence others. Don't tell me he doesn't.

In one way or another, the laws of many countries are based on the Ten Commandments, the United States included. Regardless of whether you believe in God or don't, we both know you've heard them. My question is, have you thought about them? Take a moment and read them. They are in the first seventeen verses of Exodus 20. Give them some thought as you do.

What is interesting to me is that all ten of them are about relationships. The first four are about what your relationship with God should be like. The remaining six are what your relationship with other people should be like.

God gave us much more than the "Big Ten" to follow. I reminded you of that a few paragraphs ago when we talked about Proverbs 26:4. Here is a second list for you; think of them as the second set of ten commandments. If you prefer, consider them recommendations for living a good life. If the idea of God bothers you, but you're still reading this because you believe my words may have value, try this. Instead of the word *God* in commandment seven (in the second set of ten commandments), substitute someone's name whose opinion is important to you, someone whose love you cherish. Perhaps you might want to substitute the name of your spouse, your mother, or your sister. Also, change commandment ten (in the second set of ten commandments) to "Be grateful that you are a...," then fill in the blank with whatever your professional occupation happens to be, i.e. beautician, salesmen, animal trainer, librarian, teacher, pilot, stay-at-home spouse, computer programmer, taxicab driver, or retiree. Like the Ten Commandments found in Exodus, their focus is upon relationships. You have to search for them, but the second set can be found in 1 Peter, Chapter 4.

The Second Ten Commandments?

1) Be clear-minded and self-controlled.
2) Love each other deeply, because love covers a multitude of sins.
3) Offer hospitality without grumbling.
4) Use whatever gifts you have received to serve others.
5) Clothe yourself with humility *(there's that word again)*.
6) Be alert.
7) Speak as if God is listening to every word you say *(trust me, he is)*.

8) Do not be eager for money, but be eager to serve in all things.
9) Rejoice in your sufferings.
10) Praise God that you bear the name Christian.

I placed the "Second Ten Commandments?" on the bulletin board located outside of my office door. Someone kept taking them down. I never knew who was doing it but suspect Saul was the responsible party.

One morning, as I walked down the hallway toward my office, a student was following closely behind me. He noticed the paper on which they were printed was wadded up and lying on the floor in front of my door. My student picked up the paper, smoothed it out as best he could, and placed it back on my bulletin board. That simple act touched me in an indescribable way. I left that piece of paper hanging there in all of its wrinkled glory so Saul, or anyone else who felt inclined to look, could see it. I'm sure that whoever removed it was really offended by that. Another time it was taken down, torn into small pieces, which were then wadded up together into a ball, and the remnants were stuffed under my office door.

There is supposed to be a separation of church and state, but my boss never said anything to me about what was on my bulletin board. Let me give the Sauls of the world a tidbit of advice. You are not my judge jury and executioner. You are not a member of the bulletin board police force. We share the same job title. If my supervisor disapproves of my actions, it is his responsibility to inform me, but it isn't yours. What gives you the right to remove anything from my bulletin board? Under whose authority are you acting? Your behavior amounts to childish vandalism, reminiscent of a two-year-old's temper tantrum. Freedom of religion means even if you disagree with my beliefs, I still get to express them. Freedom of religion does not mean freedom from religion.

Let me say it another way. "Do not judge, or you too will be judged. For in the same way you judge others you will be judged, and with the measure you use, it will be measured to you." Those aren't my words. Most people would likely agree they come from an impeccable source. Jesus himself said them. You can find them in Matthew's Gospel (NIV), chapter 7, verses 1 and 2.

You may find a discussion of God to be offensive. I don't really care if my actions—or perhaps more appropriately stated, my religious beliefs—offend you. That doesn't bother me, but I care greatly if they offend my Jesus. His approval means everything to me, whereas your approval means nothing to me. What happened to my freedom of religion? Why is everyone permitted to post whatever they want, wherever they want, whenever they want, while I'm simultaneously prevented from stating my beliefs because I'm a Christian?

The words of Paul from the Bible come to my mind *(Now you might have an idea why I chose Paul and Saul for names instead of something like Bob #1 and Bob #2 or Jim #1 and Jim #2. Yup, unashamedly, I did it again. I really love my brothers. When you write a book, you can put whatever you want in it)*. In verses 19 and 20 of chapter 6, in his letter to the Ephesians, Paul (from the Bible) tells us, "Pray also for me, that whenever I speak, words may be given me, so that I will fearlessly make known the mystery of the gospel, for which I am an ambassador in chains" (NIV).

Eventually, whoever was taking the second ten commandments off my bulletin board stopped doing it. I suspect Saul was the guilty party because the behavior immediately ceased the day he retired and left the building for the last time.

There is some supporting evidence for my conclusion. A few days after Saul retired, another colleague of mine asked me for a copy of them. He'd been disappointed the last time they were removed because the paper had been "savagely ripped in a manner resembling a hate crime," and the only two people in the building when this happened were Saul and himself. I'm not going to say Saul did it, but… well, draw your own conclusion.

Until the day Saul retired, I just kept replacing the Second Ten Commandments. I continued to say "Good morning, Saul" and continued smiling at him whenever I saw him. I continued to be as cheerful and cordial as possible. I never failed to treat him with the respect and dignity he deserved as a man created in God's image.

As you might suspect, my behavior was far from reciprocated. No matter how many times he pretended I didn't exist or chose to ignore me, it never hurt my feelings. To this day, I continue to love him and pray for him and his family. It doesn't matter if Saul hates me. That isn't any of my business.

You may have seen a "Coexist" bumper sticker if you have recently spent any time on a college campus. If you haven't, it is highly likely you will, because they are becoming rather commonplace. The word *coexist* is spelled out using various religious symbols. For example, the letter "C" is often a crescent and a star representing Islam, while "I" depicts the pentagram representing Wiccans or Pagans. There are numerous variations of the symbols used, but I've never seen the "T" represented by anything other than the Christian cross. To the best of my knowledge, the only religious symbol which forms the letter "T" is a cross. I recently saw a "Coexist" bumper sticker using the rainbow color spectrum, presumably to include the LGBTQ community.

"Coexistence" sounds like a "live and let live" concept, but it is considerably different. The implication is we should accept all religions (including anti-religions, witchcraft, etc.) and alternate lifestyles. In general, people different from you. That would be fine if that were the end of it. However, it really means you must openly accept someone else's preferred religion (or atheism or agnosticism) and/or alternate lifestyles while keeping your own completely out of sight, completely out of earshot, and in the closet. This is particularly true if someone happens to disagree with your beliefs.

It seems to me that those who commonly scream for others to be tolerant of different beliefs and lifestyles are typically, and absolutely, intolerant of others, particularly Christians. They will do whatever they can, and anything they can, in order to silence them. Let me explain that a bit more curtly. The prevailing attitude tends to be, "Listen to me and pay attention to what I believe, but when it comes to Jesus, shut up."

While we're on the subject of the LGBTQ community, let me inform you of something—God does not approve! Perhaps you contend you're a man trapped in a woman's body or vice-versa, so you have made arrangements to "transgender," to have the big operation. I'm willing to bet that afterward, if you were to have a DNA test, your twenty-third set of chromosomes would not have been altered in any way!

Perhaps you have said, "I'm just not attracted to members of the opposite sex." You are my brother (or my sister) and I've already told you I love you, and God loves you also. Nothing will alter either of those two facts. Just because God loves you, don't make the mistake of believing he approves of what you're doing. His point of view on the matter is pretty clear. He calls it an abomination. If you have the courage, read about it in Leviticus chapter 20.

Have you ever heard the word *rationalize*? Let's break that word down. Think of it as three separate words: *Ration*, meaning to distribute something; *A*, meaning singular; and *Lies*, meaning not the truth. In summation, it means you are lying to yourself about something.

Warning! If you have any tolerance toward or are sharing in any part of the disgusting behavior the LGBTQ community advocates, prepare to be really upset. Previously I described something as appearing to come from the southern end of a northerly bound male bovine. Now I'll be significantly crasser. You are full of *bull poop!*

You thought you were going to get a different word, didn't you? In all honesty, the first time this paragraph was written, there was a different word there. I'm a Christian, and this is a Christian book. The original word was changed, but you get the idea.

There is a reason for telling you the word was changed. My editor would probably have asked me to, but there was no need. I changed it before she read this part. When God really matters to you, then you question your actions before taking them. You want Him to be proud of you. If he is proud of me, everyone that really matters will be. Everything falls into place when your priorities are right.

Priority one is his will. LEDRSHHIP means being a professional at all times, even with your language choices, even when you don't want to.

God doesn't make mistakes. LGBTQ is wrong no matter how you attempt justification of your actions. Regardless of the banner you stand behind to argue your point—political correctness, equal rights, coexistence, tolerance, etc.—you won't change my mind. You're not about to change God's mind either. Don't get me wrong. It isn't my place to judge you. Make your own choices. God gives you that right, and I've risked mine to preserve it for you.

If you need food, come to my home for a meal. It might be rice and beans from the church food pantry, but you won't leave my home hungry. If you need clothing, I'll provide it. We might have to take a short trip to the closest thrift store, but you'll leave with something to wear and a warm coat if you need one. My first suit came from a Salvation Army thrift store and it cost a whopping $3.00. I wore it to meet Mr. Ziglar and   Dr. Peale because it was the only suit I had. I wasn't the least bit embarrassed to wear it either, even though it probably looked like a $3.00 suit.

Come to Zeigler First Baptist Church anytime. Sunday school is at 9:30 a.m., worship service begins at 10:30. I'm there every Sunday. You're welcome to worship with me whenever you wish, but your lifestyle is disgusting and demoralizing. There is nothing good about it. There is no benefit to society from the television networks, music, or movie industries continually thrusting your garbage down my throat either. It sickens me. If you think me intolerant, fine. I'll unashamedly bear the label. Consider me a dues-paying, card-carrying, proud member of the intolerance community.

But how dare you desecrate my cross!

"Uhh, wait a minute, Gerald. What do you mean your cross? Wasn't it Jesus who died on the cross? Isn't it his cross?"

Well, yes, first and foremost, it is, but Matthew 16:24, Mark 8:34, and Luke 9:23 all record the same words originally spoken by Jesus himself. To paraphrase them, "Pick up your cross and follow me." Following Jesus means picking up your cross, more specifically following him and the examples he set for us every day, no matter what, even if the cost is losing your family, job, friends, possessions, home, reputation, or even your life.

Agreed, first and foremost, it is Jesus's cross. It is also my cross. Now you want to use it on a bumper sticker and paint a rainbow on it? It's my turn to say wait a minute! Surely, I can't be the only person on Planet Earth who has noticed that an organization preaching tolerance at all costs using the banner of "coexistence" routinely des-ecrates the most sacred religious symbol known throughout history. How would the LGBTQ community react if I were to take a can of spray paint and paint their rainbow flag all black? Tell me what the difference is. Oh, that's right. You aren't worried. You know I won't desecrate your flag, because I'm a Christian.

Now here comes the irony. Saul kept a "Coexist" bumper sticker on his office door. Take down your bumper sticker, Saul! I seriously doubt Jesus intends to coexist with your "movement (I didn't say with you)" when this Earth ends, but that isn't my call. Take it up with God. He is the one who said, "Do not have sex with a man as you would have sex with a woman. I hate that" (Leviticus 18:22, NIRV)" *(HA! Got you! Whether you had the courage to read it or not when I told you about it a few paragraphs ago, you just read it!)*

How about this one? "A woman must not wear men's clothes and a man must not wear women's clothes. The Lord your God hates it when anyone does that" (Deuteronomy 22:5, NIRV). *(Ladies, before you start throwing rotten tomatoes at me, that doesn't mean you can't wear pants).* If either of my three sisters were to put on a dress, I would immediately take them to the emergency room because some-thing serious would be wrong. I can't recall the last time I saw either of them wear one and, to be candid, I'm not certain they even own a dress. What the Bible is saying here is that men should dress in a masculine manner and women in a feminine manner. Each of my sisters is very much a lady in every respect. Should you be fortunate enough to meet one of them allow me to assure you that you'll not question their femininity, regardless of how she might be dressed. Like I said, take it up with Him, but notice his use of the word hate. If you think the garbage which the LGBTQ condones and advocates is acceptable, if you wish to live a lifestyle that God Almighty hates, then you are on your own, my friend. Good luck with that.

Getting back to Saul, I prefer to let God fight my battles for me. He is a much better warrior than me. Let me tell you something really important. It's a good thing to be on God's side when battles come your way, because God always wins. Read the book of Revelation.

Have you heard the song "Old Church Choir" by Zach Williams?[27] Zach sings, "I've got an old church choir singing in my soul. I've got a sweet salvation and it's beautiful. I've got a heart overflowing, cause I've been restored. There ain't nothing gonna steal my joy."

You are so right, Zach. Nothing is going to steal my joy—not Saul, not my boss, not my children when they think something is unfair, not the bill collectors when my change is strange or my money is funny, not my wife when we disagree about something. Saul, I don't give you permission to take my joy, no matter how many times you remove a piece of paper from my bulletin board. That is because my joy comes from Christ.

Every time I replaced the second ten commandments, I could not help it. I just had to smile because I kept remembering these words in Romans 12:20 (NIV). "If your enemy is hungry, feed him; if he is thirsty, give him something to drink. In doing this, you will heap burning coals on his head."

Being angry and holding a grudge is Saul's choice. He suffers the consequences and the loss of his own joy. Do you see yourself in Saul? Living by the second set of Ten Commandments is most assuredly a challenge, but that isn't my reason for telling you this story. Living by them is a significant personal endeavor. Should you choose to put forth the effort, it will be life-altering. I've told you about them, because keeping them should be just as much a goal in your life as keeping the original set is. Living by the second set goes to the heart of LEDRSHHIP, but you can't keep either set by yourself. You need help. Making the effort is what matters. I tell you about them to remind myself how important they are.

One day, I found the second set of ten commandments had been removed from my office door and replaced by the eleven satanic rules of the earth written by Mr. Anton Szandor LaVey.[28] I'm convinced in my mind that Saul made the trade. I cannot emphatically state my assumption is correct, but why would anyone else have

---

[27] Zach Williams, "Old Church Choir," Album: "Chain Breaker," Producer Jonathan Smith, September 23, 2016.

[28] Anton Szandor LaVey, Founder of the Church of Satan, 1966, "The Eleven Satanic Rules of the Earth," 1967.

done it, particularly considering the other events which transpired before that? As I read them, I could not help but laugh, nearly to the point of hysteria. The thing that amused me is the knowledge that God's word has an answer for each of them. Come to think of it, God's Word has an answer for *everything!* Allow me to respond to Mr. LaVey in an unusual manner.

Let's assume Mr. LaVey is sitting at a lunch counter having a burger and a malt *(I'm really telling on my age with that one; ask your grandfather if you don't understand).* While he is eating, God sits down beside him to enjoy his lunch as well, and then the two of them begin to talk. We are sitting next to them and can hear the conversation. I imagine we would hear something like this:

God introduces himself, and Mr. LaVey replies by introducing himself also. When Mr. LaVey tells God his name, God might say something like, "I know who you are, because I'm omniscient. I also know you published the 11 Satanic Rules of the earth. Would you care to discuss them *(I'm making the assumption God is rather busy here, so his responses are somewhat brief)*?"

Anton: Well, God, the first satanic rule is do not give opinions or advice unless you are asked.

God: Anton, I get where you're coming from, but perhaps you might want to consider who is giving the advice. "Listen to advice and accept discipline, and at the end, you will be counted among the wise" (Proverbs 19:20, NIV).

Anton: What about my second principle *(Notice that Anton makes no attempt to debate God's reply to the first principle. He drives right past it. He ignores it. Perhaps the reason is God's word is inarguable.)*? Do not tell your troubles to others unless you are sure they want to hear them.

God: Anton, I sent my son, Jesus, here so he could help you. He had an earthly brother, and his name was James. When he was growing up, James didn't believe Jesus was my Son, but eventually, he came around. He wrote a book too. In the fifth chapter of his book, verse 16, James made a pretty interesting statement. James said, "Therefore, confess your sins to each other and pray for each other so that you may be healed. The prayer of a righteous person is powerful and effective" (NIV). Telling others your troubles helps you.

Anton: All right, God, I could possibly concede the point that talking to someone about my problems may be therapeutic, but my third principle is when in another's lair, show him respect or else do not go there.

God: I agree with you about showing others respect, but how does seeking or offering advice show a lack of it? I made woman for man, because man needs help. All of humanity needs help for that matter. The reason I created mankind was first and foremost to glorify me, but part of the reason I allow so many of you to live on my planet is so that you can help each other. Remember this, Anton. I'm God. I'm omnipotent, and there's nothing I can't do.

Let me ask you something. If one of my children, including you, were to ask me for help, would you want me to help or would you prefer me to ignore the request? "If your son asks for a fish will you give him a snake instead? Or if he asks for an egg, will you give him a scorpion" (Luke 11:11–12, NIV)? If one of your children were to make a reasonable request, wouldn't you try to get them what they want? Why do you do that? How is offering advice, as you put it, any different from helping someone or giving them something which will help if they are in need?

Anton: May we change the subject? What about my fourth principle? If a guest in your lair annoys you, treat him cruelly and without mercy.

God: Anton, you are just too easy. You wouldn't answer my last question, but I'll answer it for you and respond to yours at the same time. "A new command I give you: Love one another. As I have loved you, so you must love one another. By this everyone will know that you are my disciples, if you love one another." Do you know who said that Anton? It was my Son. Every time I remember him saying that, I can't help but smile. You can read his words in John 13:34–35 (NIV). You love your children. That is precisely why you do your best for them. It's also why there isn't ever a justifiable reason for treating someone cruelly, my friend, regardless of what they have done.

Anton: Okay, God. Number five. Do not make sexual advances unless you are given the mating signal.

God: Absolutely right. Do you remember Moses? He led my people, the Israelites, out of Egypt and into the land I promised to give them. Do you remember the Ten Commandments I wrote down on the stone tablets with my very own finger? I gave Moses ten simple rules for mankind to live by. Do you remember the seventh one?

Anton: Perhaps, but I'm not sure I remember the proper order.

God: Most folks can't keep them in order. Don't feel bad about that. All that matters is that you try to obey them, realize you will fail because it's your nature, and ask me to forgive you when you do. The seventh rule is, "You shall not commit adultery" (Exodus 20:14, NIV). I couldn't agree with you more, Anton.

Anton: How about satanic rule number six? Do not take that which does not belong to you unless it is a burden to the other person and he cries out to be relieved.

God: I agree with you, but only partially. Commandment eight, "You shall not steal" (Exodus 20:15, NIV). What part of don't steal is it that you don't understand?

Anton: I think that was pretty harsh, God.

God: Let me level with you, Anton. I get that quite often, but it's from people who don't really understand me, because they haven't made the effort to try. I'm God. Let me say it another way and tell you the same thing I told Moses. "I am who I am" (Exodus 3:14, NIV). Let me rephrase that. I am who I am also means I will be who I will be. That boils down to I'm going to do what I need to in order to accomplish my purposes. I am also the Alpha and Omega, who is and who was and who is to come, the Almighty (Revelation 1:8, NIV).

Anton: Well, let's look at my seventh satanic rule. Acknowledge the power of magic if you have employed it successfully to obtain your desires. If you deny the power of magic after having called upon it with success, you will lose all you have obtained.

God: I told you once before, I am omnipotent. Magic does not exist. Illusionists will try to convince you magic is real, but it is only sleight of hand, trickery. Everything you have is a gift that I gave to you. We talked about James a minute ago. "Every good and perfect gift is from above, coming down from the Father" (James 1:17, NIV). When it comes to magic, think about this. "Let no one be found among you who practices divination or sorcery, interprets omens, engages in witchcraft, or casts spells, or who is a medium or spiritist or anyone who consults the dead. Anyone who does these things is detestable to the Lord" (Deuteronomy 18:10–12, NIV).

And here is another one for you, Anton: "The cowardly, the unbelieving, the vile, the murderers, the sexually immoral, *those who practice magic arts*, the idolaters and all liars—they will be consigned to the fiery lake of burning sulfur. This is the second death" (Revelation 21:8). The fiery lake of burning sulfur is not a good place to be. Trust me, you don't want to go there, Anton. Perhaps you might want to reconsider your view on magic.

Anton: Your point merits thought, God. I'm not sure I believe you, but it does merit consideration. What about number eight?

God: Let me interrupt you. I don't have to prove anything to anyone. As I said, I'm omniscient, aware of everything. That includes your thoughts. To prove my point, you're about to tell me, "Do not complain about anything to which you need not subject yourself."

My thoughts on the matter are, "Give thanks in all circumstances; for this is the will of God in Christ Jesus for you" (1 Thessalonians 5:18, ESV).

Anton: And number nine, do not harm little children?

God: Absolutely, Anton. That is so dead on. When Jesus was down here, he was preaching one day, and the children wanted to visit with him. His disciples, well-meaning as they were, tried to keep them away from him. They thought he was too busy. Do you know what my Son told them? "Let the little children come to me, and do not hinder them, for the kingdom of heaven belongs to such as these" (Matthew 19:14, NIV). I really love children. It probably isn't a good idea to hurt them. You may get much more than you bargained for.

Anton: Number ten, do not kill nonhuman animals unless you are attacked or for your food.

God: We do agree on some things, Anton. I made all of those animals and set up a very delicate balance on this planet. The animals have to eat, and so do you. The system works really well, because I designed it that way. Let me remind you of those Ten Commandments again. Do you remember those? Rule number six is, "You shall not murder" (Exodus 20:13, NIV).

Anton: Satanic rule number 11, God, my last rule. When walking in open territory, bother no one. If someone bothers you, ask him to stop. *If he does not stop, destroy him (I italicized that last part because it had been underlined in red ink. Can you say veiled threat or what? If not a threat, then at a bare minimum to me, it sounds like hatred).*

God: I have three comments to make about your last rule, Anton. Peter came to Jesus and asked, "Lord, how many times shall I forgive my brother who sins against me? Up to seven times?" Jesus answered, "I tell you, not just seven times, but seventy-seven times" (Matthew 18:22–23, NIV)! Do you honestly believe that you're perfect? That you don't annoy people?

The second is this. My son said, which means me too, "I tell you, love your enemies and pray for those who persecute you" (Matthew 5:44, NIV).

My last comment about the subject is, "It is mine to avenge; I will repay. In due time their foot will slip; their day of disaster is near and their doom rushes upon them" (Deuteronomy 32:35, NIV). I'll be seeing you, Anton. I am omnipresent too. By the way, don't forget that you'll be spending eternity with me or with someone else. Make your choice.

James once disappeared when he was two. It was the middle of winter, and heavy snow covered the ground. We searched the entire neighborhood for hours with assistance from the neighbors, and of course, we were all frantic. The washer and dryer were in a separate unheated building. We finally found him sleeping inside the dryer.

He wasn't intentionally hiding. He went out to play, got tired, and decided to take a nap. He was found safe. I think Anton, like many of us, was hiding from the truth of who God is when he wrote his eleven satanic principles. You can't hide from God. You can't run from him. You can't negate the truth of his word. You can ignore it, if you choose, but only for a limited time. He will find you, even if you are sleeping in the dryer. He knows everything about you. "Indeed the very hairs of your head are numbered" (Luke 12:7, NIV). *(In my case, that number is rapidly decreasing)*

I am going to take a short detour here, but we'll return to humility in a moment. It's doubtful we would ever be able to eavesdrop on a conversation like the one I've portrayed between Anton and God, because God isn't like that. First of all, notice all the responses came from the Bible. God has already given us the answers we need when we find ourselves talking to the Antons of the world.

I've humanized him. I wasn't trying to be flippant. God can't be humanized, because He is God. We can't put him in perspective, because we can't understand him. It seems to me that most people try to put God into a box and keep him there. That doesn't work, because he is so much more than we can comprehend.

> "For my thoughts are not your thoughts, neither are your ways my ways," saith the Lord. "For as the heavens are higher than the earth, so are my ways higher than your ways, and my thoughts higher than your thoughts." (Isaiah 55:8–9, KJV)

You have to let God out of the box you are trying to keep him in.

This isn't a great analogy, but it makes the point. I have a Miniature Schnauzer named Lizzie. She is a wonderful pet. She is cute, playful, funny, and downright adorable. She is the perfect size and a wonderful lap-warmer. When company comes over, she makes it her mission to go to everyone for a few minutes, sit on their lap if they will allow it, and welcome them to our home.

Sometimes I almost believe a little hummingbird DNA accidentally got thrown into her genetic makeup. She is often in a frenetic state which consists of zooming, zipping, and darting around the house for no apparent reason and with no discernible order.

Lizzie is constantly in search of food, even though we keep her bowl filled at all times. She is particularly adept at sharing my dinner, but don't tell her veterinarian I let her. We can't say the word *treat* aloud so we have resorted to spelling it. If we don't, she goes nuts. We can't say the dreaded "B" word either *(no not the word you're thinking, the b word in this case is "bath")*. If we do Lizzie will hide under the bed and refuse to come out!

Since our children have all left home, Lizzie is our baby, and spoiled doesn't begin to describe her. If you have a pet, you can likely relate. We have a detached carport. If it is raining, and Lizzie needs to go out, she has to be carried to the carport beneath an umbrella. We keep a pile of leaves spread out in one corner so she can do her business, should she find the weather objectionable. Once finished, she stands up on her back legs to let us know it's time to pick her up and go back inside.

As I am writing this paragraph, she is lying on a pillow which is on the footrest of my recliner and begrudgingly sharing her personal space with my lap, my legs, and my computer. She can catch a ball…6424lkjfh…just stepped on my keyboard, as you can tell, and enjoys wrestling with us and playing tug of war with her toys. She has a basketful of them and selects the one she wants to play with.

She knows several tricks and has a great vocabulary. She understands what we mean when we tell her it's time to check the mail, do you want a treat, do you need to go out, it's time to brush, it's time to eat, let's go bye-bye, do you want to play, it's time for bed, excuse me, and wait. If she is hot and wants the ceiling fan turned on, she will let us know by lying down on the floor beneath it. If that doesn't work, she will stand up and bark.

Our baby is well-fed and receives the best veterinary care, but she is totally dependent on us for her needs. She can't drive herself to the veterinarian. She can't put food or water into her bowls. She doesn't understand where dog food or water comes from, but she knows when her bowls are empty and lets us know.

Her ability to communicate with us has limitations, but she can effectively convey her needs. There are a limited number of things she can comprehend about the way we think and what we do, but she trusts us implicitly. She knows we will take care of her no matter what.

God expects us to trust him in much the same way. He expects us to be just as dependent on him as Lizzie is on us. Our intellect as humans in comparison to that of God's is comparable to Lizzie trying to understand the workings of Albert Einstein's mind. Lizzie understanding the theory of relativity is not even laughable. It is preposterous; insane, really. Imagine Albert Einstein attempting to explain his theory of relativity to Lizzie. She might be a smart dog, but nobody would expect her to comprehend. She wasn't designed to. You could probably tell me the formula of relativity, but do you actually comprehend the nuances and implied meanings? I can't tell you how my computer, cell phone, or microwave works, but I know which buttons to press to warm up a plate of leftovers. She doesn't understand things like car payments, paying for groceries, property taxes, or insurance. She doesn't know where we go when we leave the house or why we're gone, but she trusts us to come back in time to take her out.

Like Lizzie, our human perspective is too limited for us to com-prehend God. We can't understand *anything* about the way God thinks. We don't have that capability, yet we tend to humanize him. We have to realize that God is so big and so powerful that we can't even imagine how big and powerful he is.

We can't even speak his language. By comparison, our language is a poor rudimentary form of communication at best. We attempt to bring God down to our level. We attempt to compare ourselves to him. It won't work. God pales in comparison to the concept of gargantuan. Stop trying to humanize him. Stop trying to minimize him. Let him out of the box you're trying to keep him in; He won't fit.

I just finished eating a candy bar. Lizzie enviously watched me as I ate it. All she wanted was one small taste. Chocolate is bad for dogs; it can kill them or cause them to have diarrhea. Normally, we give her small tastes of what we are eating, and she has come to expect it. Lizzie didn't get any of my chocolate, even though I was well-aware of her desire. Perhaps the way she was watching me eat is as close to a prayer as our little dog can get. Lizzie didn't understand why she didn't get any candy any more than she can understand the theory of relativity. I can't explain either concept to her any more than I can explain the mechanics of my computer to you.

God knows what isn't good for us. He doesn't give us things that will hurt us, regardless of how often we might pray for them. Our perspective is similar to Lizzie's; we don't get something we want. Maybe it is similar to the way a child feels when Santa doesn't stop by.

I've noticed most people approach prayer as if there was some magic genie in a bottle, waiting to grant their every wish and desire, or as if Santa Clause is going to fulfill every whim, much like Lizzie watching me as I ate the candy. God isn't in the wish-fulfilling business. God, please give me this. God, please let me do that. God, please do such and such. God, please help my mother, brother, child, or whoever feel better. God, why did you do that? I'm not saying don't pray for those things, but God's first name isn't Santa.

Don't be fooled, and above all, don't be discouraged, because God always answers prayer. What we often fail to realize is his answers don't coincide with our schedules. My advice about prayer is simple. Consider your requests carefully. Pray for things that matter, and don't be surprised when you receive them. Be prepared for the response. My belief is God will only give you one of three different responses.

The first is yes. You asked me for this, so here it is. Let's see what you do with it. The problem is we rarely recognize the yes. We don't understand it for what is. "Opportunity is missed by most people, because it is dressed in overalls and looks like work."[29] The same is true when God gives us what we ask for. We miss the opportunity, because it doesn't announce itself.

His second answer is, "I'm sorry, Gerald (remember to substitute your name for mine). I have something better in mind for you. It might not be what you want, Gerald, but the chocolate bar you asked for is going to hurt you. It's loaded with sugar and calories. You don't need that. I'm going to give you a banana instead. Your potassium is low, and you need to eat a banana. You also need a little vitamin C, so I'm going to give you an orange to go with it."

In case you missed the inference, we're not discussing fruit or candy. If you believe we are and you're not obtuse, then one of two conditions exist. Either I'm a very poor writer *(which is entirely plausible)* or your reading comprehension skills leave much to be desired. In either case, my recommendation is to go back to the beginning and start over, give this book to a friend, or take it back to the store where you purchased it. Ask for a refund, because you're not getting anything from it.

The third answer is, "You're not ready for that yet. Be patient. Just wait a little while longer." Since God always answers, you might receive your wish. Have you ever heard this one before? "Ask and it will be given to you. Search and you will find. Knock and the door will be opened to you" (Matthew 7:7, NIRV).

Warning! Don't take that out of context. Yes, I quoted that passage once before. My apology for the redundancy, but it is such an amazing promise. Let me tell you how God has answered my prayers.

Being a teacher takes patience. I asked for it. God gave me students who required tremendous patience to work with *(I finally stopped asking for patience)*. My next request was for courage. I woke up in Iraq where people I had never met were shooting at me, where

---

[29] According to QuoteInvestigator.com, the earliest citation for this quotation, which has often been attributed to Thomas Edison, was printed in May 1921. A precursor that does not mention overalls was in circulation by 1911. The first attribution to Edison was in 1962, but he died in 1931. It is therefore unlikely Mr. Edison is the originator.

people hated me, and wanted to kill me. Then, upon returning home, I found myself standing behind the pulpit on Sunday mornings, directing worship services and a church choir. Trust me, the latter takes infinitely more courage than being in a combat zone does. My desire was to understand my students, so I prayed for understanding. My gift was students with family problems and physical challenges who taught me to be understanding.

When I asked for humility, Saul did his best to make my life miserable. The result was humility became my mainstay. I asked for help and understanding, because I wanted to become an exceptional teacher. Foreign students that had difficult to understand accents and spoke broken English as a second language were placed on my schedule. It took tremendous effort and understanding to work with them. Then something incredible happened. My colleagues elected me as teacher of the year.

It doesn't matter if you are teaching your child how to do algebra homework, soldiers how to fire and maintain a weapon, a Sunday school class full of children about Jesus, college students in their chosen profession, or subordinates what they need to know and accomplish so they can become successful in their career. It is commonplace for pupils to seek your counsel. When you teach, you're seen as the expert, the role model. I prayed for insight and wisdom in order to provide sound advice to the best of my ability. God told me about LEDRSHHIP, and then he asked me to write a book. I can't begin to tell you how much I didn't want to write a book but I read "Miracle Man,"[30] by Mr. Todd Greiner. Todd is a fellow pilot I know who survived an airplane crash while he was instructing one day. His book tells the story of what happened but it isn't the tale of an airplane crash. The story is about a man's journey with God. In his book Todd said he didn't want to write a book either until God reminded him it wasn't Todd's story, but God's story. God expects us, (you included) to tell his story. If you want a real treat read Todd's book, better yet, come hear him preach.

---

[30] Todd Greiner, "Miracle Man," August 7, 2018.

Realizing how small we are in relation to how large God is goes a long way toward recognizing humility. I did not react with humility as the Paul/Saul situation began and I did not behave with honor when I sent him that e-mail. I responded with another "H" word instead. It was hatred fueled by indignant self-righteous pride. Saul got me, so I decided to get him back. That is all I could see or think about at the time.

My actions were juvenile if not infantile. Think about it, though. I'm not sure what motivated Saul during that staff meeting, but he didn't show any humility either. Not during the meeting and not after it.

Hate will destroy you. The longer you allow it to be a part of your life and fester, the longer you allow it safe harbor, the more it will influence your life. The longer you nurture it, the more it controls you. Uh-oh, I have just violated the first satanic rule of the earth. I'll live with it.

By this point, you're probably thinking Saul's behavior sounds childish. I agree with your assessment. Refusal to let go of his anger cost him. It is the little things in life which really matter, and this is one of those things. Over the years of my employment at SIUC, perhaps fifteen people reached the point in their career where they were able to retire. My work environment always felt like a family. It was a good place to work because of the people I was privileged to work with.

When Saul retired, he was not given a retirement party. No one asked why. No one was concerned, and to my knowledge, no one said they were going to miss him. Saul was the only person who retired without a retirement party. Obviously, I wasn't the only person he had a problem with. At least I attempt to be a humble man instead of a prideful one. Do you think there may be a connection?

So why choose the names Paul and Saul? Perhaps you know already. Don't get confused. We're not talking about King Saul of the Old Testament who spent much of his time attempting to murder David, the same David that killed Goliath with a slingshot and the same David whose lineage, fourteen generations later, according to Matthew's Gospel, leads to Joseph who became Jesus's earthly father.

King Saul died. You can read about his life in 1 Samuel, his death in chapter 31. There's a lesson there, but it's something you have to figure out for yourself.

New Testament Paul and Saul were the same person. Saul's job was torturing, imprisoning, and killing Christians. He was provided resources from, and his actions were sanctioned by, the Roman government. Saul genuinely believed he was doing the right thing. Like many of us, he was likely proud of his career.

Then something happened. Saul met God, and God changed him; he became a different man. The difference was so radical that Saul became ashamed of who he had been. He was gravely embarrassed by his past and changed his name to Paul because of it. Saul became Paul. You can read about his conversion in the ninth chapter of Acts.

Paul was an apostle for Christ and became a pretty good author as well. He wrote a substantial part of the New Testament. We've been comparing three pairs of men—King Saul and David, the Paul and Saul I worked with, and lastly, Paul and Saul of the New Testament. In all three cases, each pair of men could not have been greater examples of polar opposites *(my Saul may have been bipolar as well)*.

God changed New Testament Saul's (not King Sauls) "want-to-er." Of course, we both realize want-to-er isn't a word *(there's no reason to send me an ugly e-mail regarding my grammar here; I'll just delete it)*. My point is God changed (New Testament) Saul's desires. My Paul was a kindhearted, considerate, courteous man who cared about everyone. It was a pleasure to know and work with him. My Saul, on the other hand, was…well, as an adorable animated rabbit named Thumper said, "If you can't say somethin' good about somebody, then don't say nothin' at all."[31] My apologies for the double negative and spelling errors, but it is a quotation.

---

[31] *Bambi*, Animated film produced by Walt Disney, released August 21, 1942, based on the novel *Bambi, A Life in the Woods*, originally published in Austria, 1923, translated by Whitaker Chambers, published by Simon & Schuster, 1928.

Let me reiterate my Saul and Paul, along with King Saul and David, were polar opposites. My Paul understood the values of LEDRSHHIP. It is doubtful my Saul ever will.

In the disclaimer at the beginning of this manuscript, it was stated all events described herein are recorded to the best of my rec- ollection and based upon actual events. The truth is that all events and persons described in this manuscript are a complete fabrication. Any similarity to any persons living or dead is purely coincidental.

Yuh! Right! Perhaps the preceding paragraph was included for legal reasons because the author doesn't want to face a lawsuit. Perhaps the "Paul" discussed in this book is married to an attorney. Perhaps these events are indeed factual. You are welcome to make your own conclusion, but as I said, any similarity to any persons living or dead is purely coincidental.

One of the greatest joys of my life was working for a man named Leland W. It was an absolute pleasure to know him, and I am hon- ored to call him my friend. I've never met anyone more humble. He retired a few years after what I'm about to tell you happened. I still miss working with him. I'd been working for him perhaps five or six years when these events transpired.

Leland is one of the most memorable Christian men I've ever met. He is also a minister. I was heavily entangled in some personal problems and no longer remember the details *(that happens when you get older),* but as I recall, they centered on relationships between myself and other people who were part of my life at the time. They also had the potential to threaten my employer's business, so it became necessary to disclose them.

Leland listened quietly without interruption as I explained what was occurring and the associated potential outcome. He never interrupted, got angry, or raised his voice. When I finished, he asked me a simple question, which was, "Have you talked to Him about it?"

I reluctantly had to admit I had not. The next thing he did was tell me he really shouldn't do this, because he could get in a lot of trouble. He said he was going to take off his boss's hat and put on his preacher's hat. He even gestured, pretending to take off one hat and put on another for effect. That was the first time I became aware that Leland was also a pastor.

Don't get me wrong, I had no doubt that Leland was a Christian man, but I didn't know he was also a preacher. I knew he was a true genuine Christian man when we first met. It wasn't because he went around quoting scripture or preaching or telling me how to live my life or what I was doing wrong or right or, for that matter, what I should be doing that I might not be doing. He just lived his life, by example, and for Christ. That is how I knew. *Wow!* The utter simplicity! I learned a little something about humility that day, to say the least.

When I admitted I had not talked to God about my situation, he did something so simple, it astonished me. I'm going back in time a bit with the use of this next word, but what he did was so much more than astounding, really. Flabbergasted seems to be a more appropriate description. I couldn't speak *(my wife didn't believe me when I told her this; she says my being speechless is extremely rare).*

Leland got up from his chair and came around his desk to the side where I was sitting. He dropped down to his knees and prayed for me. If you haven't heard a real Christian pray for you, then you have missed out on living.

I think this was the turning point which caused me to realize I needed God back at the forefront of my life. I still didn't do it, at least not right then or right there, but eventually, I did. Don't ask me to explain why I didn't make the effort at that moment. God was ready for me to return to him. He always was and he always is waiting for your return too. The problem is I wasn't ready.

> While it is said, today if ye will hear his voice,
> harden not your hearts. (Hebrews 3:15, KJV)

When he calls, you need to answer with urgency. You may not have another opportunity.

I can't tell you what Leland prayed that day, because I don't remember his words. What I can tell you is this: After that prayer, I knew everything was going to be fine and everything was going to work out for me. There was an amazing and indescribable feeling of peace, comfort, and protection that washed over me. It covered me with a sublime calmness that was surreal. The best word I can think of to describe it, although it doesn't quite get there, is *euphoria.*

The great thing about that experience is it eventually brought me to the point where I had the desire to pray for others. I learned by the example Leland set for me. A friend of mine gets his contact lenses from and has known one of the employees for several years at the Walmart Vision shop. One afternoon, after going to lunch my friend and I stopped on the way back to the office so he could pick up his prescription and his friend asked if they could talk.

We stepped out of the shop and into the main body of the store so we wouldn't be within earshot of her colleagues. She explained that she had just given her employer a two week notice because her mother had cancer and needed to be cared for.

I didn't think about it. It was just a reaction. I simultaneously reached for her and my friend's hand. We formed a prayer circle right in the middle of Walmart. Cash registers were ringing *(I'm telling on my age again; cash registers don't ring anymore, they beep),* people were walking around us, pushing their shopping carts full of recently purchased groceries and various newly acquired treasures. Right in the middle of the noise and the afternoon rush, I prayed aloud for that woman and for her mother. I prayed for healing guidance and comfort. I wasn't ashamed and I wasn't afraid. It was of no concern to me what anyone might think or say. It didn't matter to any of us who might be staring or casting condescending judgmental looks. It was of no consequence to either of us; it didn't matter.

That isn't the first time I've done something like that. As long as God continues to bless me with breath and opportunities to pray for others, it most certainly won't be the last either. My reasoning is simple.

For where two or three are gathered together
in my name, there am I in the midst of them.
(Matthew 18:20, KJV)

Those words were spoken by Jesus himself, and let me assure you there is nothing which can compare to being in his presence.

Since I made Jesus number one in *everything (or at least made the decision to try to keep him there)*, my life has never been better. Those feelings of comfort, love, and peace which I experienced after Leland's prayer have only become better. I've never had more fun, been more financially stable, been more confident, and my relationships with my family and my friends has never been stronger or more secure. Life just has not been the same since I made that decision. Thank you, Leland. Thank you. Leland knows what it means to be humble and what it means to love. More importantly, thank you, God. Let me say that again. *Thank you, God!*

I'm going to derail the train once again for a moment, and we'll get back to Leland soon. This isn't a story about humility, but it has a great deal to do with keeping Jesus first in your life. Just prior to my last day at work, a young lady *(we'll call her Ruth, but you have to figure out why on your own. Let me give you a hint; there are two books in the Bible named for a woman)* who had quite a bit of difficulty with one of my previous classes, several semesters earlier, saw me in the hallway. She asked if she could speak to me in private, so we went into my office and closed the door.

While enrolled in that class, she had come to me on several occasions during office hours asking for help. I was happy to provide it and grateful for her desire to be successful. It is so unfortunate, but it seems to me that when most students require assistance, they wait until it is too late to ask for it. Do you see any parallels with that statement? My class was a challenge for her, and several times during the semester, she left my office in tears.

After we sat down, she smiled one of the brightest smiles I've ever seen. Her face lit up the room. The Christmas tree at Rockefeller Center would have been dim by comparison. The "happy" was written across her face, and joy was glowing in her eyes. There was no need to ask what she wanted to tell me, because I already knew what she was about to say. At the end of class, prior to the beginning of a weekend, I often close by saying, "Go to church this weekend. You need to be there." I knew her academic progress had dramatically improved recently.

Instead of asking her what she wanted to tell me, I just said, "You seem awfully cheerful today."

Her reply was, "I am. I started going to church and putting God first. Mr. T., I can't tell you how much better my life is. Thank you for being insistent and having the courage to tell me I needed to be in church."

Like I said, she didn't have to tell me.

Let's get back to Leland again. We left him hanging a few minutes ago. I never had any doubt where I stood with him or what he expected from me. I knew he would always be honest with me, brutally so at times. He had a great way of turning a phrase. I know that occasionally, I disappointed him. I'm sure that at some point, you have disappointed someone that matters to you, and you know how humbling that experience can be. It is now a rarity, but from time to time, we get to enjoy the pleasure of each other's company when we're able to meet for lunch.

Prior to Leland's retirement, another friend of mine decided to take some sick days. He was interviewing for another position at a different university located some distance away, and the salary would have been a substantial increase. He told me about it and let me know when he was going to be absent. Then he asked me to keep it confidential and cover his schedule until his return. Of course, I agreed to help, because he was my friend. He returned without incident but was not offered the new job.

About a week after my friend returned, Leland asked me to lunch. While we were eating, he asked me if I knew anything about why my friend had been gone. I'm pretty sure he knew the answer before he asked the question, but I lied and told him I didn't. Leland said okay and then told me this story several minutes later.

One day, Leland was getting ready for church and wanted to wear a white shirt he had previously worn (*yes, you've worn something and put it back in the closet without washing it, perhaps the shirt you are wearing right now; tell me you haven't, and my response will be the same thing I've told my children and students on countless occasions: "I may have been born at night, but it wasn't last night."*). Leland got his shirt out of the closet and held it up on the hanger. Then he asked his wife Mary if it looked clean enough to wear.

Leland said he didn't even remember what Mary was doing. He said she was busy deciding what shoes to wear or perhaps putting on her makeup, but he remembered what she did. Leland said she never even looked up at him or even glanced toward the shirt he was holding. She simply answered, "If it's doubtful it's dirty, put it in the hamper." How much better would the world we live in be if we all subscribed to the philosophy of "If it's doubtful it's dirty?" Leland and Mary are some of the most humble people I've ever met.

After he told me that story, I had to come clean; there was no other option. I told him everything I knew. I sang like the proverbial canary. One of the things my dad was fond of saying when we were children was, "I'd rather you do anything other than lie to me." He said lying hurt him more than anything else we could do. I didn't really understand that until I became a father but now grasp the significance of what he meant. Nonetheless, I was always afraid of "getting in trouble," so I'd sometimes lie to my dad about things when there was a potential for punishment. Somehow, Dad always seemed to know the truth.

God always knows the truth too. You can't hide it from him and you can't fool him. He is omnipresent. My dad's words flashed through my mind as Leland told me the story of the white shirt. Old habits die hard. I was trying to stay out of trouble and, in doing so, made the situation worse because the truth will always surface.

There was no other way to say it. "Leland, I lied" was the only way out. It's extremely humiliating to admit you have lied about something to a man you respect. It's much easier to tell the truth at the onset, even if your behavior was less than honorable. Even though Leland never told me he already knew the truth, I strongly suspect he did.

> For there is nothing hidden that will not be disclosed, and nothing concealed that will not be known or brought out into the open. (Luke 8:17, NIV)

As I said, he was one of the most humble men I've ever had the privilege of knowing.

Would you like to live a long healthy and prosperous life? It's difficult to believe any relatively sane person would say, "Nope, not me, not interested." If that were true, doctors wouldn't be wealthy, and lottery ticket sales would be a thing of the past.

Have you ever gone to see the doctor? Have you ever purchased a lottery ticket? No, you say? Yeah, right, I believe you *(yes, that was absolutely a prime example of sarcasm, just in case you didn't pick up on it)*. Well, check this out. Proverbs 22:4 (NIV) tells us, "Humility is the fear of the Lord; its wages are riches and honor and life."

Once again, *wow!* The thing is there are so many verses about humility. Another one from Proverbs, this time 11:2 (NIV) says, "When pride comes, then comes disgrace, but with the humility comes wisdom."

Do you remember when we were discussing my Paul and Saul? I said pride is the enemy of humility. Have you ever heard this one? Pride goes before a fall. Isn't it interesting how often we repeat common expressions without caring, much less realizing the origin actually comes from God's Word? Can you handle one more?

> Humble yourselves, therefore, under God's
> mighty hand, that he may lift you up in due time.
> (1 Peter 5:6, NIV)

It is much more preferable to have God exalt me than my boss, my family, or my friends. What about you?

Occasionally, when traveling I discover the pilot was a former student of mine. Over the span of a thirty-year career, I've taught more than a few people to fly airplanes. Recently, as I boarded an aircraft, the pilot recognized me and called me by name. I'll not reveal his name in order to avoid embarrassing him. I stood in the jet way and talked with this young man for a few minutes before taking my seat.

The landing at the flight's conclusion was less than admirable. As we deplaned, the pilot was standing by the flight deck door. I asked him what happened, and his answer was, "I wanted to impress you, Mr. T." As a flight instructor, I was fond of telling my students not to worry about impressing anyone but simply do what you have been taught. I reminded him of my words.

As fate would have it, this same young pilot was flying the route on our return trip, and the landing could not have been smoother. As we left the plane, I asked him what the difference was. He answered that a wise man told him not to worry about impressing anyone. We both laughed.

Pride is a terrible master. Pride compromises your performance. In his book, *The End of Me*,[32] Kyle Idleman said it like this: "Pride blinds us to our own weaknesses." This young pilot finally learned his lesson; pride is the enemy of humility.

Each of us plays different roles at various times. I'm a father, brother, husband, employee, manager, friend, leader, and a teacher to name just a few. I've learned much from my students. The most valuable lesson my students have taught me is who we are depends on who we ask, which depends upon perception. The only viewpoint that matters to me is what Jesus thinks. If that is right, everything else falls into place. Others see us based on our interactions with them and the role we play in their lives. I'm not difficult to talk to, so why is it that if one of my students has a negative perception of me, they won't tell me? I believe its fear of the grade or perhaps power I have over them.

The point is, Christians *(substitute leaders or people; you fit into one of those categories if you're reading this)* need to critically and regularly examine themselves. Once again, the word *humility* comes to my mind. People involved in your life rarely tell you what they think of you. They won't be honest with you, but through his word, Jesus will. The secret is learning how to let him. In chapter 4, verse 10, Jesus's earthly brother, James, said it this way: "Humble yourselves before the Lord, and he will lift you up" (NIV).

So here is your next question, assuming you don't already have the answer. Why should you live your life with humility? The real

---

[32] Kyle Idleman, *The End of Me*, David C. Cook, Colorado Springs, CO, 2015.

reason to be humble comes from Proverbs 3:34, "He scorneth the scorners; but giveth grace unto the lowly" (KJV). I want God's grace. Don't fool yourself by lying to yourself. You want it too.

"So whether you eat, or drink, or whatever you do, do it all for the glory of God" (1 Corinthians 10:31, NIV). In case you missed the inference, let me translate. We're not talking about eating a meal. Ruth, Chad, Leland, Victoria, my anonymous sister, Paul of the Bible, and my Paul, all exemplify that verse by how they live. They understand what Mary meant when she said, "If it's doubtful it's dirty," because they share a common trait. How much nicer would this world be if we all subscribed to Mary's philosophy? It's time to take a page from their book.

Let's "give up our tall, take back our small, and make God our all." You can't do that or understand LEDRSHHIP until you learn to do one simple thing summarized by two words. We'll close the chapter with them: Be humble.

9

"I"

Integrity

The righteous man walks in his integrity;
His children are blessed after him.
—Proverbs 20:7, NKJV

The very first person who comes to my mind when thinking about integrity is Job (pronounced with a long "o"—jobe). Job experienced far worse problems than any of us ever have or will. I'm confident he would have welcomed any of my problems *(or yours, for that matter)* by way of comparison.

You remember what happened to Job, don't you? He was a wealthy man with a large family. God and Satan are having a conversation one day when God points out Job's integrity. Satan tells God Job's integrity is the result of his good fortune, so God gives Satan permission to do his worst. The only stipulation is Satan can't kill Job; he does everything but. He kills Job's livestock, his servants, all ten of his children, and gives him a horrible skin disease. Job finds himself destitute, penniless, and sitting on trash pile, scratching himself with a broken piece of pottery.

All the events of Job's misfortune occur the very same day within moments of each other, but even with all of his problems, Job never lost his patience or his integrity. The vast remainder of the book is a conversation between Job and three judgmental "friends." They believe and attempt to convince him everything that happened was his own fault. They contend God has punished him for something he did.

The problem, of course, is Job knows better. Even his wife got in on the act and asked him, "Are you still maintaining your integrity? Curse God and die" (Job 2:9, NIV). That is why we tell a patient person, "You have the patience of Job."

Job never lost his faith in God. He never stopped trusting God. He never compromised his integrity. Can you imagine how Job must have felt when his wife asked that question?

Why were Job's "friends" so unwilling to believe him, to trust him? Why were they so adamant that Job was the one in the wrong? My thoughts are they compromised their own integrity. They were "fair-weather" friends, not true friends.

Just because we might be going through a rough spot doesn't mean God has forgotten you. His sovereignty, love, and goodness remain the same. They are a constant unaltered truth. It takes patience and integrity to get through the troubles you will inevitably face. In the words of a six-year-old girl in our Sunday school class, "If you really believe, you trust God no matter what." *Wow!*

Patience is the foundation of integrity, and integrity brings about honor. You can't have one without the other, but there are differences. My first job at the age of thirteen was shining shoes in a barbershop after school and on Saturdays. We lived in small town located in central Louisiana. I'm not Cajun *(a.k.a. Coonass)* by birth but consider myself to be an honorary one. In case you're wondering, the stories you've heard about what Cajuns will eat are true *(if it moves, someone will probably cook it)*. They will serve some strange sounding dishes, but they are awfully tasty.

A visit to the bayou land isn't complete unless you try gumbo, boudin, jambalaya oyster po'boys, muffulettas, fried green tomatoes, beignets, or go to a crawfish boil. Don't forget about breakfast either. The menu isn't worthwhile, much less complete, unless it includes shrimp and grits. Yes, those are actual meals, some of the best food you will ever eat. My mouth waters just thinking about them. Every recipe starts with the same three words, "Make a roux *(sorry to repeat myself, but again, if you have to ask, you wouldn't understand the answer)*."

My only option for transportation to and from work was what military folks call an LPC—leather personnel carrier, a.k.a. boots. It was about a two-mile walk, so my first goal when I started working was to save enough money for a bicycle. The object of my desire was priced at the handsome sum of $30. It was a beautiful bicycle with a double all-chrome frame, three speeds, banana seat, roll bar—man, was it sharp!

In 1969, priced at the princely sum of $30, it was an awful lot of money for a barely teenage boy. At that time, you could buy a Coke and a candy bar from the school vending machines for 25 cents total and return the bottle to the store for the 5-cent deposit. I charged 15 cents to shine a pair of shoes.

One afternoon, when I got home from school, playing baseball with my brothers sounded like a wonderful idea and skipping work seemed like a great plan. Mom never said anything about it. I don't know if she called Dad or not but strongly suspect that as soon as we walked out the back door, she picked up the phone. What I do know is Dad came home about fifteen minutes into our game. He got out of the car and joined us for a little while. Then he looked at me and said, "Son, can I talk to you in the house for a minute? *(Rrruh-rrroh, Scooby-Doo!*[33] *Not good!)*

We went into the living room, Dad sat in his chair, and then he asked me to sit on the couch. After we sat down, he said, "I thought you were supposed to go to work today."

My response was, "Yes, sir, but I wanted to play baseball instead *(notice I addressed my father with the title of Sir. Whatever happened to that? We talked about it earlier; it's known as respect. At the risk of redundancy, it is so much easier to recognize the lack of its existence.)*."

Dad calmly stood up, walked over to me, and none to gently grabbed my left earlobe. Without letting go, he began walking.

---

[33] Joe Ruby and Ken Spears, *Scooby-Doo*, Animated TV series CBS, Hannah-Barbera Productions, 1969.

Desiring to keep my ear attached to the side of my head, I thought it prudent to walk along beside him.

We went all the way to the barbershop. I asked him where we were going but soon determined the answer to my question. Dad chose to maintain complete silence. Just before he opened the door, Dad let go of my ear, placed his hand on my shoulder, opened the door with one hand, and gently guided me through it with his other. As he did so, he whispered so softly that I had to strain in order to barely hear him say, "Son, people are depending on you."

Proverbs 19:21 comes to mind. "Many are the plans in a person's heart, but it is the Lord's purpose that prevails" (NIV). We might want to go a particular direction in life, but if God wants you to do something, save yourself some grief. Do what he wants. Eventually, he is going to get his way. If you don't believe me, read the book of Jonah. Jonah didn't just refuse to go where God wanted him to, he went the opposite direction!

But guess what? Jonah eventually went where God wanted him to anyway. Don't worry, it's one of the shortest books in the Bible, only four chapters. It shouldn't take more than ten minutes. In case you missed the inference, we're not talking about a thirteen-year-old boy playing baseball or a large fish.

The story gets better. I'd been working there for almost a year at the time this happened. Normally, I'd shine two or three pairs of shoes and make 30 to 45 cents. I made more money that afternoon than on any single day before, a whopping $6. You can't get a submarine sandwich for that anymore.

You might wonder why that total is so vividly entrenched in my memory forty-nine years later. Prior to that afternoon, my bicycle fund had grown to a massive $24. Translated another way, it took me nearly a year to save $24. That afternoon, I didn't feel like working. I wanted to have fun. I wanted to play baseball and spend time with my brothers and enjoy a perfect spring day. The sacrifice of doing what I was supposed to do instead of what I wanted to do made it possible for me to get my bicycle.

There is one more reason for my vivid recollection. $6 divided by 15 cents means I shined forty pairs of shoes that afternoon. Do you have any idea how tired or dirty a thirteen-year-old boy gets after shining forty pair of shoes in one afternoon? Let me assure you, it isn't a pretty picture.

Why was that bicycle—and why is this story—so important to me? The Bible is filled with stories about blessings from God as a reward for obedience. I was obedient, albeit reluctantly, to abide by my responsibilities. I was blessed for my obedience by receiving something I really wanted. God's promise was fulfilled. It's as simple as that. The verse which puts it into perspective for me and illustrates the point is Psalms 128:1: "Blessed are all who fear the Lord, who walk in obedience to him" (NIV). My definition of integrity is obedience to God. What is yours?

Perhaps you find it offensive for me to talk about God so much. Okay, got it, that's your right; but here's the problem: He goes with me everywhere, because he lives inside of me. In the event I've offended you, let me put it another way.

How about being obedient to the laws of your country? That means not talking or texting on your cell phone when you're driving. You know it's dangerous, but you still do it. Don't deny it; I've seen you. You almost ran over me yesterday. I'm the one behind you in the construction zone who sees you weaving all over the road. *Just put your phone down when you get in the car! Turn the stupid thing off! It isn't that difficult, and it isn't that important!*

Do you surf the internet at work when nobody is looking? Do you leave work early when the boss is gone? How about returning that extra quarter the store clerk accidently gave you in change? How about going to work when you don't want to, even if you are a thirteen-year-old boy? How about refusing to allow yourself to disappoint somebody who trusts and depends upon you? It's called integrity, and even if you don't believe in God, it's still called integrity.

I'm writing this book, because when people count on you, there is no excuse for letting them down. God has provided me with a wonderful life full of rich and rewarding experiences. I believe he is counting on me to tell you about them so you can learn something from them.

God is counting on you too. God is depending on you to be an all-in Christian. He is counting on you to live and share his message every day of your life, expending maximum effort in the process. What are you going to do about it? Just a few examples, my friend, but from my point of view, they spell integrity.

Because of that bicycle, I learned about God's promises along with the importance of responsibility, determination, and value of hard worthwhile work. There is one more thing I learned courtesy of that bicycle, but you'll need to hear another story first.

I loved to ride it; the faster the better. I was proud of myself for earning the money which allowed me to purchase my most treasured possession. It made me feel good to pedal for all I was worth and enjoy the feeling of the wind in my face. One afternoon *(not on a day I was supposed to be working)*, riding as fast as my now fourteen-year-old legs would pedal, I attempted unsuccessfully to negotiate a turn. Forget about slowing down or braking—not me! I wanted to go around that corner *fast!* The result was a collision with a low stone wall, perhaps three feet tall, which served as a fence *(in case you're curious, stone walls don't move very quickly, and they tend to be rather unforgiving)*.

There were some strands of rusty barbed wire strung above the top of the wall. As you might suspect, several things happened when the impact occurred. I badly bent the frame of my bicycle, and it also cracked in two places. My treasured bicycle was useless; it wasn't rideable. I had to push it home, totally ashamed of my foolishness. I hid it in the shed behind some junk because of my embarrassment.

Soon, Dad noticed I was walking everywhere and became suspicious. He asked me about it, but I'm confident he went out to the shed before inviting me into the living room "for a little chat."

I told Dad what happened. The three of us—Dad, me and the bicycle—made a little trip to a welding shop. The bike was repaired. Dad paid for it but expected me to pay him back and save my money to do so. Next lesson learned? You can't hide. The truth will always come to the surface, no matter how much you try to cover it up. God is omniscient.

Lord, you have seen what is in my heart. You
know all about me. You know when I sit down
and when I get up. You know what I'm thinking
even though you are far away. You know when
I go out to work and when I come back home.
You know exactly how I live. Lord, even before
I speak a word, you know all about it. (Psalm
139:1–4, NIRV)

The second thing that happened when I ran into the wall was
my left forearm got cut by the barbed wire. The little toe of my left
foot was cut where it was scraped on the pedal, and my chin bounced
off of the wall. My souvenir from the event is three small scars which
still serve me well. They are a daily reminder not to do foolish things.

One more lesson learned, courtesy of the bicycle—or more
appropriately phrased, courtesy of my stupidity on the bicycle—is
actions have consequences. No matter how egregious your actions
may be, God stands ready and willing to forgive you. It really doesn't
matter what you have done in the past. God doesn't care. What he
cares about is what's in your heart today, from this moment on. He
cares about your integrity. He will never fail to forgive you if you ask
him to, but if you aren't sincere in your request, if you aren't genuinely remorseful about what you have done, if you don't really want
to change your behavior, don't expect forgiveness.

Just because he forgives you doesn't mean your problems simply
vanish. They won't necessarily just go away. Your chin, arm, and your
toe will stop bleeding and they will heal. The scars will fade over
time, but they will never completely disappear.

Don't be fooled. You can't outsmart God.
A man gathers a crop from what he plants.
(Galatians 6:7, NIRV)

I am sure you have heard the common colloquialism "What
goes around comes around *(Nah, that never happens! An expression*

everyone uses on a regular basis founded upon scripture? Who would have thought that?)."

Don't ask me what finally happened to that bicycle or where it ended up. I kept it well into my thirties but, at some point, lost track of it. Perhaps it wouldn't fit into the U-Haul truck on one of my many moves. Eventually, the padding on the seat became worn and frayed, and the weld where it had been repaired had separated. The tires got flat and rotted, the chain rusted, and it was all scratched up. The pedals were just spindles, but an ugly, worn-out, beat up old bicycle was one of my most treasured possessions for many years. I learned about integrity from a bicycle. What will be your source of learning about integrity?

> Whoever walks in integrity walks securely
> but whoever takes crooked paths will be found
> out. (Proverbs 10:9, NIV)

Jarred's was a CD player. He was chauffeured home one afternoon sporting some new jewelry. Unfortunately, his mode of transportation was a bit questionable. He arrived in the back seat of a police cruiser. My son was fifteen at the time and living with his mom. Jarred decided he needed a new CD player but lacked the funds to pay for it. He thought shoplifting would be a viable option and decided to "make his purchase" at a store with multiple security cameras. The film was of excellent quality, and the proprietor was not amused.

When his mother told me about the situation, I spoke with him on the phone and asked what happened but knew he was lying when he answered. Jarred's explanation was that he picked a CD player up from the store shelf to look at it and then put it back. He said he was curious because it looked like the one already in his pocket. Store security mistakenly thought he had stolen his own property. I chose not to debate the matter with him over the phone because a court date was imminent, and I already knew what I planned to say once the date became known.

I'll not tell you the name of the store where my son's criminal mastermind adventures occurred. However, you might be well-advised that should you feel the need to begin a shoplifting career, Walmart probably isn't a good place to perfect your craft.

At the risk of embarrassing my son, Jarred was prohibited from shopping at Walmart for a while unless he wanted to be arrested for trespassing. How can anybody survive a total banishment from Walmart? Carolyn can't go *anywhere* without stopping there. It isn't unusual for her to stop at Walmart on her way home from Walmart.

After being informed of the court date, I told Jarred I was going to be there to defend and support him because he had been falsely accused. It was my duty as his father to take time off from work and set things right. My son wasn't going to be punished for something he had not done. A week later, after my explanation, Jarred called me back and admitted the truth.

The court ordered him to make restitution for the property he had taken. He had to save his money to do that. Fortunately, he faced no significant penalties as a result. Integrity means facing the consequences of your actions no matter how dire they may appear. I know my son was frightened. I think he was more frightened of disappointing me than he was of the potential penalties he might face. He didn't want to tell me what happened, but the truth always finds you.

Jarred learned you can't cover one lie up with another one. Jarred has become a fine young man. I am proud to be his father. Jarred is a man who understands the value of integrity. Once again, Proverbs 10:9.

"P"

Personal Courage

> Take the first step in faith. You don't have to see
> the whole staircase, just take the first step.
> —Dr. Martin Luther King Jr.

In spite of the way we were treated as children, I admired much about my father. Perhaps part of the reason I chose to serve in the army is because my father did. I'm not completely sure why I made that choice so many years ago, but part of the reason may have been an undeniable and effective way to escape my situation.

Regardless of my reasoning, army brats know a thing or two about relocation *(an army brat is a child who grows up with at least one parent, or possibly two, in the army)*. Any army brat old enough to talk will tell you they just moved or they're getting ready to.

When I began the third grade, Dad had just been transferred. My new school and home were both on the same street about three-fourths of a mile apart, and there were no side streets between school and home. This was perhaps a bit far for a third-grader to walk each day, but it was too close for bus service.

Walking to school on the first day, I made "friends" with a boy in a rather unusual way *(Of course, it was uphill both ways, and when it snowed, it was knee deep to a giraffe. Thanks, Dustin, I know your grandfather lived on the same street).* I passed a nondescript house, minding my own business, merely walking down the sidewalk. My new "friend" came up behind me and quite literally coldcocked me. I went down like a streamlined anvil attached to a bag of wet cement.

Murray was the neighborhood tyrant. He was a bully and a sixth grader who outweighed me by at least forty pounds. For some unknown reason, Murray took an immediate and extremely intense dislike of me. The feeling became mutual very quickly. To make it worse, avoidance was not an option. There were no side streets which would have allowed me to walk around his house, and he was always waiting for me.

Murray seemed to have a fondness for throwing my books in the street, yelling at me, and insulting me. He had a particular penchant for punching and then chasing me and had no reservations about performing any humiliating act he might happen to think of that day. Let me add, he had quite the imagination.

My parents and my teachers at school knew about the situation *(I informed them on a regular basis).* They tried to help, but the problem is those who protect us, God notwithstanding, can't always be there.

Soon it was time to move again. You cannot possibly imagine how overjoyed I was. I was beyond happy. I couldn't contain myself. I was ecstatic, thrilled, and jubilant. I was overjoyed. My relief was indescribable and unfathomable. The day I told my teacher I'd be leaving Murray behind has been etched in my memory ever since. I've long forgotten her name but will never forget what that sweet lady told me. She said, "Murray will always be there."

It took me several years to grasp the significance of what she meant. What she taught me was you can never outrun your problems. Murray has taken many forms in my life, but he has always been around.

Courage means diving into life full-tilt without hesitation, realizing you might fall, but always be willing to get back up and try again. It took an awful lot of courage for that little third-grade boy to walk to school every day. It takes courage for anyone to face the Murrays of their life, whatever they may be. It took courage to be cordial and smile at my Saul all those years as he tried to make my life as miserable as he possibly could. It took courage to continue placing the second Ten Commandments on my office door. It took courage for me to make the commitment to pen the words in this book which you are reading.

It took courage for Carolyn to refuse to speak to an abusive father, for Jerry to make plans to leave home when she was a young girl, for Chad to abandon the pursuit of his degree and go home to help his family. It took courage every time I signed an endorsement in a student's logbook which allowed someone I taught to fly to take the controls and solo an airplane. It really took some personal courage to board an airplane destined for Iraq, but it was my duty to go, and I did it willingly. To me, these acts of bravery do not represent "real courage." Possibly you think of courage and bravery as the same thing, but not me.

Let me explain, but you need to prepare yourself. We're going the long way around the turn again, but it won't be as bad as the first time. We're only going to make a 270-degree turn so we can change heading by 90 degrees. We found a chain saw to cut the tree down and don't have to use that dull axe again. The chain on our saw needs to be sharpened, but you have the idea.

Pastor Larry S. recently preached a sermon on God's will. I'm not sure if he was quoting from a source or if these were his own thoughts. In that sermon, Pastor Larry stated the four wills of God are absolute, permissive, conditional, and desired.

God's absolute will is something that he has determined he is going to do. It will absolutely happen. His mind is made up, and nothing is going to change it. God decided to make the earth, and he did it. He decided to send his son Jesus to earth and did it. He decided to flood the earth and start over with humanity. He did that too. He decided to lead the Israelites out of bondage and let them start over in the promised land. Once again, he accomplished his absolute will.

God's permissive will is something he allows to happen. We talked about Job earlier. As the book of Job begins, Satan tells God that Job really isn't all that. In effect, Satan contends that if God stops protecting him, Job will cease to love him, cease to honor and worship him. God then permits Satan to attack Job. The vast majority of the book happens after Satan destroys Job's family. It is a dialogue between Job and his friends. God doesn't show up again until the thirty-eighth chapter when he questions Job.

His friends tell Job the reason for his suffering is because he has abandoned God. He has sinned and done terrible things, but Job knows what his friends are telling him isn't true. He doesn't understand why he has experienced all the tragedy. He desires to plead his case to God directly and proclaim his innocence. Job's mistake lies in his assumption that God is responsible. Translation: God often gets blamed for doing things he hasn't done.

Early in this manuscript, I promised to tell you about Romans Road. Romans Road is a perfect example of God's conditional will. Think of God's conditional will as quid pro quo, a tit-for-tat. If you do this, I'll do that. What is the point of me taking the time to write this book and asking you to read it? Romans Road answers the question. Romans Road consists of four short simple verses, all taken from the book of Romans, hence the name. Well, here it is:

1) "Everyone has sinned. No one measures up to God's glory" (Romans 3:23, NIRV). There is another way of thinking about that verse. No one measures up to God's standard. That means you.

2) "When you sin, the pay you'll get is death. But God gives you the gift of eternal life because of what Jesus Christ has done" (Romans 6:23, NIRV). Call it like it is or debate it as long as you like. Death in this verse means hell. Yes, God loves you, but hell yes, he will send you to hell.

3) "But God demonstrates his own love for us in this: While we were still sinners, Christ died for us" (Romans 5:8, NIV). That means you don't have to go to hell if you don't want to (you don't want to!). You have a choice; but don't fool yourself, there are only two choices. The choice of your eternal destiny is entirely up to you. So if you don't want to

go to hell, how do you avoid it? The last verse of Romans Road answers the question.

4) "Say with your mouth, Jesus is Lord. Believe in your heart that God raised him from the dead. Then you will be saved" (Romans 10:9, NIRV). That's it. A simple and sincere prayer is all there is to it. You just have to ask for the gift.

God's conditional will—accept my gift and I'll save you. It's an amazingly simple concept. This isn't the only example of God's conditional will, but I cannot think of an example more important, poignant, powerful, or meaningful. If you come up with one, then e-mail me and tell me about it. I'm not particularly concerned about my computer crashing due to an abundance of e-mails flooding my inbox.

Jarred was driving over to the house one morning to meet me and go to church with me. My home is in a rural area. It is difficult to find if you don't remember all of the backroad turns and it had been a while since his last visit. Needless to say, he got lost so he called me for directions. I asked him, "What do you see Son?" His response consisted of one word, "Corn." You know that story has to be true because my imagination isn't vivid enough to make it up. There are numerous cornfields in the area where we live so it was obvious more information was needed than his answer provided.

This is why the story is important. LEDRSHHIP means helping your brother find his way out of the cornfield when he gets lost in it. It means knowing where to look for him. If you haven't accepted the gift of Salvation which Romans Road tells you about my friend, then you are lost in the cornfield. You can't find your way out of it alone either but the great news is Jesus knows exactly where you are, even when all you can see is corn.

The ABCs used as a priority of tasks to be performed in order are used to teach a variety of things. In first aid they stand for Airway (make sure the patient is breathing), Bleeding (stop blood from leaking), and Circulation (make sure blood is flowing). In the event of an engine failure while flying an airplane, it means Airspeed (establish glide speed), Best field (where are you going to land?), and Checklist (see if you can get the engine started again). We use the ABCs to teach children in our Sunday school class the basics of becoming a Christian. They are Admit, Believe, and Confess.

I love the simplicity of the plan of salvation. God is waiting patiently for you, but time will run out. All you have to do is say a simple prayer. It has to be your prayer and it has to be sincere, but it should be something like this: "Heavenly Father, I know I am a sinner. I believe Jesus is the Son of God. I believe he came to earth to die for my mistakes. I believe he died on a cross for me, and I can be made righteous because of his blood. I confess my sins and ask you to forgive me. I accept the gift of salvation. I accept the sacrifice of your Son, Jesus Christ. I desire to live for you and follow you. Please come into my heart. Please show me your will for my life, and help me to follow whatever that may be. Help me to live for you."

Let's pretend you're on a game show and I'm the host. I want to give you—no strings attached—a new car, a large chunk of cash, buy you some new clothes, a backyard makeover, or perhaps remodel your house. You name it. Fill in the blank with anything you would like. If you don't accept my offer, the gesture would be pointless. At the risk of being repetitive, let me say that another way. If you don't accept my gift, you leave the game show with what you brought. You leave with *nothing*.

You have been offered the ultimate gift, the gift of life. Isn't your life more important than a vacation, a remodeled bathroom, or a new appliance package? What you're experiencing on earth is not life. Let me clarify that for you. It doesn't matter who you are, how much money you have or don't have, where you work, how important your job is, what your responsible for, where you grew up, how busy your schedule is, what your culture tells you, or who your family is. *What you're experiencing on Planet Earth is not life!*

You have to be born to experience life. Seems simple enough, doesn't it? Well, consider this then:

> God's grace has saved you because of your
> faith in Christ. Your salvation doesn't come from

> anything you do. It is God's gift. It is not based
> on anything you have done. No one can brag
> about earning it. (Ephesians 2:8, NIRV)

The bottom line is *you* have to accept the gift. One more question. What is more important than your eternal soul? I love that God loves me enough to create a way for me to get to him.

That is a rather clear explanation. How do you get more direct than that? Just talk to him. Ask him for the greatest gift you could possibly ever receive, which is the gift of life; and we're talking eternal life and a retirement plan that is out of this world! Notice I did say that salvation is simple but didn't say easy or automatic. That is because putting God first in your life and living as a Christian by placing the needs of others in front of your own is counterintuitive to human nature. You can't do it by yourself. You need his help. It's a choice you make every day, moment by moment. Living your life by the principles of LEDRSHHIP isn't easy either. In my opinion, they're synonymous.

Let me *(actually the prophet Isiah, who just happened to be passing down a tidbit given to him by…well, by God)* add a little something extra to Romans Road for you. You can't earn your way into heaven. I don't know how many times someone has told me they are a "good person" and if God loves me, he won't send me to an eternity without his presence. News flash, sports fans, *yes, he will.*

> All of us have become like one who is, and
> all our righteous acts are like filthy rags; we all
> shrivel up like a leaf, and like the wind our sins
> sweep us away. (Isaiah 64:6, NIV)

Refer to Romans Road if you like. You can't do enough good things to earn your way into heaven, but even so much as a single little white lie earns you a one-way ticket to hell.

God's desired will is a little different. It is what he wants for your life. He won't make it happen. You have to look for it and spend an awful lot of time on your knees asking him what it is. The great thing is God answers "knee mail." There has only been one person that ever lived on Planet Earth who lived their life in complete harmony with God's desired will. That, of course, was Jesus.

Make no mistake. He doesn't want you to spend eternity without him either. It breaks his heart, but freewill means the freedom to choose your own path.

> The Lord is not slow in keeping his promise, as some people understand slowness. Instead, he is patient with you, not wanting anyone to perish, but everyone to come to repentance. (2 Peter 3:9, NIV)

Let me explain absolute permissive conditional and desired will from a personal perspective. I earned my first college degree in business administration from Louisiana State University. Geaux Tigers! That word is not misspelled *(If I have to explain it, you would never understand, but I'll do my best. There is nothing like the experience of sitting in Tiger Stadium on a Saturday night with 102,000 of your BFFs)*. I then began to work in retail management. It was a good career that paid fairly well, but the disadvantage was the intense amount of time required.

The greater my success, the greater the time commitment became. Eventually, my life consisted of three activities. The first was work. The other two were sleeping and eating, but only when time allowed.

Perhaps you are experiencing something similar within your current employment situation. You might be close to the point of deciding enough is enough. I understand you; I've been there. Most people don't swap horses midstream in their career, but I did. It was not my choice to live my life attempting to support a lifestyle. I did not want to live that way anymore.

My decision was to return to college and pursue an aviation career. I was determined. Nothing was going to get in my way, and nothing did. The exorbitant cost of flight training along with a second college degree was financed through student loans. As I begin the seventh decade of my life, I'm still repaying them. It's like making a car payment on a vehicle I can't drive. I refused to accept any compromise in the pursuit of my goal. It was my absolute will to accomplish what I set out to do.

When my first wife was killed at the age of eighteen in an automobile accident, it was not God's absolute will. She was not wearing a seat belt. The driver of the car in which she was a passenger ignored a stop sign at a major highway intersection. The resulting accident caused her death.

When my dad died from a heart attack at the age of forty-eight, it wasn't God's absolute will either. Dad was a heavy chain-smoker. I regularly saw him light one cigarette after another with the butt of one he had just finished. It wasn't uncommon to see him with a lit cigarette in each hand. Since Dad smoked, that means his children smoked secondhand. All of us have breathing and allergy problems as a result. He had a heart attack prior to the one that killed him. Even though his doctors repeatedly advised him to adjust his diet and quit smoking, he refused to follow the advice.

I blamed God for a long time for taking my dad and my first wife at such young ages. I was mad at God. There is nothing wrong with being mad at God. He has big shoulders; He can take it. He understands. He designed us with emotions built in and invented the emotion of mad. It is part of the package. The problem is we tend to blame God when things like this happen, but they aren't God's fault. God permits things to happen because of the choices we make.

Earlier, I relayed the advice Mom gave me when she said the most difficult thing she ever did as a parent was let her children make a mistake. When it was appropriate, I allowed my children to make mistakes. I allowed my students to make mistakes. God does the same thing, but sometimes those mistakes come with dire consequences. The reason I have to take allergy medication on a daily basis in order to breathe is a result of God's permissive will. LEDRSHHIP does not mean forcing someone to do your will because you are stronger, more powerful, or are in a position of authority over them. God doesn't impose his will on us. He gives us a choice.

As a supervisor, I've often had to make compromises. I have allowed my subordinates to take time off for special reasons, provided they performed certain tasks. Conditional will is similar to a contract. If you do this, then I will allow you to do that, but it goes well beyond a contractual agreement.

As a flight instructor, I have to teach my students how to perform various flight maneuvers. Maneuver-based training is important, but a good pilot must be able to do much more than perform a given list of maneuvers to standard. Maneuvering an aircraft well is not the only skill set required to be a safe pilot.

Pilots recognize other pilots, even if we don't know them personally. There is just something about the way we think and act which allows our colleagues to easily identify us. Don't ask me to explain, prove, or quantify it, but it's true. The same thing applies to Christians. I recognize my Christian brothers and sisters just like you recognize members of your own family. It doesn't matter if I've never seen or even met them before.

On the way home from Iraq, we landed in Germany around 3:00 a.m. local time. All of the local stores at the airport were closed and there wasn't much to do except attempt to sleep in an airport terminal. If you have ever attempted sleeping in a chair at an airport, you know how ineffectual the effort. I leisurely strolled around for a little while to stretch my legs and then returned to the gate. After I'd been sitting there about ten minutes, the pilot walked up from where he had been and set down across from me.

I wasn't wearing a crisp white shirt with epilates on the shoulder. I didn't have on a necktie, and there were no wings or aviation insignia on my lapel. I was wearing my US army uniform, the same uniform everyone on the plane was wearing. There was nothing visible about me which identified me as a pilot. I looked like any other soldier on his way home from Iraq. As he sat down, the pilot asked me, "Who do you fly for?"

We engaged in conversation for a while. Another soldier sitting next to us was intently and quite obviously eavesdropping. Eventually, he asked the pilot why we were being delayed. The pilot said because we needed fuel and he had to wait for fuel services to open. He then said he didn't really want to go swimming in the middle of the Atlantic.

It isn't enough to just be able to take off, land, maneuver, and navigate an aircraft. You must also be able to make decisions based on the situation you are in. I want to fly with the pilot who knows how to make the right decision. I want to fly with the pilot who refuses to swim in the Atlantic Ocean. What about you?

In addition to teaching maneuvers, the FAA also requires me to utilize Scenario-Based Training (SBT). The idea is to enhance aeronautical decision-making (ADM) skills. I purposefully place my students in scenarios or circumstances they could realistically face, then give them corresponding constraints a pilot might normally encounter. Rarely is there only one correct course of action. It isn't the particular choice they make which is important. Determining and executing a reasonable and valid course of action allowing successful extrication from the situation is what matters. God's conditional will is like SBT. When you do this, the result will be that.

Have you ever played chess with someone whose abilities vastly exceed your own? It can be both embarrassing and humbling. I would not even classify myself as an amateur. I still have difficulty remembering how all the pieces are supposed to move on the board. Imagine if I were to attempt to play a game with a grand master. Why would I be so soundly defeated? I submit it would not only be due to the master's superior skill.

Success in a game of chess depends on being able to see what your opponent is planning to do well in advance. I do not have that skill. This thing called life, which we are privileged to enjoy for a few years, was invented by Jesus. He is the grand master of all grand masters. You will not beat him at his own game, because he knows every possibility and exactly what you are thinking. Conditional will—when you do this, God does that.

My desire was for my children to go to college and establish themselves in a worthwhile career. It was not important to me what they chose to do with their lives as long as it was something they could become successful pursuing. I could not make them go to college. They chose to, and I'm happy about that, but it was their decision. It was their decision to choose whatever career path they wanted to pursue. I was not able to, nor would I have attempted to, exercise any control over that choice.

It was my desire for my subordinates to be prepared for taking my place upon my retirement, to become successful in other areas within the industry. They sought my advice on how to accomplish that. I let them know what they needed to do in order to prepare for success. Some listened and some didn't. I let them know of my willingness to help but also made sure they realized I can't do it for them.

Pastor Seth S. is a wonderful pastor and a gifted public speaker. He has a way of personalizing biblical principles in a way people can easily identify with. It is easy to relate to his messages. In many respects, that's exactly what I'm attempting to accomplish with this book. A man in his early thirties tends to talk about his family while discussing his experiences. We like to talk about things we know about. It seems to me the best preachers use personal experiences to convey biblical truths.

Seth is a master at this. In my opinion, he should be awarded an honorary doctor of divinity. I consider him to be a close personal friend, because we share what I believe to be a common work ethic and because he is my Christian brother.

At one point during the pursuit of his aviation goals, he was a flight student of mine. Later when he was no longer my student, I had the privilege of administering his commercial pilot check ride. He passed, and his performance was exemplary.

Instead of being happy about accomplishing this incredible achievement, he was depressed. He told me he didn't understand why. He knew he should be experiencing incredible joy after reaching this crucial aviation milestone but could not understand why he felt something was missing. He knew something was wrong but didn't know what.

He later told me that on his way to the car after completing the check ride, he prayed about it, and God answered. The answer was not what he expected. If you are willing to lay it on the line, God will tell you what he wants. You may not get the answer you want, but don't ask for the answer unless you are ready to go where he wants and do what he asks.

God's answer to him was, "Flying isn't what I want you to do. You can continue pursuing an aviation career if that is your choice, and you will be very successful, but I'm not going one step further with you. You will be on your own. I want you to preach instead."

I'm grateful that Seth recognized God's call and chose to follow it. He understands the importance of following God's desired will. He understands from a personal perspective the importance of obeying God, no matter the cost. That is the moral of this next story, which was a part of his sermon one Sunday morning.

Seth was taking his two children to school for the first day of the year. His son was starting kindergarten, and his daughter was in the first grade. If you have children, I don't have to explain this; you know how it works. For the first day of school, you buy your kids new clothes, new shoes, new backpacks, new school supplies, new this, new that, and new everything.

It had rained the day before. After they got out of the car, Brother Seth was walking his children up to the school building, and there was a large fresh puddle on the sidewalk. He told his children to follow him and walk around the puddle. His daughter did, but his son didn't. His son had on brand-new shoes. New shoes tend to have slippery soles. His son decided he wanted to jump into the puddle. It wasn't a little or timid jump. It was a take a few steps back and make a running full steam ahead jump, as hard as you can jump, to make as large a splash as possible jump.

You can probably guess what happened. Because the soles of his shoes were slick, when he landed in the puddle, he lost his footing, fell, and hurt himself. He got cold because his new clothes were now dirty and wet. Of course, he began to cry. Seth picked up his son and wiped away the tears. As his son sniffled and whimpered, he held him and settled his daughter in school for the day.

Afterward, Seth took his son home, got him changed, and drove him back to school which caused him to be late for work. Seth was our interim bi-vocational pastor at the time because we couldn't afford to pay him a full-time salary. We still can't afford a full-time pastor.

The point of his story is we should follow the desired will of our Father. The 2001 edition of *The Strongest Strong's Exhaustive Concordance*,[34] tells us the word *follow* is mentioned eighty-six times in the Bible. That doesn't include references to *followed*, *followedst*, *followers*, *followeth*, and *following*. When God mentions a single word that many times, my only conclusion is he thinks it is rather *important*.

When we choose not to follow and decide to jump into the puddle instead, things don't usually work out very well for us. Jesus knows the dangers of the puddle. He can see what we can't. He knows the puddle looks inviting and fun but also knows when our shoes are slippery. He knows that if we chose not to follow him, we will fall as a consequence. In case you missed the inference, we aren't really talking about a little boy falling after jumping into a puddle.

We have an instruction book for life, and it's called the Bible. It's a huge mistake to use it like a side-view mirror in heavy traffic. We tend to glance in our mirror only when we want to change lanes and ignore it the rest of the time. We try to go through life without following the directions *(Did you ever try to put a swing set, bookcase, or a desk together without following the instructions? How many times did you get something in the wrong place?)*. The Bible needs to be our primary focus. We tend to set out on our own and jump into puddles. The result is that we fall, and it's often an unpleasant experience.

The good news is that when we fall, Jesus is going to pick us up, clean us up, and set us back on the course of life. He will wipe away the tears. He will wipe away the sniffles, give us clean clothes, and make it better for us, but it is so much easier if we listen and obey first. I imagine that he gets rather tired of picking us up, but he is always ready and willing to do it over and over again. If we follow his instructions, we can avoid the pain and problems which come as a consequence of not listening in the first place.

---

[34] James Strong, LL. D, STD, *The Strongest Strong's Exhaustive Concordance of the Bible*, Zondervan, Grand Rapids, Michigan, 2001.

God has plans for all of us.

> "For I know the plans I have for you,"
> declares the Lord, "Plans to prosper you and
> not to harm you, plans to give you a hope and a
> future. Then you will call on me and come and
> pray to me and I will listen to you. You will seek
> me and find me when you seek me with all your
> heart." (Jeremiah 29:11–13, NIV)

If there is anyone I want to listen to me, it is my Jesus. If there is anyone I want to find, it is my Jesus. Seth made the decision to follow God's desired will for his life.

I think Jesus did a much better job of teaching the same lesson my third-grade teacher did on the night he was betrayed when he prayed in the garden of Gethsemane.

> Father, if you are willing, take this cup from
> me; yet not my will, but yours be done. (Luke
> 22:42, NIV).

Jesus was certainly a courageous man. He faced the cross willingly, head-on, and without hesitation. How could any man have that kind of courage? The simple answer is no man could have. Jesus wasn't just any man, though. Jesus is God. Jesus knew what was coming. He knew what the game plan was before he even got to earth. He was aware of the torturous death and humiliation that awaited him. Agony doesn't begin to describe it.

So here is Jesus, who is really God incarnate, and the creator of creation. He knows what's coming and he drops to his knees. Then he says, "Hey, Daddy, I'll go through this if You really want me to. If there is any other way around it, I would really prefer to skip the whole thing, but whatever you want, Dad. I'm willing and I will do whatever you want, but are you sure, Dad? Isn't there another option? I have unlimited power. I could just come home right now if I want and we could give up on these hard-hearted, hateful, inconsiderate humans. We can just forget about them. I know you wouldn't be upset with me, but if you insist, then bring on Murray."

All right, here we are. The tree has been cut down and the fire has been built, but this time we're toasting a bagel *(Can you tell I like to eat?)*. Bravery is defined as having a courageous attitude which means courage is the result of bravery, the outward manifestation of bravery. It is how you act, because you are brave to begin with. Earnest Hemingway said, "Courage is grace under pressure."

Think about the two thieves who were crucified beside Jesus. Both were able to talk to him. One man recognized who Jesus was, but the other man didn't. One recognized his punishment was just, while the other believed he had been treated unfairly. One was sincere in his repentance, but the other man didn't care. What did Jesus tell the thief who acknowledged him?

> Jesus answered him, "Truly I tell you, today you will be with me in paradise. (Luke 23:43, NIV)

Talk about grace under pressure!

Bravery means facing your Murray. It means looking your King Saul in the eye and saying, "Go for it, dude, bring on your worst, hit me with everything you've got!" Courage means facing your Gethsemane. Real courage is asking God what his will is for you and complying with the answer. "Where do you want me to go? What do you want me to do? Where do You want me to work?" Real courage is a willingness to submit your life to God's desired will without question. The heart of true courage lies in trusting God to take care of your needs, concerned only about following and believing in his plan for you, regardless of what that may happen to be.

Courage is the story of Daniel told in Daniel chapter 6. Daniel was thrown into the lion's den because he refused to stop praying to God. God sent an angel who kept the lions' mouths closed. Courage is the story of David facing the giant, Goliath, armed with only a slingshot and his faith in God which is told in 1 Samuel chapter 17. God took out Goliath.

If you trust him, God will fight your battles. You can count on him to win. Courage is the story of three Hebrew boys told in the third chapter of Daniel. Shadrach, Meshach, and Abednego refused to worship the statue of King Nebuchadnezzar, because that would have meant disobeying the first commandment found in Exodus 20:2: "You shall have no other gods before me" (NIV). They were thrown into the furnace but trusted in God. God rescued them.

The Bible is filled with stories of courage which go well beyond bravery. Forget about Murray. You are not going to get away from him. Either you'll learn how to fight Murray or he'll be taking your lunch money away from you the rest or your life. The real question is, have you faced your Gethsemane? Once you learn to face Gethsemane, Murray becomes inconsequential.

Conclusion
(Love)

Love is patient, love is kind. It does not envy, it does not boast, it
is not proud. It does not dishonor others, it is not self-seeking, it
is not easily angered, it keeps no record of wrongs. Love does not
delight in evil but rejoices with the truth. It always protects, always
trusts, always hopes, and always perseveres. Love never fails.

—1 Corinthians 13:4–8, NIV

I consider myself extremely fortunate to have been allowed to fly
airplanes for more than thirty years. Many have made this statement,
but my job is the greatest in the world. The amazing feeling—not to
mention adrenaline rush—of leaving the earth in my machine and
safely bringing it back to land again, and the incredible view which
accompanies the experience, is indescribable. To appreciate the satisfaction and joy, you simply have to do the same thing.

If you are a pilot, you understand what I am saying. If you are
not, then you don't and it is inexplicable. The love of flying is one
thing, but if you think about it, everything in this book is about
the idea of love. Prepare yourself for a few "love" stories in this conclusion so we can tie everything together. Consider an analysis of
LEDRSHHIP; it is really a different way of spelling love.

Explaining the concept of LEDERSHHIP is a monumental undertaking, well beyond gargantuan. It's probably similar to offering a sneezing hippopotamus a handkerchief.

I don't have to see God to know he exists any more than I need to stand in traffic to know it will hurt if I get run over by a bus. It isn't necessary for me to put my hand into a raging fire to know that will hurt either. If you want to stand in front of a moving bus or burn your hand, then go ahead. Don't expect me to do the same, but be my guest. Tell me how it works out for you.

I see God everywhere I look, but that doesn't mean I'm able to describe him unless it would be with the word *love*. In 1 John 4:8 (NIV), we're told, "Whoever does not love does not know God, because God is love." Love can be used as a verb or a noun; in this sense it is a specific verb. John is telling us about the benevolent love of Jesus. He is informing us that Jesus is charitable, gracious, considerate, thoughtful, accommodating, and kindhearted. In short, God is inclined to do good things for us. He wants to make our lives better. You can walk past the Salvation Army Kettle and drop in a dollar. You can give without loving. I can't walk past the same kettle without dropping in a dollar. I cannot love without giving; it is impossible to love without giving. Jesus puts his love for us into action. He does things for us, even when we are unaware or unconvinced. If you really want to be successful in this life, learn to love your co-worker that detests you, your supervisor who takes advantage of you, the employees who work for you and talk about you behind your back. Learn to love the drudgery of the details of your job. John also tells us what Jesus Himself said about it. "No one has greater love than the one who gives his life for his friends" (John 15:13, NIRV). A few days later, Jesus willingly went to the cross.

Let me give it to you straight. That kind of love is impossible for me to understand, and so is that level of humility, but it should be our goal to emulate that standard as best we can. I can't love the way Jesus does but can accept his incredible gift based simply on faith. Jesus expects us to put forth our best effort in attempting to love our brothers the same way he loves us. This begs the question, "Who is my brother?" In case you have missed the inference, we aren't discussing siblings.

The short answer is that everyone is my brother. Let me translate that for you in case you missed the point. Everyone is *your* brother. *Everyone!* That means you are my brother, and it also means I'm your brother. We both have a responsibility to each other.

I love God. I'm not ashamed of it; I'm proud of it. If I say, "I love God," it means I must also love you. That statement must hold true at all times. I must love you, even if and while you are choosing to hate me, regardless of your actions or how you treat me. I still love you. It doesn't matter if I don't want to or if I don't like you, I still love you. I've made up my mind to love you just as you are, faults and all, no matter what you've done or will do, because Christ commands me to. No matter what you say about me or do to me, I'll continue to love you. It's just that simple. I'm far from being there, but I want to be like Christ and love like Christ. There is nothing you can do about it. You can't change my mind. You'll never convince me of anything different.

Since you are my brother and I love you, it means you can count on me to help when you need assistance, but that also means I'm your brother, and you should come to my aid when help is needed. Ever hear this one? Family takes care of family. Or perhaps, family loves family. How much should you love me?

One day, a lawyer asked Jesus a question. The attorney wasn't exactly being straightforward. It isn't my intent to alienate the entire legal profession, but there are many jokes which are not in the best taste regarding lawyers *(the best ones are told by attorneys)*. This particular fellow was trying to trap Jesus. His was deceitful and wanted to turn Jesus's own words against Him. The question was, "Teacher, which is the most important commandment in the law?"

Jesus replied, "Love the Lord your God with all your heart and with all your soul. Love him with all your mind. This is the first and most important commandment. And the second is like it. Love your neighbor as yourself." (Matthew 22:36–39 NIRV) Let me translate that for you. Put God first, everyone else next, and yourself last.

Huh? Wait! What? Rewind! Hold the phone, dude! Just one darn cotton pea-pickin' minute, buddy! Let me get this straight. You're saying I have to love my boss who treated me unfairly and cost me that promotion I should have had? My former spouse who tried to take everything I own? My Saul, my Murray, the mugger who took my wallet, and the jerk that was driving drunk and killed my child the same way I love myself? You can't possibly be serious! That is beyond preposterous! It's insanity!

Nope, I'm not saying that. Jesus is. I'm just the messenger. Believe me, I have trouble with it too. It isn't a request, though. It isn't negotiable. It's a command.

Sometimes I get to fly above the clouds. On the darkest day, I have the privilege of seeing a breathtakingly beautiful blue sky, stark white clouds below me *(pilots refer to this as an undercast),* and sunshine so brilliant it hurts my eyes. Words can't begin to describe the breathtaking splendor of God's earth. I love that experience. This usually happens around 5,000 feet of altitude. A mile is 5,280 feet.

Here is the point. On the dreariest day, sunshine is less than a mile away. Christians *(leaders, if you prefer)* need to see things from more than one perspective. They need to think outside of the box and find the good. Better yet, just get rid of the box. The good is always there, but the trick is in knowing where to look. Christians love finding the good.

Here is a short poem I wrote. I'll explain why that is the only introduction I'm going to give you after you read it.

The Mall

She's been in the mall only five minutes
But already knows every store that's in it.
Give me some money. Can we get a pet?
Why haven't you bought me anything yet?
I'm going to go try on some jeans.
I need some new clothes.
No, I'm sorry, but I don't like those.
Your taste is awful, get with the times.

We've got to hurry, they close at nine.
Can we stop and eat? How about a treat?
I'm really tired. Will you rub my feet?
Where did I see that blouse before?
I don't remember. Was it this store?
Where's the makeup? The jewelry counter?
Please don't embarrass me should friends I encounter.
I brought cash but I've long since spent it.
My credit cards are all maxed to the limit.
It drives me nuts. It makes me fuss.
Sometimes it even makes me cuss.
But I would not trade even one single minute.
For when we get home, she hugs me tight,
And says, "Dad, I love you, sleep well, goodnight."

I'll admit to not being the world's greatest poet, but I'm rather proud of that piece. Be honest with yourself. What did you think as you began reading it? Perhaps your thoughts were along the lines of, *This poor sap must be married to a shrew or something. What an ungrateful woman!* It kind of fools you at the end, doesn't it?

I wrote that for my daughter on September 17, 1998, after she and I spent an afternoon shopping. Life can be like that. It can fool you until the very end. Are you letting the reality of eternity fool you? I love life with all of its twists, turns, and surprises; and I really love my daughter.

Somebody who was not fooled about life was the Apostle Paul. Paul got it right. In his Roman prison cell, Paul wrote a letter to the church in Philippi. In the first chapter, verse 27 (NIV), he discusses the attitude a Christian *(leader?)* should have: "Whatever happens, conduct yourselves in a manner worthy of the gospel of Christ."

My take is that he's really saying no matter what challenges we face, no matter what interrupts our plans, how frustrated we may become, or what obstacles are in our way, we should respond to all situations with a Christ-like attitude, regardless of whether you believe Christ was, who he claimed to be, or not. He also tells us a few verses later in chapter 2:5 (NIRV), "You should think in the same way Christ Jesus does." Paul loved Christ, loved being a Christian, and loved living for Christ.

At the risk of embarrassing them, let me tell you some stories about Magen and Jarred when they were little. When my daughter was almost two years old, and before my son was born, I was staining the deck while her mom was at work. Magen was watching and wanted to help. She was insistent *(there's that word again)* and repeatedly kept asking. Moms and dads, if you don't already know, you are most assuredly going to identify with what I'm about to say next. It is incredibly difficult to deny an insistent two-year-old who has her heart set on something.

When everything was finished except for the deck floor, I decided to let her help. Have you ever watched a two-year-old with a paint brush and deck stain? It is quite an amusing sight. I'm laughing at the memory as I recall it. Needless to say, she got more stain on herself than the deck. Soon it was time to get cleaned up and go pick up her mom. Not considering my words or the potential for their impact, I told her, "Let's get you cleaned up. If Mom sees you like that, she'll shoot both of us." Next was a bath, followed by dressing in clean clothes, and finally the trip to retrieve her mom.

About halfway there, Magen suddenly became withdrawn and despondent. I knew something was bothering her, but she refused to answer when I asked what was wrong. When her mother walked out of the office and got in the car, my daughter started crying and shaking. She literally screamed, "Mommy, don't shoot me!"

I felt almost as tall as the knee of a common housefly! It was humbling to realize how literally my child took an everyday colloquialism, an expression which I've used countless times—and you have undoubtedly used as well thinking nothing of it—and how much those simple words terrified her. I love my daughter and the simplicity of the way children think.

A child's interpretation of events is quite literal. If you are a parent or if you have been around a young child, you understand how simple their world can be. I love the simplicity with which children view their surroundings.

Another story about the literality of children occurred in our Sunday school class a few weeks ago. A six-year-old boy was visiting our class, and we asked him to complete a carbonless three-copy visitor contact form. He completed it, but I couldn't read the last copy, so one of the other children told him he had to press really hard. He stood up and put the form on the table. Then he put his palm on the form and started pressing downward with all the muscle he could muster. No doubt you have witnessed something similar.

Jesus really loves children. I think perhaps part of the reason He does is because of the innocent and simplistic view they have of life. Have you read *Heaven is for Real* by Todd Burpo?[35] If you haven't, you need to. It's a great book!

Lack of understanding between different cultures can cause miscommunication. After a harrowing day, a student pilot who spoke English as a second language with an accent, making comprehension difficult, was making the control tower operator's job rather challenging. The airspace was busy, it was late in the day, and everyone was tired. The situation had the potential to quickly become dangerous.

Airborne at the time, I was monitoring tower frequency. After the student pilot landed, the tower controller needed to determine where to direct this young man. Did he want to continue practicing takeoffs and landings? Did he want to taxi to the ramp? If so, then to which ramp did he need to go? The controller needed him off of the runway to make room for other departing and landing aircraft. The student pilot stopped on the runway because he was confused and didn't know what to do next which was creating a frustrating and hectic situation.

The tower controller asked him to, "Say intentions."

The student pilot replied, "I wish to become a pilot."

Are you stuck on life's runway? Are you confusing a flurry of activity in the world around you for accomplishment? Does the hectic schedule of your life deter you from communicating with those you love, and more importantly, does it keep you from communicating with God? Have you heard the expression "work smart, not

---

[35] Todd Burpo, *Heaven is for Real*, Thomas Nelson Inc., Nashville, TN, 2010.

hard?" Confusing activity for productivity is a tremendous waste of time.

The student took the controller literally, and while he did nothing incorrectly, his actions still caused problems. At the same time, his reaction brought some much-needed levity into a tense situation. The controller used proper phraseology with his communications, but the pilot did not comprehend.

Leaders need to understand their communications don't always portray the desired intent. Perhaps the person you are talking with understands you differently than you would believe. They might interpret what you are saying literally, almost the way a child would. We need to have childlike faith. We need to have childlike understanding of Jesus while simultaneously being serious about our salvation. We can't take him or our salvation for granted. His communication with us is extremely clear and straightforward. His word leaves no room for doubt.

> The grass withers and the flowers fall, but the word of our God endures forever. (Isaiah 40:8, NIV)

On more than one occasion, Jesus told us to follow him. Don't take my word for it. Go to a Bible concordance and look up the word *follow*. The instructions "Follow me" are concise. The verse that sums it up for me, though, is John 12:26: "Whoever serves me must follow me; and where I am, my servant also will be. My father will honor the one who serves me" (NIV). I don't know about you, but I can think of nothing better than being honored by God.

Seth's daughter followed her dad's instructions, and she went right to school without any consequence. His son didn't follow, and he got hurt. I love that story and the lesson it teaches. I'm thankful to have heard it in our church. I love my former pastor and his family. I love my current pastor as well, but he doesn't tell many stories. I love that God takes care of me and protects me, even when I choose not to follow, even if I jump in the puddle. Thank you, Brother Seth.

> To this you were called, because Christ suf-
> fered for you, leaving you an example that you
> should follow in his steps. (1 Peter 2:21, NIV)

I went to work early one morning while my children and their mother were still sleeping. At 8:00 a.m., my work telephone rang (pre-cell phone days), and the local sheriff's office suddenly wanted my immediate attention. The officer asked me if my son's name was Jarred. "Yes, it is. Why do you ask?" I answered.

She described a boy (my son) who was sitting on her lap in the Sheriff's office. Jarred woke up and left the house while his mother was sleeping. He wandered around the neighborhood wearing nothing but a diaper and got lost. He was only about two-years-old at the time, and it was winter.

Fortunately, a woman that lived in the neighborhood and was on her way to work saw him on the sidewalk. She noticed him walking alone and crying. She realized the situation wasn't normal, so she picked him up and drove him to the sheriff's office. I never had the opportunity to thank her, because she requested her name be kept anonymous. Perhaps she will read this book and know how grateful I am.

Jarred decided to set out on an adventure that morning. When you don't follow in the Father's footsteps, you might not fall in the puddle, but you could become quite lost and never realize the dangers you might face.

I had no idea my son was lost until that phone call. I shudder to think what might have happened had it not been for the selfless service of a complete stranger who owed me or my son nothing, the kindness of Jarred's Good Samaritan. Even though I never met this woman, I love her for what she did.

When I picked him up at the Sheriff's office, I don't know who was happier. The relief I felt when I saw my son sitting there is impossible for me to explain. So was the joy on his face when he saw me. I'll never forget his expression.

On one occasion, I decided to run away from home. That isn't an uncommon thing for a child to do, but it's usually done by a youngster, perhaps between five to ten years old. Jarred was not running away from home. He was exploring the neighborhood and got lost. I was running away. I was not coming back; I was serious. Based on some of the things you have read, I'm sure you can understand why I might want to.

I was a junior in high school at the time. My plans were not very well thought out, and I didn't get very far. I made it to the home of one of my teachers who then went to work. Of course, he called Dad from school, and then Dad came to get me.

It is almost impossible for me to describe, but I distinctly remember the look on my father's face when he knocked on that door. It was a simultaneous plethora of emotions consisting of joy, relief, love, sadness, hurt, and disappointment. The look on Jarred's face when I picked him up was eerily similar.

When you are lost, when you're not following in his footsteps, Jesus, our heavenly Father, is going to look for you. How joyful he must be when you return to the path he has forged for you. If you have lost your path without realizing it, perhaps because you might have never been on it in the first place. How joyful you will feel once you return to your Father. How happy God must be when you find your way home. I love my Jesus. I love that he has shown all of us the way.

Mark 10:15 (NIV) tells us, "Truly I tell you, anyone who will not receive the kingdom of God like a little child will never enter it." Yes, I believe the Bible, literally, absolutely, without question, and entirely. I believe Moses parted the Red Sea *(but he had permission from his supervisor first),* the earth was created in six days, the great flood covered the whole earth, Methuselah lived to be 969 years old, Jesus came to earth as the result of immaculate conception, he was born to a Virgin, he died on a cross, and came back to life—and all the other stories you read about in God's word. I accept these things on faith. I love reading the Bible and love to study it.

Before you say anything about the impossibility of somebody living to be 969 years old, let me tell you that I'm not obtuse. A man who was 969 years old would definitely be an old man. How could the heart continue beating that long? What about the kidneys and the liver? How would the bones not become so brittle that they would simply shatter *(I'm only in my sixties; I already have arthritis, and my body reminds me of a garage sale. Some things work, some things don't, and some things I don't even recognize anymore)*? I've heard the argument that God measures time differently than we do and can tell you where to find it.

> But do not forget this one thing, dear friends: With the Lord a day is like a thousand years, and a thousand years are like a day. (2 Peter 3:8, NIV)

It really doesn't matter to me how God measures time. Faith allows me to trust that God will reveal to me what he needs me to know when he needs me to know it. God expects that childish faith and trust. Anything less is to dishonor him. Jesus loves me. He loves you. He loves it when we have that childlike faith. He loves it when we trust him and his word without question.

I had the pleasure of taking Jarred for his airplane flight when he was five. It was an incredible experience for each of us. I'm confident the greater joy was mine because of the wonder and excitement showing in his eyes. Thirty plus years ago, I can still remember the beaming look on his tiny face *(It's not little anymore. Sorry, son, but I'm trying to write a book here. You're bigger than I am now.)*. The excitement of knowing he was going to fly with Dad was something he talked about for days before it finally happened.

Shortly after takeoff, for a reason only a five-year-old could explain, he began to play with things. It wasn't a good idea. One of the things he thought might be fun to play with was the fuel shut-off valve. He turned it *off!* Let's just say things got very quiet very quickly in that airplane. I'll not ever forget the terrified look in his eyes when that happened either *(That was the moment I learned the importance of giving all of my passengers a thorough preflight safety briefing. Let me assure you, it was a lesson never forgotten)*. My son taught me something incredibly valuable that day. I love my son. Jesus gives us a very thorough prelife briefing. He expects us to constantly read it. In case you haven't guessed by now, I love my Jesus.

At the conclusion of one semester, a student of mine gave me a gift. It is a cap with the word *retired* and the US Army logo on it. I love that simple cap, because it means Bob was paying attention in class about what is important to me. People pay attention to how you live your life and they can be extremely observant. It really isn't the cap I love but the thought that Bob cared enough about me that he wanted to make me happy. I love Bob for being that considerate *(the Scotch was pretty good too; thanks, Bob. No, not my brother Robert, a different Robert.).*

On my last day of work, I had to turn in my keys and the equipment which belonged to the university I had been using. This included an iPad. After everything had been turned in, I began cleaning out my desk and found the iPad charger. It was about the size and shape of a small ring box. I gathered it up along with a few other things I had also not returned and jaunted off to the office of the department chair's administrative assistant. I had many conversations with her over the years and knew she was a Christian based upon those interactions.

I walked into her office, held up the charger, and said "I have something for you."

She said, "It looks like a diamond ring box. I didn't know you cared that much."

She was kidding, of course, and I knew that because I knew her. I responded with, "I love you, Sis, but there are limitations."

We both got a good laugh out of it, and I finished out the day. On my way home, as I replayed that conversation in my mind, something occurred to me. The love of Jesus has no limitations. That is what makes it so very special. I love the people I had the opportunity to work with for so many years, and I love that my Savior loves me completely, absolutely, and unconditionally.

While we were teenagers, we lived next to a gasoline station. Robert and I were going bowling one Friday evening. He was ready, and I wasn't, so I handed him some money, the keys to my car (my very first car, by the way, a red two-door 1970 Ford Galaxy with black interior), and asked him to drive over next door and fill up. A few minutes later, he came back into the house and told me he had ruined the transmission because the car wouldn't move. Have you noticed most gas stations have a short concrete post in front of their pumps and the pumps are usually on an elevated concrete island? That hasn't always been the case.

It wasn't the transmission. My brother had backed into the gas pump. Now, let me tell you, my friend, that was exciting. There is nothing like the experience of seeing a gasoline pump impaled by the bumper of your car *(I'm not suggesting Robert singlehandedly changed how gas stations locate their pumps, but perhaps he contributed. Thank you for reminding me of that, Robert. I told you I would find a way to get this in here. It's just too good of a story to be left out.)*.

Fortunately, the incident wasn't worthy of a Hollywood production. The fire department was not called, there were no explosions or stuntmen, and no significant damage was done. We jacked up the car and pried the bumper loose with a crowbar. Then we were able to push the car away from the fuel pump. The owner of the gas station knew both of us, and he was very forgiving.

We went bowling, and life went on. Robert was afraid I would be angry. He was worried that the car was damaged. We were both ecstatic that it had not been. Mostly, I was grateful he had not been hurt. Cars can be repaired, bumpers can be bent back into shape, and gasoline pumps can be repainted, but brothers can't be replaced. A good brother is hard to find.

I love my siblings. I love that Robert was worried about how I'd feel if he damaged something belonging to me, which he knew I worked hard for and valued. The thing to remember is nothing belongs to me. It all belongs to God. He just lets me use what he thinks I need. His judgment is pretty good.

The Soldier's Creed[36] is a standard of behavior, the army values by which all United States Army personnel are expected to live. All branches of service have their own version. At the beginning of this book, I told

---

[36] Task Force Soldier's Warrior Ethos Team, "The Soldier's Creed," Authorized by Army Chief of Staff General Erik K. Shinseki, May 2003, Approved by Army Chief of Staff General Peter Shoomaker, November 13, 2003, Published in *Infantry* magazine, December 22, 2003.

you those values are LDRSHIP, and my version of it is LEDRSHHIP. US Army personnel are taught the Soldier's Creed during basic training. The words are poignant and humbling. Soldiers stand at attention when reciting the Soldier's Creed. Every single time I recite, hear, or read these words, they never fail to bring a tear to my eye.

Soldier's Creed

I am an American Soldier.
I am a warrior and a member of a team.
I serve the people of the United States, and live the Army Values.
I will always place the mission first.
I will never accept defeat.
I will never quit.
I will never leave a fallen comrade.
I am disciplined, physically and mentally tough, trained
and proficient in my warrior tasks and drills.
I always maintain my arms, my equipment, and myself.
I am an expert and I am a professional.
I stand ready to deploy, engage, and destroy the enemies
of the United States of America in close combat.
I am a guardian of freedom and the American way of life.
I am an American Soldier.

The first time I donned a uniform to serve this great country was September 17, 1974. The last time I removed my uniform was December 13, 2013. While I no longer physically wear my uniform *(it wouldn't fit now)*, the reality is I'm always in uniform. Once a soldier, always a soldier. I love being a soldier, because I love the core values soldiers live by.

I've had the honor of serving with many incredible soldiers and leaders. The greatest soldier, the greatest leader I have ever served or served with, is my Jesus. I've taken some liberties with the Soldier's Creed and modified it as my own personal Christian Creed. There is nothing of which I'm more proud than being able to tell you I'm a soldier in God's army.

CHRISTIAN'S CREED

I am a Christian.
I serve the risen Jesus Christ, Son of the One, the only, the true,
living, omnipotent, omniscient, and omnipresent, eternal God.
I live by his word and his rules.
I will always strive to place his goals first.
I will always strive to never compromise my Savior's values.
I will never fail to forgive.
I will never fail to love my brother.[37]
I am physically and mentally tough and proficient in his word.
I will always maintain my mental and Christian discipline.
I will always live up to the responsibility and trust Jesus
has vested in me by adopting me into his family.
I am an expert and I am a professional.
I stand ready to deploy where Jesus asks, whenever Jesus asks,
and do whatever Jesus asks, no matter when Jesus asks.
I am a guardian of peace, love, and the Christian way of life.
I am Christ's servant and slave.
I am a Christian.

In case you haven't figured this out yet, I love my Jesus and I love
being a Christian. That also means I love you, no matter who you
are, no matter where you are, and no matter what you have done. I
love doing my best to live by the values of LEDRSHHIP.

I've only given you a thumbnail sketch of what living as a
Christian should mean. To sum it up, to live as a Christian or to
be a good leader means being grateful, disciplined, patient, content,

---

[37] You are my brother, by the way.

faithful, hardworking, willing to do what is right—no matter the cost—forgiving to a fault, having a positive attitude, never accepting less than your personal best, a willingness to face your challenges head on without excuses, humble; and above all, to have an attitude of sacrificial love for everyone.

If this is what living each day as a Christian means, it also means the antithesis of being a Christian is to be the opposite. That is a pretty tall order. To understand the magnitude of the challenge, let's answer the question, "What are people really like (meaning, what are you really like)?"

I apologize for once again quoting the Apostle Paul, but he has so much to say, and better still, he agrees with me *(Sorry, that was rather braggadocios on my part. A better way of saying that would be I agree with him.)*.

In his second letter to Timothy, chapter 3, verses 2–5 (NIV), he tells us, "People *(which means all of us, you included)* will be lovers of themselves, lovers of money, boastful, proud, abusive, disobedient to their parents, ungrateful, unholy, without love, unforgiving, slanderous, without self-control, brutal, not lovers of good *(meaning lovers of evil)*, treacherous, rash, conceited, lovers of pleasure rather than lovers of God."

Does this sound like anyone you know? Does it sound like you? If I'm honest with myself, I must admit it sounds like me.

This brings me to the conclusion that being a Christian is the opposite of being human. That is probably one of the reasons it is so unpopular. It's a monumental challenge for a human being to not behave as human being, which shouldn't be confused with a human being who is misbehaving. You may believe the two concepts are the same thing, but I disagree *(the children I raised, along with an occasional student, have provided me with numerous examples of misbehaving humans!)*.

Being a Christian and living the principles of LEDRSHHIP within any profession is a pretty high bar. You can't accomplish it just by claiming the title. I can't clear that hurdle by myself, neither can you. I do better on some days than on others, and I'm constantly trying to get better but just can't get there by myself.

I'll leave you with one last verse that should offer you some encouragement and comfort. It is Philippians 4:13: "I can do all things through Christ who strengthens me" (KJV). The catch is you must want to *(you really have to want to)* and have to ask for his help.

Let me reiterate that living as a Christian isn't easy. It is far from a bed of roses *(Who came up with that one anyway? Last time I checked, roses have thorns and they hurt.)*. The concept of salvation is simple, but you cannot live as a Christian by yourself. You just can't. Jesus expects you to, so what is the answer? Yes, I said this before and I apologize for being repetitive, but you have to want it. Let me repeat that. *You really have to want it.* It has to be an all-consuming desire.

Like Dad, everyone needs to sometimes pause, take a step back and, in a loud voice with raised fist and all the enthusiasm they can muster, exclaim, "Behold, I come!" Then with full confidence, wade right into whatever challenges you are faced with. You never know what the outcome will be if you don't try.

You see, there is a little more to that story than I first told you. I grew up addressing the lady he fell on as Mom. That's how they met. As Paul Harvey said on numerous occasions, "And now you know the rest of the story."[38] I love my mom and my dad, faults and all.

A chicken and a pig were talking about opening a restaurant. The chicken suggested putting ham and eggs on the menu. The pig said, "No thanks. I would be committed, but you would only be involved."

Dad was good at whatever he did. I think it was because he had the courage to be committed to whatever task he pursued.

Being a Chreaster just doesn't cut it. That isn't enough. Before you ask, a Chreaster is someone who comes to church for Christmas and Easter but only if they don't have anything better to do. Gentlemen, I would be willing to bet and give you ten to one odds that when you first began dating your wife, you did not have the following conversation: "Sweetheart, I really like where this is going.

---

[38] Paul Harvey, American broadcaster, *The Rest of the Story*, a Monday through Friday radio program which began as newscasts during WWII, Premiered as a series on ABC Radio Networks May 10, 1976–2009, Paul Harvey Jr., *The Rest of the Story*, Bantam Books, Doubleday, New York, NY., 1977.

I think we have the potential to make it long-term. Let me tell you what I'm willing to do. I'll come over and visit with you every Sunday morning for about an hour.

"I might miss more Sundays than I show up, because I like to sleep in on weekends. I have to cut the grass and Sunday is a great day for fishing. The golf course isn't usually crowded on Sunday, so if I can get a good tee time, I won't be there. Otherwise, I'll show up about 11:00. Expect me to look at my watch periodically to make sure I'm not going to be late for lunch. If you start talking, I might nod off from time to time, but at 12:00, I'm leaving. Let's try it and see where this goes."

The idea is ludicrous; it's beyond preposterous! It doesn't merit consideration, but is that any different than the way we approach God or the way you're approaching LEDRSHHIP?

> Not forsaking the assembling of ourselves together, as the manner of some is; but exhorting one another: and so much the more, as ye see the day approaching. For if we sin willfully after we have received the knowledge of the truth, there remaineth no more sacrifice for sins. (Hebrews 25–26, NIV)

What God is saying here is simple. It amounts to *show up!* Life takes commitment, not just involvement; so does being a Christian, so does LEDRSHHIP. If you're planning on going to heaven, but you're a Chreaster, consider this. I love being in church because I love being around God's people; I love the sense of family and belonging, the atmosphere, the fellowship. If you think you don't need to go to church all the time, or perhaps believe the occasional Sunday morning is good enough, you might want to reconsider.

When you get to heaven, who do you expect to be there? The answer is God's people, those same people you are avoiding now because you don't want to come to church. Don't bet the bank that Jesus and you will be the only occupants. If I invite you to my home for a dinner party and you don't like my friends, you probably aren't going to have much fun.

I'm in church every time the doors are open. I have my own keys to the building, because sometimes I have things to do, so the doors can be opened. This is what God said about it:

> I know your deeds, that you are neither cold
> nor hot. I wish you were either one or the other!
> So, because you are lukewarm—neither hot nor
> cold—I am about to spit you out of my mouth.
> (Revelation 3:15–16, NIV)

When we were eating dinner, Dad would occasionally ask each of us what we learned in school that day. It wasn't something he did all the time, but it was often enough for us to expect the question. I've used this tactic with my students more times than I can count, because it is an effective barometer. Through this simple question, it became possible for me to determine whether my efforts had been worthwhile or if I'd been wasting my time. You purchased my book, and I'm grateful to you. Thanks. You read the book and, hopefully, you enjoyed it. I hope it meant something to you and had an impact on your life.

This is one of my last questions, and it is an important one. What did you learn? If you didn't learn anything by reading this, then you wasted time which you can never get back. If the words in this manuscript don't make a difference in your life, then reading them was a pointless endeavor. Perhaps you have remembered some of your own "snipories" as you read mine.

Send me an e-mail and let me know. Tell me about them. Perhaps if I get enough of them, we can publish *Snipories, Volume 2*. I'd love to hear from you. If you want me to pray for you, regardless of what your needs are, let me know. God can take care of them.

My e-mail address is flynprof@yahoo.com. I'll respond, but don't expect me to tweet, post, or snap when you chat. Social media is the ruination of society. I have no "Pinterest" in your "Instagram;" and it drives me up a "Wall." Yes, I have a Facebook page but don't know my password. Don't bother following me, because it would be a boring proposition.

I'm the wrong person to be following anyway. Try following Jesus instead. My personal life is my private business between God, my family, and myself. You don't need to know where or when I go on vacations, what kind of music I like, what I ordered for dinner, where my favorite restaurant is, or what movie I choose to watch. Don't hold your breath waiting for a picture of what I ate for dessert. If that is what your life is all about, you need a life. I'll be happy to pray for you if you ask.

In my opinion, the book is usually much better than the movie. I'm not sure if that holds true with *The Case for Christ* by author Lee Strobel.[39] In this case, the movie and book tell the same story but from different perspectives, so there probably isn't a fair way to make a comparison. The movie is based on the book, which in turn is based on true events. Regardless, both are exceptional and well worthwhile expenditures of your time. I highly recommend them. In both, Mr. James Dixon was sent to prison for a crime he didn't commit.

In the movie, wrongful imprisonment is partially because of an article written and published in the Chicago Tribune by Mr. Strobel. He eventually realized his error, told Mr. Dixon that he missed the truth, and then apologized to him. Mr. Dixon's reply was, "You missed the truth because you didn't want to see it."

In the book, which I believe to be the more truthful account, Mr. Strobel simply reported on the facts as any good reporter would. However, his mind was made up regarding Mr. Dixon's guilt prior to writing the article based on the facts he was presented with. His article had no bearing on the outcome of the trial. After realizing there were alternate reasons for the facts presented, Mr. Strobel also realized Mr. Dixon was innocent. Mr. Strobel states in part:

> "One reason the evidence looked so con-
> vincing was because it fit my preconceptions.
> When police told me the case was airtight, I took

---

[39] Lee Strobel, *The Case for Christ*, Zondervan, Willow Creek Resources, 2016.

them at their word. But when I traded my biases for an attempt at objectivity, I saw the case in a whole new light. I allowed the evidence to lead me to the truth, regardless of whether it fit my original suppositions."

The book and the movie make the same point and begs the question, how do you see Jesus? What is the perspective you are using? What are your preconceptions? What do the lenses of the glasses you are using look like? Is your mind already made up based upon your preconceptions or what someone else has told you?

Do you have eyes but fail to see and ears but fail to hear?... Do you still not understand?"
(Matthew 8:18,21, NIV)

I recently went to a medical appointment at a doctor's office I had not previously visited. As I was completing the pre-appointment paperwork, the intake specialist asked me if I was employed. Out of habit, my response was yes. I'd only been retired about a month when this happened.

Is what you tell yourself about God how you really feel? Or is it something you automatically respond with? How many times have you responded with "Fine" when someone asks, "How are you?" Are your thoughts about God just as habitual? Are your beliefs about Jesus based on your own research? Or are they something you tell yourself without any thought, reasoning, or consideration? Do you really want to gamble your own eternity based on what somebody else said?

Yes, there is a fish on the back of my truck, and I know (notice the use of the word *know*) Jesus is coming back. He told me so. He told you the same thing. You may have missed it, but that doesn't mean he didn't say it. My task has been accomplished because the information has been relayed.

If you choose to think of me as a religious zealot, then by all means, feel free to do so. I don't care. No matter how hard you try, no matter what you say to or about me, and regardless of what you do to me, you will never succeed in any attempt to hurt my feelings. I withhold my permission for you to insult or anger me. That is because when Jesus returns, I'm going to go with him. He told me that also. Did he tell you?

You can't frighten or worry me.

> The Lord is with me; I will not be afraid.
> What can mere mortals do to me? (Psalms 118:6, NIV)

I am Gerald Andrew Thornhill Jr., and by grace through faith in Jesus Christ, the Son of God, I have been born again. I have delivered the message as instructed. Do with it what you will. If you don't like the message, don't fool yourself into a disbelief regarding the validity. God's word has been relayed.

Should you choose to disregard it, then do so at your own peril, but let me remind you of something in the fifty-fifth chapter of Isaiah, verse 11. "My Word that goes out from my mouth will not return to me empty, but will accomplish what I desire and achieve the purpose for which I sent it." It's your future and eternity. As far as eternity is concerned…well, it's eternity.

Stop me if you have heard this one *(Translation: stop me if you believe this one)*. If there is a loving God, then he won't send me to hell. Well, you are almost right, but you're missing an important part. The truth is God doesn't send anyone to hell. He merely grants your request to go.

"What's that?" you say. "I never asked to go to hell. Why would I ask to go to hell? I would have to be crazy!"

Let me explain.

God is Holy and cannot tolerate sin. He can't be around it or even look at it. One of the last things Jesus said as he hung on the cross was, "My God, My God, why have you forsaken me?" (Matthew 27:46, NIV), which is actually a quote from Psalms 22:1. God turned his back on Jesus.

> For he made him who knew no sin to be sin
> for us that we might become the righteousness of
> God in him. (2 Corinthians 5:21, NKJV)

I did not want to fire my brother from his job, but there wasn't any choice. My hand was forced. If you are thinking I'm a good person so I won't go to hell, then think about this. Wrong is wrong and God can't tolerate it. The only way out of hell is by trusting Jesus to get you to heaven. If you insist you don't believe in him, then how can you trust him?

Have you ever broken even one of the Ten Commandments? Perhaps you're thinking, *I haven't cheated on my spouse. I'd never even consider it.* Not so fast, my friend. Read Matthew 5:28 (NIV). "But I tell you that anyone who looks at a woman lustfully has already committed adultery with her in his heart."

Gentlemen, do you expect me to really believe that when you see an attractive woman, you don't look? I know better, because I'm a man just like you are.

Ladies, you look too. Granted, you are more subtle about it, but don't try to deny what I'm saying, because I've seen you. Don't misunderstand what I'm saying either. Just because you're already guilty, don't think that gives you license to do something physical like it won't matter. It does matter, and someone is keeping score.

Maybe you're thinking, *I haven't murdered anybody. I'm certainly not guilty of murder.* Hold the phone, dude. Wait just a second. What about Proverbs 23:7? "For as he thinks in his heart, so is he" (NKJV).

Do you expect me to really believe you have never thought about getting even with someone because of something they did to you? Go back and reread what I said about my Saul and my Paul.

Remember that one about not stealing? You never took anything that didn't belong to you, not even a candy bar from the store when you were a kid *(I'm guilty of that),* or taken advantage of the copier at work for personal use *(I'm guilty of that one too)*? Have you ever called in sick when the only thing wrong was a severe case of "workitis," meaning you just wanted to take a day off? Maybe you went shopping, took the kids to an amusement park, played golf, or took your spouse to a movie. It doesn't really matter the activity and it's likely the break was sorely needed, but you got paid for being at work. That is theft, my friend.

Let's see. We've talked about adultery, murder, and theft just now. We talked about lying, coveting, and taking God's name in vain some time ago. By my count, that makes six out of ten so far. I could review the remaining four, but why bother? Discussing them won't prove anything. You should already be crying, "Uncle!"

Let's make the assumption that starting today you never break even one of the Ten Commandments again for the rest of your life. The problem is you can't fix this fact. You're already guilty. Your ship has sailed, brother. Actually, it didn't make it out of port because it sank dockside. You doused it with gasoline, struck a match, lit it on fire, torpedoed it while it was burning, watched as it went down, and danced a jig on the dock as the last of the mast disappeared into the depths.

I recently backed into another vehicle. The accident was my fault. My insurance paid the cost of repairing the vehicle I damaged, but the $500 deductible in order to repair my truck came out of my pocket. That didn't include the citation for "improper backing resulting in an accident." It would have been nice to get into a time machine and refrain from putting my vehicle into reverse.

My truck has been repaired, but it still cost me $700 when the deductible, the ticket, and the cost of going to "traffic school" are all calculated into the total *(I was the oldest attendee which didn't help my ego)*. I'm a working man. Seven hundred dollars is an appreciable sum of money for me and my family. I'd like to have it back.

Fortunately, my insurance company understood, and my premium did not increase. Once a decision is made and the action has been taken, you become responsible for the consequences. You can't undo the past sins you have committed any more than I can unwind a stupid decision of backing up without looking into my rearview mirror.

Since God can't tolerate sin, not even from his own Son, you are condemned at the outset, and it's just that simple. Pardon me while I repeat myself—it is what it is. The only way out is with Jesus.

> Jesus saith unto him, "I am the way, the
> truth, and the life: no man cometh unto the
> Father, but by me." (John 14:6, KJV)

Unlike his Uncle James, my son, Jarred, is indeed a man of few words. Although he doesn't say much, when he tells you something, it is important. After reading a rough draft of this manuscript, his critique consisted of four words, and I quote, "Dad, it ain't bad."

That left me somewhat perplexed. His statement was confusing. Did he mean my book was excellent, horrible, or somewhere in between?

Placing God in your life the way you should "ain't bad," but you will never know what that means until you put him where he belongs. Let me assure you of this one thing: If you make the effort, you will be immeasurably happy with the choice.

We are finally here. We've arrived at the conclusion of the conclusion and it comes down to a rather trite but none-the-less true, and very appropriate phrase. Denial isn't just a large river in Egypt. You can believe or disbelieve. You can choose to believe in Jesus or you can choose to believe in evolution, the Big Bang theory, atheism, agnosticism, or whatever else you want. No matter how you characterize your choice, you are either with Jesus or you aren't. Let me summarize evolution for you. Goo plus zoo plus you equals evolution. None of my relatives ever swung from a tree.

It is entirely your choice, but keep this in mind: Should you choose disbelief, you will eventually change your mind.

> "As surely as I live," says the Lord, "every
> knee will bow before me; every tongue will
> acknowledge God." (Romans 14:11, NIV)

Those aren't my words. That is a direct quote from Jesus who just happened to be quoting from Isaiah 45:23. "Before me, every knee will bow; by me, every tongue will swear" (NIV). Note the word *will*. You have a decision to make which *will* result in the writing on your wall *(no, that isn't your Facebook wall)*.

In case you are wondering, that isn't an archaic expression of unknown origin. It is a great story well worth reading found in the fifth chapter of Daniel. The handwriting on the wall roughly translates to you have been measured and found wanting. When it is my turn to meet Jesus I don't want to hear I have been measured and found wanting. My very last question is, has reading this book caused an epiphany? Have you experienced a great Revelation causing a new Genesis? Or is this *the end*?

ABOUT THE AUTHOR

Captain Gerald A. Thornhill Jr. (US Army, Retired) has lived a life of service. He enlisted in the United States Army in 1974 and served as an infantryman until 1978. After his service, Captain Thornhill pursued and completed an associate degree, two baccalaureate degrees, and ultimately, a master of science degree in aviation safety from Central Missouri State University. While pursuing flight training, he rejoined the military in the Missouri Army National Guard and subsequently the United States Army Reserve.

Captain Thornhill held two company commands and served one combat tour in Taji, Iraq, at Camp Cooke in 2003 and 2004. During his military career, Captain Thornhill was recommended for the Bronze Star, decorated with three Army Commendation Medals, the Global War on Terrorism Medal, and many others.

While a member of the Army Reserve, Captain Thornhill served in his civilian life as an educator. He has been an FAA advanced ground instructor since 1994 and certificated flight instructor since 1995. He has given flight instruction in the St. Louis area and at Southern Illinois University, Carbondale. He retired from SIUC as an assistant chief flight instructor in February 2018.

He has taught numerous students to fly several different types of aircraft along with FAA-approved ground classes at both SIUC and John A. Logan College in Carterville, Illinois. He has given more than 5,000 hours of flight instruction and innumerable hours of ground instruction throughout his career. He was named Teacher of the Year by the department of Aviation Management and Flight at SIUC in 2017.

Captain Thornhill's professional life has been built on serving the needs of the nation and the aviation community through education. He continues to serve his community as the music director and as a Sunday school teacher at First Baptist Church in Zeigler, Illinois. He lives in Mulkeytown, Illinois, with his wife, Sheila, and their Miniature Schnauzer, Lizzie.